the

isease Series

se

M.D.

AU

Recent Titles in
Biographies of D

Parkinson's Disea
Nutan Sharma

Depression
Blaise A. Aguirre,

Diabetes
Andrew Galmer

Stroke
Jonathan A. Edlow

AUTISM

Lisa D. Benaron

Biographies of Disease
Julie K. Silver, M.D., Series Editor

GREENWOOD PRESS
Westport, Connecticut • London

Library of Congress Cataloging-in-Publication Data

Benaron, Lisa Dorothea.
  Autism / Lisa D. Benaron.
    p. cm. — (Biographies of disease, ISSN 1940-445X)
  Includes bibliographical references and index.
  ISBN 978-0-313-34763-4 (alk. paper)
  1. Autism—Popular works. I. Title.
  RC553.A88B457 2009
  616.85′882—dc22   2008028537

British Library Cataloguing in Publication Data is available.

Library of Congress Catalog Card Number: 2008028537
ISBN: 978-0-313-34763-4
ISSN: 1940-445X

First published in 2009

Greenwood Press, 88 Post Road West, Westport, CT 06881
An imprint of Greenwood Publishing Group, Inc.
www.greenwood.com

Printed in the United States of America

∞™

The paper used in this book complies with the
Permanent Paper Standard issued by the National
Information Standards Organization (Z39.48–1984).

10 9 8 7 6 5 4 3 2 1

First, I want to acknowledge the parents and family members of children with autistic spectrum disorders. Their love for their children propels them past the visible shock and grief at the time of diagnosis to become their children's teachers, advocates, and rooting sections. I am continuously moved by the strength and dedication they show during their journeys.

I also want to acknowledge Jake, my daughter's half-brother, who started me on my journey with autism fifteen years ago. Despite all that I have learned, it is still heart wrenching to realize that I will never fully understand how Jake experiences life from deep within his wordless world of autism. I used to have dreams in which he could talk so he could tell me everything I yearned to know. Now that dream is a reality for the parents of many children with autistic spectrum disorders who are increasingly finding their voices through effective early intervention.

To my mother, Dodi Benaron, I offer my profound gratitude for encouraging me to be an independent thinker and instilling in me her love of words.
Finally, this book is dedicated to my eleven-year-old daughter, Molly, who selflessly encouraged me during the long hours I spent at my laptop. She has a writer's soul, and I look forward to reading her stories and poems for many years to come.

Epigraphs

The greater the ignorance, the greater the dogmatism.
Sir William Osler, Physician (1849–1919)

To be humane, we must ever be ready to pronounce that wise, ingenious, and modest statement "I do not know."
Galileo Galilei

If a man begins with certainties, he shall end in doubts; but if he will be content to begin with doubts, he shall end in certainties.
Francis Bacon

Contents

Series Foreword

Every disease has a story to tell: about how it started long ago and began to disable or even take the lives of its innocent victims, about the way it hurts us, and about how we are trying to stop it. In this *Biographies of Disease* series, the authors tell the stories of the diseases that we have come to know and dread.

The stories of these diseases have all of the components that make for great literature. There is incredible drama played out in real-life scenes from the past, present, and future. You'll read about how men and women of science stumbled trying to save the lives of those they aimed to protect. Turn the pages and you'll also learn about the amazing success of those who fought for health and won, often saving thousands of lives in the process.

If you don't want to be a health professional or research scientist now, when you finish this book you may think differently. The men and women in this book are heroes who often risked their own lives to save or improve ours. This is the biography of a disease, but it is also the story of real people who made incredible sacrifices to stop it in its tracks.

Julie K. Silver, M.D.
Assistant Professor, Harvard Medical School
Department of Physical Medicine and Rehabilitation

Preface

The study of the autistic spectrum disorders (ASDs) presents a unique opportunity to sort through a mystery as the facts are still emerging. The groundwork has been painstakingly laid by pioneering professionals starting in the forties with an intensified effort over the past two decades. Instead of reading the headlines and watching the news shows to try to understand autism, anyone with enough interest to think carefully about what is and is not known for certain can formulate his own hypotheses and follow along as doctors, psychologists, scientists, and educators, spurred on by tireless advocates, race to solve the puzzle.

The ASDs are much more common than was originally thought. By now, the vast majority of people in the United States and other developed countries are aware of at least one acquaintance or relative dealing with a child who has been diagnosed with an ASD. If ASDs have not directly touched your life yet, it probably will not be long before you are personally drawn into the mystery.

Individuals committed to understanding the ASDs are desperately needed in a wide variety of fields, including medicine, psychology, genetic research, and other areas of scientific investigation, education, speech therapy, occupational therapy, social work, and early child intervention. By the time students heading for any of these careers finish their training, much more will be known about autism, but it is unlikely that the mystery will be completely solved.

The goal for this book is for readers to be familiar with how our understanding of autism has developed over the years, how it is changing, and which questions still need answers. With a solid background, it will be possible to watch the developments in the field of ASDs with a knowledgeable perspective degree of understanding that most bystanders do not have.

New understanding of the causes underlying ASDs and how best to treat or even prevent ASDs will be welcomed by all. The findings will surely be fascinating but most likely will not be surprising to those who have thought carefully about the ASDs and followed closely as the mystery is unraveled.

Presenting a synthesis of all there is to know about autistic spectrum disorders is a daunting task. As research in the field has exploded over the past decade, it has become increasingly difficult (if not impossible) to be an expert in all facets. I could not have put this work together without the assistance of the experts who generously responded to my questions and were kind enough to review sections of the manuscript. I extend my deepest gratitude to the following individuals: Frances Page Glascoe, Nancy Wiseman, Deborah Fein, Diana Robins, Amy Wetherby, Ami Klin, Irva Hertz-Picciotto, Ron Huff, Natacha Akshoomoff, Shirley Korula, Isaac Pessah, Judy Van de Water, and Judy Rapaport. Thank you for your passionate dedication to your work and for sharing your insights with me. Finally, I thank my editors, Kevin Downing and Dr. Julie Silver, for their faith in me.

Introduction

QUESTION: WHAT DO THESE SIX INDIVIDUALS HAVE IN COMMON?

Donald T.'s Story: Odd Language

Donald T. wasn't like other children his age. While most one year olds were struggling to come up with a few simple words such as "hi," "bye-bye," "doggie," "kitty," "mama," and "dada," Donald could already sing several different songs with surprising accuracy. By the time he was two, he was able to recite short poems and learn the Twenty-third Psalm by heart. He quickly memorized the entire alphabet backward and forward and could count to one hundred with ease (tasks most kindergarteners, and even most adults, cannot accomplish). He developed the seemingly impossible ability to spin unlikely objects: blocks, pans, or any round object he came across would balance and twirl improbably at his touch. Watching the object whirl, Don jumped up and down in ecstasy. His speech was odd, consisting primarily of words that bore no obvious connection to his activity or environment: "chrysanthemum"; "business"; "the right one is on, the left one is off"; "Through the dark clouds shining." He showed no interest in playing with other children and seemed oblivious to the comings and goings of most people, even his parents. If a child approached him to play, he retreated from them, content to be left alone.

Fredrick W.'s Story: Minimal Language

Fredrick W. was six years old when he was brought to see the psychiatrist because of his unusual and unpredictable behavior. If a person tried to interact with him, he might withdraw or he might attack. At his appointment, he wandered around the room seemingly unaware of the three professionals who had gathered to evaluate him. He sat down on the couch suddenly and then lay down on the floor. Tense at first, his facial expression changed to a dreamy look once he was comfortable. He did not respond to any questions or commands, except for the occasional parrot-like repetition of words that had been directed to him. Objects completely absorbed his attention, while the people in the room were nothing more than unwelcome intruders into his self-directed exploration. Fredrick did not cooperate with attempts to test his intelligence, but he did demonstrate an uncanny ability to complete puzzles; showing no concern as to whether the pieces were right side up or not, he worked purely by the shape of the puzzle piece.

Richard M.'s Story: No Language

Richard M. was brought to see the doctor when he was three years and three months of age because his parents thought he might be deaf. He had started imitating word sounds when he was younger but then stopped for no reason that his parents could discern. He no longer used any words but often made unusual shrill sounds. "Ee! Ee! Ee!" he would cry out when excited or upset, his utterances directed to no one in particular. At the hospital, the astute intern immediately noticed that Richard was able to follow simple directions, even when they were given out of his line of sight. Requests such as "lie down" or "sit up" were followed by Richard. His doctors knew right away that he could not be deaf, but they did not know how to explain his detachment from those who sought to interact with him. Richard was not interested in the typical toys that attracted other children his age. In the exam room, he rejected a number of toys in favor of a small box that he threw repeatedly, as if it was a ball. Turning the lights on and off fascinated Richard, and he would do whatever it took to reach the light switch. If he had to crawl over people or furniture, he did so without hesitation, barely seeming to notice anyone who happened to be in his way. If someone tried to prevent him from reaching his goal, he went into a screaming rage that lasted as long as it took to get the object of his desire. Once he had whatever it was that he wanted, his tantrum stopped instantly, just as suddenly as it had started.

Harro L.'s Story: Lack of Conversational Skills

Harro L. was referred by the staff at his school at eight and a half years of age because he was "unmanageable." He was a small child with a faraway gaze, often appearing to be lost in thought, and then, suddenly and unexpectedly, he would laugh to himself for reasons unknown to those around him. Something about him gave the impression of an older, dignified adult rather than the boy that he was. Although he was quite capable of expressing himself, there was something odd about his word choices. It was not possible to have a real conversation with Harro; he preferred talking on and on about subjects of interest to him alone, without giving the listener a chance to respond. When spoken to, he often did not respond. His teachers felt that he could do better in school if he just tried, but he never did his homework, or, for that matter, most things he was asked to do. Harro talked back to his teachers, unconcerned about the consequences. "This is far too stupid for me," he would say if that was what he thought. His teachers were at their wits' end.

K.'s Story: Lifelong Struggle

K. was a calm baby who seemed always to be smiling. Nothing seemed to bother him; he seldom cried. He started to talk at the usual time (around one year of age), stopped for a while, and then started talking again at age three. He kept to himself when around other children. If another child took his toy, he did not protest. He referred to himself as "he" or "K." until he was five years old, but otherwise his language use did not seem unusual to his parents. As a toddler, he was fascinated by his large collection of toy cars and trains, playing with these toys above all others and stopping only when forced to give them up. He noticed instantly if any of his prized cars or trains were missing or out of place. As he grew older, he continued to be fascinated with all modes of transportation. He read everything he could on the subject, watched cars and trains whenever he had the opportunity, and took trips in his free time to see trains of particular interest. Except for his fellow train enthusiasts, he had no social contact with anyone except his parents. He attended a private school, performing well in subjects that required a good rote memory but struggling with comprehension of abstract ideas. K.'s attempt to be a soldier was cut short; he was discharged after a brief stint because of his clumsiness and his peculiar ways. K. was able to find employment doing routine clerical work. As time went on, he became more and more aware that he was different. K. wanted to be like other men, to have a wife and a social life, but he had no idea how to go about it. As he struggled with his exclusion from the normal social world, he grew sad and anxious. Finally, at the age of twenty-eight, he sought help from a psychiatrist.

Temple Grandin's Story: A Successful Career

Temple was a beautiful child, with blue eyes and brown hair. There was nothing in her appearance to suggest that she was different from any other baby. In fact, she seemed like a very good baby; she was quiet and seldom fussed, but something was not quite right with Temple. Around six months of age, she stopped being cuddly. She stiffened when held. By nine months of age, she fought to avoid being held, clawing at her mother like a wild animal trying to free herself. When she didn't start talking on time, her mother worried that she might be deaf, but tests showed otherwise. Her first words did not emerge until after her third birthday, and even then she struggled to get them out. There were times when she said words as clear as could be, like the time she said, "Ice. Ice. Ice," when the car window shattered as her mother sideswiped a trailer, distracted for a brief moment by Temple throwing her hat out of the car window. Random sounds, something as innocuous as a noisemaker at a birthday party, would drive her into a frenzy of distress, kicking and screaming on the floor, although other loud sounds went largely unnoticed. Left to herself, she could spend hours tearing up paper and watching the pieces fall to the ground or letting sand slip through her fingers while she watched with intense concentration. She had a talent for spinning coins and jar lids. She often sat on the floor, repetitively spinning in circles, deep within her own world. Her eye contact was poor, and her voice had a flat, monotone quality that was distinctly odd. At age three, she was evaluated by a neurologist who suspected brain damage and recommended only speech therapy.

Temple's mother was not content to accept the diagnosis of brain damage. She enrolled Temple in a small private school that was supportive, accepting her oddities while continually working to help her learn and improve. With her mother's patient guidance and involvement, Temple kept up with the class work. However, life at school was not easy for Temple. She annoyed the other children with her constant questioning and fixations. When she became fascinated with the gubernatorial elections in fourth grade, she talked almost nonstop about election buttons, posters, and bumper stickers, much to the dismay of the other students. She was teased and bullied, labeled with unkind nicknames such as "Chatterbox" and "Tape Recorder" because of her propensity to go on and on about topics in which no one else was interested.

The situation became harder for Temple once she entered seventh grade in a larger, more chaotic, and less supportive school. Expelled after two and a half years because of her temper outbursts, her mother found a better environment for her at a boarding school for gifted children. Still, Temple did not fit in. Although her language had improved, her speech still sounded odd. Try as she might, she still could not dress like the other students. She was labeled with names like "Buzzard Woman" and cried when a classmate told her that boys did not like her because she had "no sex appeal." Fortunately, Temple found a mentor at her high school who changed her life. He helped her focus her interests into a career plan and supported her as she progressed through college and on to graduate school. A fascination with cattle chutes, developed during the summer of her junior year in high school at her aunt's ranch in Arizona, eventually led to her successful career designing feedlots and meat-processing plants. Temple lives alone and has chosen a celibate life because the social rules of dating and relationships are simply too mystifying for her.

Question: What Do These Six Individuals Have in Common?

Answer: They all have autistic spectrum disorders.

The first three vignettes are based on case histories provided in Dr. Leo Kanner's 1943 report that first brought attention to the condition that he later called infantile autism (Kanner 1943).

The fourth case description is taken from a translation of Hans Asperger's original 1944 paper (Frith 1981), written just one year after Kanner's paper (without any knowledge of Kanner's work), describing a "new" syndrome that he independently titled "autistic psycopathy."

The fifth case is based on a description provided by Lorna Wing, an eminent British psychologist who brought Asperger's previously obscure paper to mainstream attention in 1981, coining the term "Asperger syndrome" (AS) in the process.

The sixth individual profiled is Temple Grandin, Ph.D., a highly intelligent adult with high-functioning autism (HFA). The vignette is a compilation of information provided by Temple Grandin in her first and second books, *Emergence: Labeled Autistic* and *Thinking in Pictures*. Temple is arguably the best-known adult with HFA in the world as a result of her prolific writing, lecturing, and countless television interviews on news programs and popular talk shows. Her books and media presence have added greatly to public awareness that a childhood diagnosis of autism need not be viewed as an inescapable sentence to an unfulfilling life. Dr. Grandin has a successful career as an associate professor at Colorado State University in the department of animal sciences, where she has excelled in the design of livestock-handling facilities. She attributes her success to her ability to "think in pictures" combined with her in-depth understanding of the instinctual basis of animal behavior (read her book *Animals in Translation* for an in-depth look at the basis for animal behavior and find out why she finds animal behavior easier to understand than human behavior).

THE AUTISTIC SPECTRUM: SIMILAR SOCIAL DEFICITS WITH WIDE DIFFERENCES IN LANGUAGE AND INTELLECTUAL ABILITIES

These six vignettes illustrate the tremendous range of language abilities (from no recognizable words to fluent speech) and intellectual abilities (from mentally retarded to highly intelligent) seen in individuals with autistic spectrum disorders (ASDs). Because the abilities of individuals with ASDs vary so greatly, professionals have tried to find a way to divide the spectrum into separate diagnostic groups that serve as a shorthand for their level of impairment. Autistic disorder (autism), high-functioning autism (HFA) Asperger's syndrome (AS), and pervasive developmental disorder-not otherwise specified (PDD-NOS) are the most current diagnostic labels. Instead of helping to make the autistic spectrum more understandable, the division into separate diagnostic categories has obscured the interconnectedness of these related disorders, creating the appearance of solid borders between conditions that are not used to stratify the ASDs truly separable.

Clinicians attempting to base a diagnosis on the current system are forced to take a complex situation and choose one label over the others, giving the impression of diagnostic certainty in a field that has not evolved enough to merit certainty. The current rules used to assign a specific ASD diagnosis will be discussed in Chapter 4, but the reader should realize up front that the labels used in the past, those used currently, and the diagnostic classifications that will prevail in the future are all works in progress, proposed and then refined over time as more information is gathered in an attempt to further our understanding of individuals similar to those originally described by Kanner and Asperger.

TERMINOLOGY CHOICES FOR THIS BOOK

In this text, both the terms ASDs and pervasive developmental disorders (PDDs) will be used in an essentially interchangeable manner to describe individuals with autistic disorder, Asperger's disorder, and PDD-NOS. The terms autistic disorder and autism are used interchangeably. The labels AS and Asperger's disorder are interchangeable. AS will be used preferentially in this book, except when references are made to the *Diagnostic and Statistical Manual* classification system in which "Asperger's disorder" is the official label that was chosen. AS is preferred by most individuals with AS, who point out that they are different but not disordered. Common usage is to omit "syndrome" and "disorder" and simply refer to individuals with "Asperger's."

The term "intellectual disability" (ID) is the preferred term for mental retardation (MR). The meaning is the same: individuals with MR or ID have intelligence quotients (IQ)s that fall below the low average range (less than 70). ID is preferred because it does not have the derogatory associations that are associated with the MR label (almost every child has heard the word "retard" hurled at kids on the playground as the ultimate insult, and it is long past time for this pattern to end).

Although boys with classic autism outnumber girls approximately 4:1 (see Chapter 5 for more complete information on sex ratios in ASDs), it is inaccurate to think of ASDs as a problem that only affects males. To promote awareness of ASDs in females, personal pronouns for both sexes (he and she) will be used throughout the book.

The description of individuals with autism as "autistic" has been avoided as much as possible in deference to individuals with disabilities of all types who object to being described by a diagnostic label. A person who has autism is, first and foremost, a person; autism is the challenge that person must face.

CONTROVERSIES IN ASDS

Increased awareness of the ASDs and the increasing frequency of diagnosis have propelled the ASDs into the spotlight as one of the most pressing mysteries confronting medical science. Controversy surrounds almost every aspect of the ASDs, from the rules used to diagnose ASDs, through attempts to accurately determine the true incidence of ASDs and clarify how the numbers are changing over time, to the contentious disagreements about the causes of these disorders and how to best treat children with ASDs. For those just beginning the study of ASDs, there is a danger of getting lost in the highly publicized, emotionally charged debates over controversial issues. Before diving headlong into the fray surrounding the "autism 'epidemic'" and whether or not vaccines or mercury plays a part in the increasing incidence of ASDs, it is important to start with a solid understanding of the core characteristics of the ASDs and how our conceptions of ASDs have changed over time.

Armed with the knowledge you are about to gain, you will be able to form your own opinions, based on careful consideration of the field. It is not possible to accurately assess what you hear on the news or read on a website unless you have a solid base of understanding. Whether you are a college student, parent or relative of a child with an ASD, teacher, speech therapist, psychologist, or someone with curiosity and interest in the field, you will be a valuable resource for anyone trying to sort out the massive amounts of information available on the topic. If you are a student and the mystery tugs at you, there are a wide array of careers to choose from that will allow you to contribute to the cause.

1

Autism, AS, and the Evolution of the Concept of the ASDs

To fully understand what is currently meant by the term "ASD," it is best to go back to the first published description of autism and work to the present conception of the ASDs. Knowing where the field of autism has been helps in the understanding of where the field is going.

Although autism clearly existed before Dr. Leo Kanner published his initial report in 1943, his original description of the disorder marks the first recognition of autism as a distinct developmental disorder. To look farther back in history at the fate of the children (and adults) who suffered under the misunderstanding of their condition long before anyone had ever heard of autism, see the Sidebar entitled "Autism through the Ages."

KANNER'S AUTISM

In 1943, Leo Kanner, chairman of the newly formed Department of Child Psychiatry at Johns Hopkins Hospital in Baltimore, published an article entitled "Autistic Disturbances of Affective Contact" in a journal called *Nervous Child* (Kanner 1943, p. 217). Kanner's initial descriptions of eleven children (eight boys and three girls) still stand as an impressive and insightful description of the qualities common to children with autism.

Autism through the Ages

In her book, *Autism: Explaining the Enigma*, Uta Frith, a Ph.D. psychologist, provides in-depth accounts of several historical figures who fit the profile for autism. Dr. Frith prefaces the stories with her remarks that "autism is not a modern phenomenon, even though it has only been recognized in modern times. In view of the short history of psychiatry, and the even shorter history of child psychiatry, we know that a disorder recently described is not necessarily a recent disorder." Historical accounts of individuals who were thought to be prophets, with odd speech and unusual behaviors, date back to the beginnings of Christianity. In medieval Russia, they were revered as "holy fools." Their "life outside society, guilelessness, and indifference to social conventions," along with their unintelligible remarks and echolalia, are all features that suggest possible ASD.

In 1799, a five-year-old boy was admitted to a mental asylum in England. Records from the doctor caring for him indicate that he "never engaged in play with other children or became attached to them, but played in an absorbed, isolated way with toy soldiers." Scholars have reviewed the historical accounts of this child's life and are in agreement that he most likely had autism.

The "Wild Boy of Aveyron" is one of many stories about feral children ("feral" means untamed or uncultivated and is used to describe children raised in isolation from normal society). The boy, appearing to be somewhere around twelve years old, was found in a forest in central France in the late 1700s. He did not speak or respond to questions. He was given the name "Victor" and was brought to live with a physician named Dr. Itard, who took it on himself to educate the boy. Although Victor was initially thought to be deaf because of his lack of response to spoken language and unexpected loud sounds, it soon became clear that he could hear.

A description written by Dr. Itard in 1800 could easily apply to an autistic child today: "His affections are as limited as his knowledge; he loves no one; he is attached to no one; he shows some preference for his caretaker, but as an expression of a need and not out of a feeling of gratitude; he follows him, because the man is concerned with satisfying his needs and appeasing his hunger." Victor's story was made into a movie by Francois Truffaut (1969) entitled *The Wild Child* based closely on Dr. Itard's writings. The behavior of the boy and the way he learns from Dr. Itard are quite typical for a child with autism. Watch the movie and decide for yourself whether the wild child was autistic.

Ranging in age from two to ten, the children were brought to him after an exhaustive search for answers. Many of the children had been incorrectly diagnosed with MR or schizophrenia as the underlying explanation for their unusual behaviors. Three of the eleven had no spoken language when Kanner evaluated them (all but one went on to develop the ability to use words to communicate). The remaining eight spoke to varying degrees, but all of the speaking children used language in ways that were distinctly unusual.

Both Kanner and Asperger used the word "autistic" in the title of their seminal papers, but neither of these two early pioneers in the field can be credited with introducing the term into the psychiatric lexicon. A Swiss psychiatrist, Ernst Bleuler, introduced the concept in 1909 for reasons that had nothing do with ASDs. Bleuler derived the word from the Greek word "autos," meaning "self." He used the term to describe the marked withdrawal schizophrenic patients demonstrate when they retreat into a self-contained existence filled with delusions and hallucinations. (Bleuler had a knack for introducing words into the psychiatric nomenclature; he is also responsible for the term schizophrenia.)

Kanner observed that the children in his study all exhibited what he called "extreme autistic aloneness," the tendency to ignore, shut out, or fail to respond to input coming from the surrounding social environment. Shortly after the publication of his 1943 paper, Kanner proposed the name "early infantile autism" for the syndrome he first described, a diagnostic label that was used in the United States until 1980, when it was replaced by "autistic disorder."

Kanner's decision to use the word "autistic" to name the newly described disorder had an unfortunate consequence. The absorption with the inner world, seen in both autistic children and schizophrenics, led many clinicians to conclude that early infantile autism was a childhood form of schizophrenia—an incorrect theory that prevailed into the early seventies. Indescribable harm was done to the families who suffered under the false accusation that the autistic child's withdrawal was the fault of "refrigerator mothers"—ambivalent, withholding mothers whose inadequate attachments to their children drove them into isolated inner worlds. Starting in the sixties, momentum built toward the unequivocal conclusion that autism is a neurodevelopmental condition with a biologic basis independent of parenting style (see the Sidebar entitled "False Accusations").

In *Autistic Disturbances of Affective Contact*, Kanner described the birth history, medical issues, and developmental history for each of the eleven children in his case series from early childhood through preadolescence (the oldest child he followed was only eleven years old at the time he wrote his initial paper). In 1971, Kanner published a paper providing a thirty-year follow-up on the original eleven children (for details, see Chapter 10).

The first sentence in Kanner's 1943 report reads, "Since 1938, there have come to our attention a number of children whose condition differs so markedly and uniquely from anything reported so far, that each case merits—and, I hope, will eventually receive—a detailed consideration of its fascinating peculiarities."

From his meticulous descriptions of the eleven children (the first three are encapsulated in the Introduction to this book as Donald T., Frederick W., and

> ### False Accusations: The "Refrigerator Mother" Theory of Autism
>
> Kanner observed that many parents of children with early infantile autism seemed reserved and withholding. He wrote, "In the whole group, there are very few warmhearted fathers and mothers." A psychologist named Bruno Bettleheim (who has since been largely discredited) promoted the theory that maternal ambivalence was the root cause of autism in a book called *The Empty Fortress*. He popularized the stigmatizing term "refrigerator mothers" (Kanner is reported to have been the first to use the term, although he later retracted). Bettleheim recommended that children with autism should be taken away from their mothers for their own good.
>
> Although it now seems beyond comprehension that anyone would believe that autism is caused by deep-seated issues arising in early childhood relationships, virtually every psychiatric condition was attributed to parent-child relationships in the 1940s and 1950s, when Freudian psychoanalytic theory was in its heyday. To learn more about the devastating impact of these false accusations, go to the PBS website to read firsthand accounts from the five mothers chronicled in the 2002 film *Refrigerator Mothers* (http://www.pbs.org/pov/pov2002/refrigeratormothers/index.html). The film is available for purchase from the Kartemquin Films website.
>
> Kanner's observations that many of the parents lacked social warmth was almost certainly due to social qualities that are part of the broader autistic phenotype (see glossary).

Richard M.), Kanner was able to extract a list of what he called the "essential common characteristics" of the syndrome he was attempting to describe. The central characteristic, still recognized today as the core feature of an ASD, is the "inability to relate themselves in the ordinary way to people and situations."

Kanner acknowledged differences amongst the children with regard to the severity of their disturbance, their specific interests and behaviors, and their developmental course, but he was absolutely clear in his conviction that the pathognomonic feature of autism is the child's peculiar social relatedness ("pathognomonic" is a medical term that means the essential or defining characteristic of a particular condition).

The requirement for unusual social interactions as the core feature of ASDs cannot be overemphasized. Studies have shown that even typically developing (TD) children engage in hand flapping, pursue unusual interests, and show obsessive desire for sameness. Unless there is a significant impairment in the individual's social connectedness that is present across all environments, an ASD diagnosis does not fit. Dr. Hans Asperger, another pioneer in the ASD field, also emphasized the stability of behavior across different environments:

"Thus, apart from its distinctiveness, it is its constancy that makes autism a highly recognizable entity."

Kanner's group of children had severe limitations in their awareness of and interest in social interactions that persisted during the many years he followed their progress, albeit in a less severe form for most of the children as they grew up. As toddlers, each of the children Kanner described barely responded to their parents' social cues. Children who demonstrate a profound lack of interest in the social environment around them are typically described as aloof (meaning distant, removed, or remote). An aloof child often seems oblivious to the presence of other individuals in the surroundings, interacting with others only when they have a need to do so or if it serves them in some way.

All eleven children described by Kanner were aloof when he first evaluated them, vastly preferring to interact with objects over people and becoming easily annoyed or upset by any efforts made to join into their self-directed play. He attributed their preference for objects to the fact that objects are predictable and do not intrude on their aloneness. (Kanner could well have offered the same explanation for the strong interest in computers shown by many individuals with ASDs—see the Sidebar entitled "Computers and ASDs"). The use of the terms "Kanner's autism" or "classical autism" is a common shorthand way to indicate that the child with autism has the aloof nature that Kanner described.

Although "autistic aloneness" is the central component of autism, Kanner noted many other distinctive features that tended to cluster together, including highly specific types of language oddities; failure to respond when called by name; play that was extremely repetitive, often involving objects that would not interest a typical child; a strong preference for sameness; distinctive motor mannerisms that often occurred during periods of excitement; unusually strong reactions to noises; and rapid mood shifts that are all seen with astonishing regularity in individuals with autism.

In addition to his descriptions of the behavioral features of autism, Kanner offered his observations and thoughts about the heritability, onset, and medical correlates of autism and issues related to intelligence. In the ensuing sixty years, most of Kanner's conclusions have been confirmed, while others either have required slight modification or remain controversial. His observation that there was a higher than expected number of family members with obsessive behaviors and anxiety disorders was confirmed by numerous studies and has provided an important lead in the search for genetic causes of autism. Researchers have added several other mental health conditions to the list of commonly encountered traits in family members referred to as the "broader autistic phenotype" [BAP] (see Chapter 6 for further discussion).

Computers and ASDs: A Match Made in Heaven

A December 2001 article in *Wired* magazine entitled "The Geek Syndrome" focused on the high-tech culture of California's Silicon Valley. The author proposed that ASDs were increasing in Silicon Valley because people with AS were meeting and mating with other people with AS within the confines of their respective technology-laden workplaces. There may be some truth to that theory but not enough to explain the increasing prevalence of ASDs all across the United States.

The tech fields do seem to have a draw for individuals with HFA/AS. Tony Attwood, an Australian psychologist who travels widely speaking about AS, emphasizes that individuals with ASDs can use their orderly thinking styles to find satisfying work in fields that require an ability to reason in an organized and systematic way.

There is another advantage to working in high-tech fields: the work does not require interpersonal skills. In the *Wired* magazine article, the benefits of techie work are expounded: "Autistic people have a hard time multitasking—particularly when one of the channels is face-to-face communication. Replacing the hubbub of the traditional office with a screen and an e-mail address inserts a controllable interface between a programmer and the chaos of everyday life. Flattened workplace hierarchies are more comfortable for those who find it hard to read social cues." Attwood comments that computers "are an ideal interest for a person with Asperger's syndrome . . . they are logical, consistent, and not prone to moods."

His belief that the disturbance in relating to others is innate or inborn (present "from the beginning of life") has been confirmed for children with known genetic causes of autism but is still a point of contention for the children with autism who do not show signs of autism until an average of 14–18 months (see Chapter 5 for more information about the "late-onset" or "regressive" subtype of autism).

Kanner felt that it was significant that the children in his case series were physically indistinguishable from TD children. Since Kanner's time, autism has been associated with many genetic syndromes and medical conditions, with approximately 10–20 percent of individuals with autism demonstrating physical features that are commonly seen in individuals with other developmental disabilities. That still leaves 80–90% of children with autism who fit Kanner's profile for physical appearance.

Finally, Kanner disagreed with the professionals who looked upon many of the children as "feebleminded" (a term that was replaced by "mentally retarded" and may soon be changed to "intellectual disability"). The children demonstrated skills that would not be expected in children with low intelligence, most commonly consisting of impressive abilities to memorize information and prowess with puzzles and other tasks requiring spatial problem solving. The presence of an uneven pattern of intellectual strengths and weaknesses has been observed repeatedly and is now commonly referred to as "splinter skills."

Finally, the observation that all of the autistic children in his series came from highly intelligent families may have been true for the parents who found their way to see Kanner at the prestigious Johns Hopkins hospital in the forties, before autism was widely recognized, but the observation is not true of the population as a whole. Autism cuts across all intelligence, socioeconomic, and ethnic barriers.

Given the fact that Kanner based all of his conclusions on observations of only eleven children over a time frame of just a few years, it is astonishing how little our core conception of autism has changed since that time. The fine art of description of clinical cases, as much a literary feat as a scientific one, has largely been lost in medical writing. Kanner's eloquent descriptions will stand for years to come as examples of the enviably astute powers of observation shown by the early giants in the medical and psychiatric fields by such notable contributors as Sir William Osler and Sigmund Freud.

Kanner laid the groundwork for understanding autism as a condition primarily defined by the inability to relate to people in the typical way. He was the first to note that the social disconnect was accompanied by communication oddities and preference for restricted and repetitive behaviors. The co-occurrence of problems in these three areas is still the basis for a diagnosis of autistic disorder.

HANS ASPERGER'S LONG-OVERLOOKED CONTRIBUTION

No discussion of autism would be complete without giving Dr. Hans Asperger his due. Asperger, an Austrian pediatrician based in Vienna, described four boys with social oddities in a 1944 paper published only in the German language. Although Asperger's work was published a year after Kanner's influential paper appeared in the U.S. medical literature, he was not aware of Kanner's work (not a particularly surprising situation given that World War II was in full swing in Europe, eventually leading to the destruction of Asperger's clinic). The full translation of Asperger's original paper is difficult to track down but can be located in Uta Frith's book *Autism and Asperger Syndrome* (Frith 1981, p. 37). Like Kanner's original paper, it is well worth the read. Asperger felt that the children in his case series had a unique disorder separate from Kanner's autism. However, a careful read of the paper reveals that all four of Asperger's patients easily meet the current criteria for autistic disorder rather than AS.

Asperger's paper languished in relative obscurity for decades. As a result, the "discovery" of autism was credited to Kanner, until a British psychologist named Lorna Wing brought Asperger's article to the attention of the non-German-speaking world. In 1981, Wing, the mother of an autistic child, published a paper entitled "Asperger Syndrome: A Clinical Account" based on Asperger's translated work (Wing 1981).

Asperger did not name the syndrome after himself; it was Wing who first proposed the name "Asperger syndrome." In her landmark paper, Wing summarized Asperger's observations and added her own perspective based on her accumulated clinical experience. She proposed three key features to differentiate AS from Kanner's autism:

1. Individuals with AS had relatively intact speech development (although she acknowledged that their speech was often socially inappropriate and they had persistent difficulties understanding complex meaning).
2. Children with AS were likely to make odd, one-sided social approaches, whereas children with autism were more often aloof.
3. Children with AS tended to amass facts on particular topics of interest rather than play repetitively with odd or unusual objects.

Wing noted that both children with AS and those with autism shared many other core traits, including difficulties using conventional gestures, unusual eye contact, few or unusual facial expressions, and odd-sounding vocal intonation. Although articles on AS in the mainstream press often emphasize that motor clumsiness is a feature of AS but not autism, there is no real basis for that generalization. In fact, Lorna Wing was astute enough to recognize early on that many children with autism also demonstrated motor awkwardness. Studies done since then show that motor awkwardness (sometimes referred to as "dyspraxia" or motor-planning problems) occurs at an equal frequency in AS and the other ASDs.

Despite Lorna Wing's success at bringing AS to the attention of researchers in the autism field, it took over ten years until AS was formally recognized as a separate diagnostic category in the *International Classification of Disease, Tenth Edition* (ICD-10) and *The Diagnostic and Statistical Manual of Mental Disorders, Fourth Edition* (DSM-IV).

The debate about whether AS is a distinct entity from autistic disorder started in earnest with Wing's 1981 paper and continues to this day. As the knowledge about autism and AS increases, more and more professionals have come to the conclusion that the effort to make a distinction between AS and HFA is ultimately futile and of limited utility. The discovery of a single gene defect that caused autism in one brother and AS in the other drives home the point that AS and autism are manifestations of the same underlying brain abnormality.

Multiple studies comparing groups of high-functioning individuals with autism (autistic individuals with normal intelligence who had early language delays but went on to develop functional language skills) to individuals diagnosed with AS (individuals with normal intelligence who did not demonstrate significant delays in early language acquisition) have consistently failed to demonstrate reliable differences between the two groups (Howlin 1997). AS, as currently defined, is not a valid construct. It makes little sense to continue to make the diagnostic distinction, but professionals are mandated to do so until the accepted rules governing diagnosis change (see Chapter 4 for the current system used to separate autism from AS).

BEYOND ASPERGER'S AND AUTISM: THE BEGINNING OF THE AUTISTIC SPECTRUM CONCEPT

In his seminal paper, Asperger wrote, "Once one has learnt to pay attention to the characteristic manifestations of autism, one realizes that they are not at all rare in children, especially in their milder forms." Asperger was right. For every individual diagnosed with autism, there are others who have similar deficits in social understanding who do not meet the criteria for a diagnosis of autism. The recognition of the existence of less obvious forms of autism created a dilemma for the professionals charged with the task of diagnostic evaluations: What diagnosis should be given to the individuals with variants of Kanner's classic autism?

Evolution of the DSM Classification System for ASDs

Over the years since Kanner first proposed the term early infantile autism, a confusing procession of diagnostic categories related to autism has been developed, revised, discarded, or replaced. Each adjustment to the available diagnostic labels for autism and related conditions came with specific rules governing usage as the experts struggled to devise a useful way to identify classic autism and its variants. A cursory inspection of the myriad diagnostic labels and categories that have come and gone makes it clear that developing a logical diagnostic system to make sense of autism and its variants has been a difficult, imprecise, and sometimes contentious process (see Table 1).

Kanner's First Diagnostic System

In 1956, Dr. Kanner and his colleague, Dr. Eisenberg, developed the first set of criteria that could be used by qualified professionals attempting to diagnosis

Table 1
Evolution of the DSM Diagnostic Class and Categories Related to Autism

DSM version:	DSM-I (1952)	DSM-II (1968)	DSM-III (1980)	DSM-III-R (1987)	DSM-IV (1994)	DSM-IV-TR (2000)
Changes made to DSM-ASD categories:	Autism not included	Autism not included	Autism introduced as one of the PDDs	Changes in criteria result in over-diagnosis of PDDs	Changes made to diagnostic criteria improve the accuracy of diagnosis	Explanatory text revised but no changes in the diagnostic criteria
Changes made in childhood Schizophrenia category:		+Schizophrenia, childhood type added (ASDs misdiagnosed as schizophrenia)	Childhood schizophrenia deleted			
Changes made in autism subcategories:			+PDDs: a new class of childhood-onset disorders	PDD categories condensed	PDD categories expanded	PDD categories retained without changes
		1. +Infantile autism, full syndrome	1. +Autistic Disorder	1. Autistic disorder	1. Autistic disorder	
		2. +Residual infantile autism	2. +PDD-NOS	2. PDD-NOS	2. PDD-NOS	
		3. +COPPD	COPPD deleted	3. +Asperger's disorder	3. Asperger's disorder	
		4. +Residual COPPD	Concept of a residual form abandoned	4. +Rett's disorder	4. Rett's disorder	
		5. +Atypical PDD	Atypical PDD subsumed under PDD-NOS	5. +CDD	5. CDD	

+ indicates that the diagnostic class or category appears in the DSM for the first time. COPPD = childhood onset pervasive development disorder; CDD = childhood disintagrative disorder; PDD = pervasive development disorder; NOS = not otherwise specified.

autism. Culled from Kanner's initial clinical descriptions and accumulated experience, the proposed criteria consisted of five features modified from his original descriptions (only the first two criteria were designated as absolute requirements for a diagnosis of autism): (1) a profound lack of affective contact with other people ("affect" refers to the outward expression of feeling or emotion); (2) an anxiously obsessive desire for the preservation of sameness; (3) a fascination for objects, which are handled with skill in fine motor movements; (4) mutism, or a kind of language that does not seem intended to serve interpersonal communication; and (5) the retention of an intelligent and pensive physiognomy ("physiognomy" is an outdated word used to describe the facial appearance of a patient) and good cognitive potential manifested, in those who can speak, by feats of memory or, in the mute children, by their skill on performance tests.

These criteria served as the only available diagnostic system for many years. Autism was not even mentioned in *DSM-I* (published in 1952) or *DSM-II* (published in 1968). The only diagnosis in *DSM-II* that came close to describing the disconnect from the social world seen in autism was "schizophrenia, childhood type." As a result, many children with autism were incorrectly diagnosed with childhood schizophrenia for lack of a better category.

Michael Rutter's Diagnostic Criteria

In 1978, Michael Rutter, an influential British child psychiatrist who continues to make major contributions to the field, proposed a set of diagnostic criteria that synthesized Kanner's work with the knowledge that had been gained in the intervening twenty years. He proposed a simplified diagnostic system with four essential features: (1) onset by two and a half years of age; (2) impaired and distinctive social development; (3) impaired and distinctive communication; and (4) unusual behaviors including, but not limited to, resistance to change, unusual responses to the environment, and motor mannerisms. Although Kanner described repetitive motor mannerism in his 1943 paper, for example, "jumping up and down in ecstasy" while watching a spinning top, Rutter was the first to call them "motor mannerisms" and include them in the diagnostic criteria. Rutter's criteria were used in the United Kingdom for most of the early studies of autism.

Synching the *DSM* with the *ICD*

Around the same time as Rutter proposed his criteria, the World Health Organization published criteria for autism in the 1979 *ICD-9*. The American Psychiatric Association (publishers of the *DSM*) made a commitment to develop criteria for the diagnosis of autism that would be compatible with those in the *ICD-9*. To accomplish that task and to make other changes that were long overdue, the American psychiatric classification system needed a drastic overhaul. Although there is now an updated version of *ICD-9* (*ICD-10*), the codes in the *DSM-IV-TR* continue to reflect *ICD-9* categories.

New Paradigms in the Evolution of Psychiatry: The *DSM-III*

The field of psychiatry in the United States underwent a major shift from highly theoretical models of developmental and mental health disorders toward a scientifically based categorization system with the implementation of the *DSM-III*. Dr. Robert Spitzer was the driving force behind the overhaul in his role as the head of the task force charged with revising the *DSM-II*. Spitzer called for a sweeping effort to develop a classification system that would facilitate clear communication amongst clinicians (independent of their theoretical orientation). Perhaps more importantly, Spitzer seized the opportunity to develop the *DSM* for use as a framework for research so that psychiatry could evolve as a science. To start the move toward evidence-based practice, Spitzer relied on the consensus of experts who used the limited research that was available at the time to construct an orderly diagnostic system that utilized patterns of symptoms that clustered together to created diagnostic categories. The goal was to form groups that were homogeneous (i.e., groups of affected individuals who all shared the same basic constellation of symptoms). His goal was to base future versions of the *DSM* on solid empirical evidence ("empirical evidence" refers to information that is gathered through observations and data collection).

Validity and reliability are the two key pieces of statistical information needed to determine if diagnostic criteria achieve the goal of dividing disorders into useful categories. "Validity" is a measure of whether or not a diagnostic category is truly separable from related categories. "Reliability" refers to whether or not clinicians using the specified criteria arrive at the same diagnosis.

THE PDDS

The *DSM-III*, published in 1980, officially recognized autistic disorder for the first time as part of a new class of disorders called the PDDs. The PDD category was intended to describe childhood conditions that shared, to varying degrees, "distortions in the development of multiple basic psychological functions that are involved in the development of social skills and language."

When the PDDs were first introduced as a class of disorders, there were five diagnostic labels to choose from: infantile autism, full syndrome; residual autism; childhood onset pervasive developmental disorder (COPDD); residual COPDD; and atypical pervasive developmental disorder.

Successive Revisions

In 1987, the PDD category was reorganized for the revised edition of the *DSM-III* (referred to as the *DSM-III-R*). Based on information gathered on the validity and reliability of the *DSM-III* criteria, the categories were reshuffled. COPDD and atypical pervasive developmental disorder were collapsed into a single category, PDD-NOS. The "full syndrome" and "residual syndrome" qualifiers were dropped, leaving only two categories in the PDD group: autistic disorder and pervasive developmental disorder not otherwise specified (also called "atypical autism").

PDD-NOS

"Not otherwise specified" (NOS) is a term that was added into the *DSM-III-R* as a replacement for the "atypical" designation used previously for a variety of conditions; it was not invented just for the PDDs. If an individual appears to have a condition that is closely related to a class of disorders (e.g., the PDDs) but does not meet the full criteria for any of the specific diagnoses within the category (e.g., autistic disorder), the NOS term is used. NOS is also used if there is uncertainty about whether or not the individual truly fits into the category or if there is something atypical about the course, such as late onset.

The specific rules used to decide whether PDD-NOS is the best-fit diagnosis for a child will be reviewed in Chapter 4. For now, it is enough to know that determining if a child's behaviors are severe enough to meet the threshold for a diagnosis of autism or are better described as PDD-NOS is a subjective process despite attempts to make the process more uniform.

Parental reaction to a PDD-NOS diagnosis spans the range from relief to frustration. Many parents receive the diagnosis with more relief than is warranted, interpreting PDD-NOS to mean that their child does not have autism (when the diagnosis is intended to indicate that the child has a closely related condition). Other parents are frustrated with the vague-sounding diagnosis that leaves them feeling as if they are stuck in limbo.

A significant factor fueling the dissatisfaction with the PDD-NOS diagnosis is that the diagnosis is used by professionals in widely uneven ways. Although some professionals do not make a diagnosis of PDD-NOS unless the individual is very similar to an individual with autism, others use the diagnosis if there is any hint of a resemblance to a child with autism. One clinician's autism may be another clinicians PDD-NOS or vice versa, and that is disconcerting to both parents and professionals.

Asperger's Disorder Added to the PDDs

AS was added to the *ICD-10* in 1992. Asperger's disorder was introduced into the *DSM* for the first time in 1994 with the release of the *DSM-IV* (see Table 2 for a comparison of the *ICD-10* and *DSM-IV* nomenclature).

Members of the panel charged with creating the diagnostic criteria for AS were not in complete agreement as to the validity of the AS category or the criteria to use for diagnosis. In the end, a decision was made to give the Asperger's disorder label to individuals with normal intelligence and no history of language delays when they demonstrate the same qualitative types of social deficits and restricted and repetitive behaviors seen in autism. A hierarchical rule mandates a diagnosis of autism instead of AS if autism can be given (autism trumps AS if adequate criteria are met for autism). (More information about the rules used to diagnose AS can be found in Chapter 4.)

Diagnostic chaos resulted from this somewhat arbitrary way to carve out the AS category. As a result, there has been extreme variability in the way professionals use the Asperger's disorder label. Many professionals assign a diagnosis of AS to any individual with PDD characteristics who has normal intelligence in the absence of language delays without even considering HFA as a diagnostic possibility.

Studies have demonstrated that at least one-third of individuals diagnosed with AS meet the criteria for a diagnosis of autism. Peter Szatmari, a prolific

Table 2
Comparison of the *ICD-10* and *DSM-IV* Classification Systems for ASDs

ICD-10	*DSM-IV*
Childhood autism	Autistic disorder
Atypical autism	Included under PDD-NOS
Rett's syndrome	Rett's disorder
Other childhood disintegrative disorder	Childhood disintegrative disorder
Overactive disorder associated with mental retardation and stereotyped movements	No corresponding *DSM-IV* category
Asperger's syndrome	Asperger's disorder
Other pervasive developmental disorder	Included under PDD-NOS
Pervasive developmental disorder, unspecified	Included under PDD-NOS

researcher in the psychiatry department at McMaster University in Canada, feels that the majority of individuals given a diagnosis of AS could be given a diagnosis of HFA under the current rules, making the attempt to separate AS from autism futile.

SIMILAR BEGINNINGS, DIFFERENT ENDINGS: RETT'S DISORDER AND CHILD DISINTEGRATIVE DISORDER

A controversial change was made to the PDD category in the *DSM-IV* with the addition of two other conditions, Rett's disorder and childhood disintegrative disorder (CDD), bringing the PDD category officially up to a total of five separate conditions. Although the *DSM* uses "Rett's disorder," most medical references to the disorder use "Rett disorder" or "Rett syndrome").

Both Rett syndrome and CDD are much less common than the other PDDs. Rett syndrome occurs only in females (there are males who have the mutated gene responsible for Rett syndrome but their developmental problems do not follow the Rett syndrome course). The most widely quoted statistic for the prevalence of Rett syndrome is one case per 10,000 female births. Advances in genetic diagnosis have revealed that the rate is probably much higher than previously suspected—approaching one case per 2,000 female births. CDD, also known as Heller's syndrome or disintegrative psychosis, is much less common than Rett syndrome. Only four hundred cases of CDD have been reported. CDD is rare in children who are diagnosed with ASDs. Out of every 100,000 children with one of the ASDs, only two meet the criteria for CDD.

Children with Rett syndrome may initially look like they have a regressive form of an ASD as they go through a sudden period of rapid loss of language and social connectedness. Eye contact is preserved, but the children often seem to be in another world. Children with CDD may also look like children with ASDs in the early toddler years. Both Rett syndrome and CDD are easily separated from ASDs over time because the conditions evolve quite differently from the ASDs.

Both conditions start out with a period of normal development, lasting between five to thirty months for Rett syndrome and at least two but less than ten years for CDD. The average age for onset is 6–18 months for Rett syndrome and 3 years for CDD. The main feature distinguishing Rett syndrome and CDD from the ASDs is the loss of previously acquired motor skills after the onset (usually more severe in Rett syndrome). In Rett syndrome, a characteristic pattern of midline hand movements (called "motor stereotypies") along with a slow-down in head growth both signal the clinician that an ASD is not the correct diagnosis. In CDD, the child undergoes a profound change from normal language, self-help skills, and cognition to a much lower functional level. Following the change, basic skills such as toileting are lost and subsequent development of skills proceeds slowly. Although loss of speech is seen in the regressive subtypes of ASDs, the child usually has no more than a five- or six-word vocabulary before the language regression and other functional skills are not affected. Widespread loss of skills is not seen at any time in autism, AS, or PDD-NOS. Any mistake in diagnosis should be easily recognized as the clinical course of Rett syndrome or CDD plays out (see Tables 3, 4, and 5 for the *DSM-IV* criteria for autistic disorder, PDD-NOS and AS).

Proponents of leaving Rett syndrome and CDD in the PDD category feel that evaluators need to keep these two conditions in mind to avoid making a diagnostic mistake. Recent studies have shown that the gene that causes Rett syndrome may be one of the many genes that play a part in causing the ASDs. Whether or not Rett syndrome and CDD stay in the PDD category remains to be seen. The important point to take away is that, when people refer to the ASDs, they mean autism, PDD-NOS, and AS; Rett syndrome and CDD are not included.

DSM-IV-Text Revision

The latest version of the *DSM*, released in 2000, is a "text revision" of the *DSM-IV* (*DSM-IV-TR*). No changes were made to any of the diagnostic categories. Changes were made to the text that accompanies the criteria to bring the descriptions up to date with our current understanding and to help clinicians using the manual.

Future Revisions of the DSM

Continual reassessment is ongoing to determine whether the separate diagnostic categories are "valid constructs," meaning that the specific diagnostic labels actually describe separable conditions that exists independently. The result of these studies influences whether or not a diagnostic category stays or goes. Additional refinement of these issues will undoubtedly influence the shape of the upcoming *DSM-V*, due out sometime around 2011–2012. The category at greatest risk for deletion or significant modification is Asperger's disorder, based on insufficient evidence proving that it is a valid construct since its inclusion in 1994.

ASDs Emerge into the Diagnostic Lexicon

Evidence is mounting that the ASDs cannot be reliably separated into discrete categories that will remain separate over the life span of the child.

Table 3
DSM-IV-TR Diagnostic Criteria for 299.0 Autistic Disorder

A. A total of six (or more) items from (1), (2), and (3), with at least two from (1), and one each from (2) and (3):

(1) qualitative impairment in social interaction, as manifested by at least two of the following:

    (a) marked impairment in the use of multiple nonverbal behaviors such as eye-to-eye gaze, facial expression, body postures, and gestures to regulate social interaction

    (b) failure to develop peer relationships appropriate to developmental level

    (c) a lack of spontaneous seeking to share enjoyment, interests, or achievements with other people (e.g., by a lack of showing, bringing, or pointing out objects of interest)

    (d) lack of social or emotional reciprocity

(2) qualitative impairments in communication as manifested by at least one of the following:

    (a) delay in, or total lack of, the development of spoken language (not accompanied by an attempt to compensate through alternative modes of communication such as gesture or mime)

    (b) in individuals with adequate speech, marked impairment in the ability to initiate or sustain a conversation with others

    (c) stereotyped and repetitive use of language or idiosyncratic language

    (d) lack of varied, spontaneous make-believe play or social imitative play appropriate to developmental level

(3) restricted, repetitive and stereotyped patterns of behavior, interests, and activities, as manifested by at least one of the following:

    (a) encompassing preoccupation with one or more stereotyped and restricted patterns of interest that is abnormal either in intensity or focus

    (b) apparently inflexible adherence to specific, nonfunctional routines or rituals

    (c) stereotyped and repetitive motor manners (e.g., hand or finger flapping or twisting, or complex whole-body movements)

    (d) persistent preoccupation with parts of objects

B. Delays or abnormal functioning in at least one of the following areas, with onset prior to age 3 years: (1) social interaction, (2) language as used in social communication, or (3) symbolic or imaginative play.

C. The disturbance is not better accounted for by Rett's Disorder or Childhood Disintegrative Disorder.

Reprinted with permission from the Diagnostic and Statistical Manual of Mental Disorders, Fourth Edition, Text Revision.

Table 4
DSM-IV-TR PDD-NOS 299.80 Pervasive Developmental Disorder Not
Otherwise Specified (Including Atypical Autism)

This category should be used when there is a severe and pervasive impairment in the
development of reciprocal social interaction associated with impairment in either
verbal and nonverbal communication skills, or with the presence of stereotyped behavior, interests, and activities, but the criteria are not met for a specific Pervasive Developmental Disorder, Schizophrenia, Schizotypal Personality Disorder, or Avoidant
Personality Disorder. For example, this category includes "atypical autism"—presenta-
tions that do not meet the criteria for Autistic Disorder because of late age at onset,
atypical symptomatology, or subthreshold symptomatology, or all of these.

*Reprinted with permission from the Diagnostic and Statistical Manual of Mental Disorders, Fourth Edi-
tion, Text Revision.*

Kanner's single category diagnosis (infantile autism) has been expanded and
contracted over the last 60 years to include as many as five different diagnostic
categories in the *DSM-III* or as few as two in *DSM-III-R*. This process is not
unique to ASDs. In any effort to develop a diagnostic system there is an active
tension between attempts to group like conditions together (as Kanner did
with infantile autism) and efforts to gain precision by splitting the group into
related but separable conditions. This process has played out in medicine over
and over and is a necessary exercise to establish the most useful balance
between those who wish to "lump" similar conditions together and those who
try to "split" the conditions. The struggles with diagnostic systems in the
DSM are not limited to the ASDs. There is a current backlash in psychiatry
that is moving the field away from the rigid adherence to categorical diagnoses
towards the recognition of spectrum disorders in a variety of conditions,
including obsessive-compulsive spectrum disorder, bipolar spectrum disorder,
and even schizophrenia spectrum disorder.

There are two main lines of evidence that are leading inextricably to the conclusion that it is time to abandon the strategy of splitting the ASDs into AD,
PDD-NOS, and AS in favor of lumping the ASDs together: diagnostic stability
for any specific PDD category is not as good as previously thought, and the agreement on the most appropriate categorical diagnosis is poor amongst clinicians.

Kanner realized that the behaviors of the children he described in his series
changed as time went on but he did not suggest that the underlying diagnosis
should be changed. Instead, he considered the children to have infantile autism with widely variant developmental trajectories that were influenced by a
multitude of factors. The current *DSM*-based diagnostic system used for diagnosing the PDDs works quite differently. A 2006 study from the University of

Table 5
DSM-IV-TR: Diagnostic Criteria for 299.80 Asperger's Disorder

A. Qualitative impairment in social interaction, as manifested by at least two of the following:

   (1) marked impairment in the use of multiple nonverbal behaviors such as eye-to-eye gaze, facial expression, body postures, and gestures to regulate social interaction
   (2) failure to develop peer relationships appropriate to developmental level
   (3) a lack of spontaneous seeking to share enjoyment, interests, or achievements with other people (e.g., by a lack of showing, bringing, or pointing out objects of interest to other people)
   (4) lack of social or emotional reciprocity

B. Restricted repetitive and stereotyped patterns of behavior, interests and activities, as manifested by at least one of the following:

   (1) encompassing preoccupation with one or more stereotyped and restricted patterns of interest that is abnormal either in intensity of focus
   (2) apparently inflexible adherence to specific, nonfunctional routines or rituals
   (3) stereotyped and repetitive motor mannerisms (e.g., hand or finger flapping or twisting, or complex whole-body movements)
   (4) persistent preoccupation with parts of objects

C. The disturbance causes clinically significant impairment in social, occupational, or other important areas of functioning.
D. There is no clinically significant general delay in language (e.g., single words used by age 2 years, communicative phrases used by age 3 years).
E. There is no clinically significant delay in cognitive development or in the development of age-appropriate self-help skills, adaptive behavior (other than in social interaction), and curiosity about the environment in childhood.
F. Criteria are not met for another specific Pervasive Developmental Disorder or Schizophrenia.

Reprinted with permission from the Diagnostic and Statistical Manual of Mental Disorders, Fourth Edition, Text Revision.

Michigan looked at stability of diagnosis between the initial evaluation at age two and follow-up evaluations at ages five and nine (Lord 2006). The study was done to answer the question of how sure clinicians can feel about ASD diagnoses at various ages. Overall, 33 percent of the children in the study were given a different diagnosis at age nine. AD was by far the most stable diagnosis. Of the children who received a diagnosis of AD at age two, 89 percent continued to be appropriately described by a diagnosis of AD at age nine. Children who received an initial diagnosis of PDD-NOS were much more likely to shift from one category to another: 50 percent moved up to autism,

40 percent continued to be best described by a diagnosis of PDD-NOS, and 10 percent moved off of the spectrum entirely. Other researchers have shown even higher rates of changes in the best-fit diagnosis over time. The fluidity of diagnosis suggests that there are no firm boundaries between the ASDs. If autism is viewed as a spectrum disorder, the results make more sense: for children diagnosed with an ASD before age two, the vast majority continue to have an ASD at age nine.

The second argument in favor of moving from a splitting strategy to lumping is that there is excellent agreement amongst clinicians experience in diagnosing ASD when they are asked to decide if an individual does or does not have an ASD. Conversely, the agreement is poor when clinicians are asked to compare their categorical diagnoses (AD, PDD-NOS, or AS). To acknowledge the nonstatic nature of the diagnostic labels, many clinicians are starting to describe their diagnostic impression as a "best-fit" or "best-estimate" diagnosis. The current diagnostic system for ASDs is not functioning optimally; adopting the spectrum disorder conception appears to be a reasonable way to address the current problems. The point that should never be forgotten is that one clinician's best-fit diagnosis will not necessarily align with another's, and there is no clear correct answer in many situations. Classic autism is easy for all to agree upon, but the dividing lines between autism and PDD-NOS, AS and HFA, and PDD-NOS and a non–spectrum disorder remain subjective. The current classification system must be followed until changes are made, but it needs to be recognized for what it is—a highly imperfect system.

Adverse Consequences of Maintaining the Categorical Approach to the PDDs

There is little gained but a great deal lost attempting to parse out autism, PDD-NOS, and AS. Parental and professional time is poorly utilized agonizing over the minute details that might land one individual in the autism category and another into the AS or PDD-NOS category at any specific point in time.

The idea of the autistic spectrum is increasingly becoming the preferred way to think of the PDDs as more and more professionals acknowledge that the potential for differences of opinion and unclear dividing lines make the categorical diagnoses imprecise. Attempting to draw lines where no clear borders exist does not benefit the system or the individual.

Undoubtedly, the worst consequence of making distinctions between the various PDDs is that the final diagnosis chosen by the clinician has serious repercussions with regard to the availability of support services. Although some forward-thinking states may provide identical services for children with any of the ASD diagnoses, many states provide specific government-funded services to those with autism but not to individuals with a diagnosis of

PDD-NOS or AS. There is absolutely no empirical evidence to support the notion that diagnostic categories determines intervention needs.

The tragic result of relying on categorical diagnoses to guide access to services is that many individuals in need of assistance miss out. The cracks in the system are easy to fall through. Although it is generally true that individuals with AS function at a higher level than individuals with autism or PDD-NOS, that generality cannot be extended to each and every person in the separate PDD categories. An individual with AS may look good on paper yet be unable to work or live alone without substantial supports in place, functioning no better in real life than a person with PDD-NOS or autism. A categorical diagnosis should never be used as a proxy for the extent of disability from a PDD. Limiting services based on the differentiation between categorical diagnoses that have been shown to have a high degree of variability over time and from clinician to clinician makes no sense. The money saved by limiting services for individuals with PDD-NOS and AS is false economy over the long haul.

THE EVOLUTION OF PSYCHOLOGY: FROM INTELLECTUALIZATION TO BIOLOGIC CAUSATION

Ideas about childhood mental health and developmental issues have evolved greatly since Kanner almost single-handedly introduced child psychiatry as a viable specialty with the publication of the first textbook on the subject in 1935. Over the intervening years, our understanding of the mind has moved away from the highly theoretical models of the psychoanalysts to a more scientifically based conception focused on observable behaviors. These conceptual changes are reflected in the successive versions of the *DSM*. Mental and developmental disorders are increasingly being recognized as neurologic phenomena that are governed by the same genetic and biological principles as those that control the development and function of other aspects of health. With time, it is likely that the *DSM* classification system will evolve to reflect our improved understanding. In the future, the diagnosis of ASDs may be based on measurable biologic features referred to as "biomarkers." Accelerated brain growth starting in the first year of life, abnormal levels of brain-related growth hormones in newborns, and markers of immune system activation are all potential leads currently under investigation for use as biomarkers. In the future, the DSM may evolve away from using descriptions of observable behavior clusters to a diagnostic system divided by the underlying biologic causes of the condition.

2

Screening for ASDs: Past, Present, and Future

I n the world of human disease, screening is the process of systematically looking to uncover the presence of an unsuspected disease before harm has been
caused, or at least as early as possible. Colonoscopy and mammography are
two well known from examples of screening tests. The goal for all screening is to
allow for the earliest possible intervention with the hopes of achieving the best
possible outcome ("outcome" is synonymous with "prognosis" in medical terminology). In the area of child development, screening is meant to accomplish the
same thing: identifying children with developmental problems at the earliest opportunity so that intervention can be started, with the goal being to achieve the
best possible prognosis.

Screening and early detection of all developmental delays are crucial for children because early intervention (EI) has been shown repeatedly to help children
function at a higher level. The existence of a large body of studies proving that EI
improves outcome in a cost-effective manner is the reason that the federal government continues to provide funding for programs such as Head Start and Early
Intervention. Unfortunately, the current screening practices in the United States
fall far short of the ideal. According to the CDC, 17 percent of children have
some type of developmental problem, yet less than 50 percent of these children
are identified by healthcare providers before they reach school age, resulting in

delays in identification and lost time for EI. Other developmental experts give the current system even lower marks, estimating that up to 80 percent of developmental and behavioral problems are not detected by primary care providers (PCPs).

ASDs are receiving quite a bit of attention lately, with a good deal of emphasis on early identification. The reason for the push is simple: evidence is mounting that the earlier an ASD is detected, the better chance there is for the child to do well. Early access to appropriate developmental services for ASDs can make an enormous difference in the quality of the child's life. Studies have shown that children with ASDs who receive EI services before age three and a half have better outcomes than children who are not recognized until age five (when most children start kindergarten). More recent studies have shown that children with ASDs who start EI before age three do even better. Two small pilot studies by independent researchers (Amy Wetherby at Florida State University and Sally Rogers at the University of California, Davis M.I.N.D. [Medical Investigation of Neurodevelopmental Disorders] Institute) showed improvements in the core behaviors of ASDs in children who received behavioral therapies before age two and a half (in Wetherby's study, the average age was eighteen months). As the age of diagnosis continues to come down, it is likely that upcoming studies will reveal that intervention started at the first sign of an ASD (perhaps as early as twelve months of age) will result in outcomes that are better still.

HOW WELL IS THE CURRENT SYSTEM IDENTIFYING ASDS?

Before autism became a household word in the twentieth century, most children with ASDs were not diagnosed until age five or older (higher-functioning children with ASDs were diagnosed much later in childhood, if they were diagnosed at all). A 1997 survey of almost 1,300 families of individuals with autism demonstrated that the average age of diagnosis was not until age six, despite the fact that most parents felt there was something wrong by eighteen months. Less than 10 percent of children were diagnosed when the parents first expressed their concerns. Ten percent were told to return if worries persisted or told that their child would "grow out of it." At a mean age of forty months, 40 percent had been given a formal diagnosis, 25 percent were told not to worry, and 25 percent were referred to a third or fourth professional for additional evaluation (Howlin 1997).

Even with the increased public awareness of ASDs, many children in the United States are still not been diagnosed until after their fourth birthday. A 2006 study using data from the CDC's Metropolitan Atlanta Developmental Disabilities Surveillance Program 2000 found that the average age that children with autism were first evaluated was at age four years, but the average age of diagnosis with an ASD was not until thirteen months later, when they were over five years old. Most children were first diagnosed with language delays or general developmental delay before their ASD was definitively diagnosed. Fortunately, there is strong evidence that the average age at diagnosis of an ASD is coming down, with the majority of children now receiving a diagnosis between the ages of two to three and a half (with reliable diagnoses made by experienced clinicians as early as eighteen months). Experts in ASDs and parents of children with ASDs both share the vision that ASDs can and should be detected as early as possible (see the comprehensive treatment of screening issues available at http://www.first signs.org/screening/asd.htm). Putting an effective system in place to promote early identification of ASDs requires that we take a look at the past, present, and future of developmental screening with specific attention to what has gone wrong with the early identification of ASDs and how the process can be improved.

GENERAL DEVELOPMENTAL MONITORING AND SCREENING IN THE HEALTHCARE SETTING

By far the most common source for developmental monitoring for U.S. children has been the child's pediatrician (a doctor who specializes in the care of children). Family practice doctors also participate in the care of a great many children, as do nurse practitioners and physician's assistants. All of these healthcare providers serve as PCPs.

The PCP who follows the child regularly is charged with the responsibility of detecting any developmental problems. The developmental areas regularly monitored are gross and fine motor abilities (e.g., sitting, crawling, walking, and the ability to manipulate small objects in a coordinated way), speech and language acquisition, and indicators of intelligence (referred to as "cognitive" abilities). Up until very recently, social and emotional development has not been monitored as well as the other developmental areas, but the increasing awareness of ASDs is motivating PCPs to correct that oversight.

A child who is not progressing as fast as expected in any developmental area should receive a more detailed developmental evaluation, but that does not always happen—at least not in a timely manner. How well PCPs perform their developmental monitoring responsibilities is highly variable, a fact that most parents should find disturbing. The adequacy of developmental monitoring depends entirely on the priorities set by the PCP and their personal ideas about what constitutes adequate attention to the task.

There are three general strategies commonly used to detect developmental issues. PCPs have always had a free hand in choosing which one to use (which is a large part of the reason that the detection of developmental issues has been sub-optimal). By far the most common approach (but clearly not the best method) has been for the PCP to ask pertinent questions about the child's developmental progress at regularly scheduled visits called "well-checks" or "well child visits." This method of developmental monitoring, referred to as "developmental surveillance," is popular amongst PCPs because it is based completely on their clinical judgment—the intuitive sense of whether or not a child has a significant problem developed over years of training and experience. The drawback of this method is that it depends entirely on the questions that the PCP chooses to ask. In the busy office setting with time pressures and the need to provide information on an ever-growing array of topics (e.g., immunization safety, dietary advice, and video and TV exposure) in addition to addressing all of the other parental concerns, the PCP usually asks only a few basic questions about the child's development. Often the questions are preprinted on the office note with check boxes for the PCP's use to document whether or not development is proceeding as expected. Review of the PCP records during ASD evaluations reveals that the boxes are frequently left blank or, worse, checked off as normal when that is not the case. It has been shown that parents often do not bring up their concerns if the PCP doesn't ask. The result is that far too many well-checks are completed without adequate attention directed to the child's developmental issues.

A more thorough developmental screen can be obtained by using a standardized general developmental screening tool designed to detect problems in the important developmental areas. For a test to be "standardized," it must be given to a large number of subjects with and without developmental problems to establish the borders between typical development and developmental delays (DD). For a standardized test to be appropriate for use, researchers must show that the instrument does a statistically acceptable job identifying the problems it was designed to detect.

Standardized general developmental screening tests can be used in one of two ways: administered only when the parent or PCP has a concern (referred to as "selective screening") or given to all children at all of the scheduled well-checks (referred to as "universal screening"). Universal screening is the strategy that is endorsed by the American Academy of Pediatrics (AAP) because it is unequivocally the best method for developmental monitoring, allowing for early intervention for a wide variety of developmental issues including, but not limited to, ASDs. Despite long-standing recommendations to use universal screening, pediatricians and other PCPs have not adjusted their office practice to incorporate universal screening, with less than 30% of pediatricians using any form of standardized testing. Although general developmental screening tests do not specifically screen for ASDs, a study of the Pediatric Evaluation of Developmental

Status (PEDS) test demonstrated that 78 percent of the children with an ASD scored in the range indicating that further evaluation was indicated. Not surprisingly, the failed items were in the sections that assessed language and social behaviors. General screeners do not identify the cause of the DD but they do alert the PCP to ask more in-depth questions, pay closer attention to the child, and obtain additional evaluations, vastly increasing the probability that an ASD diagnosis will be considered if appropriate. Unfortunately, PCPs balk at the use of standardized developmental tests because of their incorrect beliefs that testing is too time consuming and costly and their firm belief that they can do just as well by using their clinical judgment.

Clinical Judgment versus Standardized Testing

How well does clinical judgment fare? Not very well. A 2007 study published in the journal *Pediatrics* showed that pediatricians using clinical judgment at the twelve- and twenty-four-month visits failed to refer 67.5 percent of children who had developmental delays that were significant enough to qualify the children for free developmental intervention services provided by a federally mandated program called Early Intervention (Hix-Small 2007). That is an alarmingly high miss rate.

All available evidence points to the conclusion that much more good than harm comes from the use of standardized developmental screening tests. Although PCPs worry that too many unnecessary referrals result from the use of standardized developmental tests, their concerns are unfounded. What they should be worrying about is how many children with developmental delays they are missing by not using standardized tests. The "wait-and-see" approach is no longer a viable option for childhood developmental issues; too much is lost during the delay in recognition of significant developmental issues.

EFFORTS TO IMPROVE THE EARLY IDENTIFICATION OF ASDS: INCREASING AWARENESS OF EXPECTED SOCIAL-EMOTIONAL DEVELOPMENT

Instead of waiting for PCPs to make the long-hoped-for move to universal screening, a variety of innovative approaches have been developed to try to increase the early identification of ASDs. Two promising approaches that do not require standardized testing include efforts to educate parents and PCPs on the important language and social developmental milestones that can yield early clues to ASDs and the development of red flags list for ASDs.

Learn the Signs: Expanded Social and Language Developmental Milestones

In response to the incomplete review of development conducted by many harried PCPs, the CDC launched a program called "Learn the Signs. Act Early," available on the Web at http://www.cdc.gov/ncbddd/autism/actearly. The initiative aims to empower parents to follow their own child's progress and encourages them to bring concerns to their PCPs attention. The site provides a comprehensive list of developmental milestones that includes the usual questions about motor and cognitive development but also includes expanded lists of expected social, emotional, and language milestones (areas often given short shrift by healthcare providers). The milestones are listed for three time points in the first year (at three, seven, and twelve months) and then yearly up to age five.

The social-emotional milestones are particularly useful to alert parents to behaviors that should be present in children. Oftentimes, parents (particularly if the child is their first) do not realize that the child is not reacting to social situations in the expected manner. A twelve-month-old child who is not shy or anxious with strangers or does not cry when the mother or father leaves the room might be thought of as easygoing or good natured to someone who is not aware of the expected social-emotional developmental milestones. A more worrisome interpretation of these behaviors is that the child is failing to demonstrate the expected attachment to her parents. Parents might not notice if their twelve month old does not repeat sounds or gestures for attention or extend an arm or leg to get help when being dressed if they have not been told to expect that social behavior.

Language delays are almost always noted by parents, but often they are convinced by their PCP to wait far longer than necessary to have the child's language evaluated. Although most parents are aware that the age that most children use their first simple words (e.g., dada, mama, and uh-oh) is approximately twelve months of age, fewer parents realize that there are other important signs to monitor besides the use of first words. Long before a child's first word emerges, infants are trying to learn language. At seven months, the infant's effort to learn language allows him to learn to respond to his own name, use his voice to express pleasure (cooing, laughing) or displeasure, make sounds in response to sounds directed to him by adoring parents, start to recognize what "no" means, and babble joyful chains of consonant sounds (e.g., ba-ba-ba-ba or da-da-da-da) A child who has no words at twelve months but pays attention to spoken language and responds appropriately does not raise concerns nearly as much as a child who displays limited interest in or understanding of language.

The social-emotional and language development checklists developed by the CDC work together to showcase the myriad ways that infants and toddlers engage socially. At the bottom of the milestone lists for each age is a section called "Developmental Health Watch" that clearly lays out which missed milestones should prompt the parent to contact their PCP. In addition, the CDC website contains a section on how to talk to a healthcare provider about developmental concerns that is likely to be of great assistance to concerned parents.

The CDC campaign strongly emphasizes the point that loss of previously acquired language skills and/or appropriate social responsiveness comprises extremely worrisome signs that merit immediate attention. Although the most commonly recognized form of regression is loss of language, recent research has revealed that there is often a social regression—a drawing inward—that can occur without noticeable speech regression. Approximately fifty percent of individuals with ASDs undergo a loss of social relatedness, language regression, or both. Regression is a worrisome sign because loss of communication and social skills (without loss of motor abilities) is rarely seen in other developmental conditions (see Table 6 for the "Learn the Signs. Act Early." listing of behaviors that might be seen in children, adolescents, and adults with ASDs).

Red Flag Indicators for ASDs

"Red flags" for ASDs are behaviors that should alert parents—or anyone else interacting with the child—that they should consider an ASD as a possible explanation for the child's atypical development. The lists are intended to prevent the bottleneck that can occur when worried parents are unable to move forward with an evaluation because their PCP is not convinced that their concerns are valid (most PCPs are unaware of the studies showing that parents are right about 80% of the time when they suspect a developmental problem). There are many different red flag lists that have been compiled by various panels of experts and groups dedicated to early identification of ASDs.

In 1999, a panel of experts convened by the American Academy of Neurology and the Child Neurologic Society recommended immediate evaluation for an ASD if a child failed to meet any of the following expected developmental landmarks: babbling by twelve months, use of gestures (e.g., pointing and waving) by twelve months, single words by sixteen months, two-word spontaneous (not echolalic) phrases by twenty-four months, and any loss of any language or social skills at any age (Filipek, 1999).

First Signs, an organization devoted to improving the early identification of ASDs, used these guidelines to formulate the first widely distributed red flag list. Based on the work of Stanley Greenspan, a pioneering developmental

Table 6
CDC "Learn the Signs. Act Early." Indicators of a Possible ASD in Children and Adults

A child or adult with an ASD might

- not play "pretend" games (pretend to "feed" a doll)
- not point at objects to show interest (point at an airplane flying over)
- not look at objects when another person points at them
- have trouble relating to others or not have an interest in other people at all
- avoid eye contact and want to be alone
- have trouble understanding other people's feelings or talking about their own feelings
- prefer not to be held or cuddled or might cuddle only when they want to
- appear to be unaware when other people talk to them but respond to other sounds
- be very interested in people, but not know how to talk, play, or relate to them
- repeat or echo words or phrases said to them, or repeat words or phrases in place of normal language (echolalia)
- have trouble expressing their needs using typical words or motions
- repeat actions over and over again
- have trouble adapting when a routine changes
- have unusual reactions to the way things smell, taste, look, feel, or sound
- lose skills they once had (for instance, stop saying words they were once using)

Contact your child's doctor or nurse if your child experiences a dramatic loss of skills at any age.

Note: When considering the possibility that an adult might have an ASD, it is important to remember that signs of an ASD must have been present during early childhood. Adapted from the ASD Fact Sheet available at: http://www.cdc.gov/ncbdd/autism/actearly/autism.htl

pediatrician, two very early indicators of abnormal social development were added to the list: no big smiles or other warm, joyful expressions by six months; and no back-and-forth sharing of sounds, smiles, or other facial expressions by nine months. Loss of speech or babbling or loss of social skills at any age (regression) as an ominous sign was emphasized.

The red flags were welcomed by daycare providers, early childhood educators, and PCPs because of the ease of use. There was no test to administer, no forms to fill out, and no scores to calculate; all that was needed was the list and observation. With the red flags in hand, the parent has justification to insist on an evaluation, even if the PCP would rather wait and see. Although red flags for ASDs are a powerful tool to get the message out to the public, the utility of the list was limited by the absence of research supporting its use. The lists were devised with credible information, but no studies were done to answer the question of how well the red flags

Table 7
Red Flags Proposed by the First Signs Organization

The following red flags may indicate a child is at risk for an autism spectrum disorder, and is in need of an immediate evaluation.
In clinical terms, there are a few "absolute indicators," often referred to as "red flags," that indicate that a child should be evaluated. For a parent, these are the "red flags" that your child should be screened to ensure that he/she is on the right developmental path.

Red Flags of Autism Spectrum Disorders:
If your baby shows two or more of these signs, please ask your pediatric healthcare provider for an immediate evaluation.

Impairment in Social Interaction:

- Lack of appropriate eye gaze
- Lack of warm, joyful expressions
- Lack of sharing interest or enjoyment
- Lack of response to name

Impairment in Communication:

- Lack of showing gestures
- Lack of coordination of nonverbal communication
- Unusual prosody (little variation in pitch, odd intonation, irregular rhythm, unusual voice quality)

Repetitive Behaviors and Restricted Interests:

- Repetitive movements with objects
- Repetitive movements or posturing of body, arms, hands, or fingers

Wetherby, A., Woods, J., Allen, L., Cleary, J., Dickinson, H., and Lord, C. Early indicators of autism spectrum disorders in the second year of life. *Journal of Autism and Developmental Disorders*, (2004) 34: 473–93. Based on research at the Florida State University FIRST WORDS® Project. Used with permission from Amy Wetherby and First Signs, Inc.

fared in the quest for early identification of children with ASDs. To address this problem, the First Signs red flags were updated in March 2008 to reflect research on the early signs of ASDs in children twelve to twenty-four months of age conducted by Amy Wetherby and colleagues at Florida State University (see Table 7).

EFFORTS TO IMPROVE THE EARLY IDENTIFICATION OF ASDS: ASD-SPECIFIC SCREENING TESTS

Numerous standardized screening tools have been developed specifically for ASDs. A complete discussion of the available screening tests is not possible without a working knowledge of a few basic statistical concepts. The worth of a screening test is judged by its performance in three important statistical parameters: sensitivity, specificity, and PPV.

Sensitivity refers to the percentage of individuals with a condition (in this case an ASD) who will be detected by the screening test. The idea is to identify as close to 100 percent of the target population as possible. Tests that approach that goal are considered to have "high" sensitivity (high sensitivity is a desirable feature).

Specificity is a measure of how sure the clinician can be that the condition is not present when the test says it is not likely. High specificity ensures that most individuals who pass the test do not have ASD. Because it is not possible for any screening test to get it right 100 percent of the time, researchers consider 70 percent or greater sensitivity and specificity as the minimum for an acceptable test. The best screening tests have sensitivities and specificities closer to 80–90 percent.

PPV tells how likely it is that the child has an ASD if the screening test is positive. This is sometimes referred to as the "correct hit rate." A high PPV means that most children with ASDs are correctly identified by a positive screen (true positives are correctly identified) and most children who do not have an ASDs get negative results (true negatives are correctly identified). For a test to have a high PPV, there should be very few false positives (children who do not have ASDs that the test identifies as at-risk for ASD) and very few false negatives (children who really do have ASDs that the test fails to identify). A child is said to have "passed" the screening test if the test indicates a low probability of an ASD (also called a "negative" screen). The test is "failed" if the results suggest a high probability of an ASD (also called a "positive" screen).

Many screening tests for ASDs have been developed and piloted over the years. Two of the most widely known screening tests are the Modified Checklist for Autism in Toddlers (M-CHAT) and the Social Communication Questionnaire (SCQ) (see Table 8). Despite the extensive research that has gone into developing these screening tests, their use in a systematic way is not yet commonplace in general practice.

A 2004 survey of practicing pediatricians indicated that only 8 percent had used a screening test for ASDs. There are high hopes that the AAP guidelines for screening and diagnosis of ASDs, rolled out with great fanfare in the fall of 2007, will dramatically increase that number (Johnson, 2007). The AAP guidelines were widely hailed as a breakthrough in the fight for early identification of ASDs. The guidelines continue to recommend universal screening for general developmental issues at every well-check but take the significant step of recommending universal screening for ASDs at the eighteen- and twenty-four-month well-check visits. The idea behind the two separate

Table 8
Modified Checklist for Autism in Toddlers (M-CHAT)

Please fill out the following about how your child usually is. Please try to answer every question. If the behavior is rare (e.g., you've seen it once or twice), please answer as if the child does not do it.

1. Does your child enjoy being swung, bounced on your knee, etc.?
2. Does your child take an interest in other children?
3. Does your child like climbing on things, such as up stairs?
4. Does your child enjoy playing peek-a-boo/hide-and-seek?
5. Does your child ever pretend, for example, to talk on the phone or take care of dolls, or pretend other things?
6. Does your child ever use his/her index finger to point, to ask for something?
7. Does your child ever use his/her index finger to point, to indicate interest in something?
8. Can your child play properly with small toys (e.g. cars or bricks) without just mouthing, fiddling, or dropping them?
9. Does your child ever bring objects over to you (parent) to show you something?
10. Does your child ever look you in the eye for more than a second or two?
11. Does your child ever seem oversensitive to noise (e.g., plugging ears)?
12. Does your child smile in response to your face or your smile?
13. Does your child imitate you? (e.g., you make a face—will your child imitate it?)
14. Does your child respond to his/her name when you call?
15. If you point at a toy across the room, does your child look at it?
16. Does your child walk?
17. Does your child look at things you are looking at?
18. Does your child make unusual finger movements near his/her face?
19. Does your child try to attract your attention to his/her own activity?
20. Have you ever wondered if your child is deaf?
21. Does your child understand what people say?
22. Does your child sometimes stare at nothing or wander with no purpose?
23. Does your child look at your face to check your reaction when faced with something unfamiliar?

©1999 Robins, Fein and Barton. Used with permission.

M-CHAT scoring Instructions: A child fails the checklist when 2 or more critical items are failed OR when any three items are failed. Yes/no answers convert to pass/fail responses. Below are listed the failed responses for each item on the M-CHAT. Bold capitalized items are CRITICAL items.

1. No	6. No	11. Yes	16. No	21. No
2. NO	**7. NO**	12. No	17. No	22. Yes
3. No	8. No	**13. NO**	18. Yes	23. No
4. No	**9. NO**	**14. NO**	19. No	
5. No	10. No	**15. NO**	20. Yes	

If a child passes the M-CHAT, yet the parent and/or physician is still concerned about an ASD, the child should receive follow-up. (Given that no screening instrument can have 100% sensitivity, this is necessary to avoid missing cases.)

If a child fails the M-CHAT, the M-CHAT Follow-up Interview is recommended. This structured interview elicits details and examples of the child's behavior; use of the Interview reduces the false positive rate of the M-CHAT.

Free downloads of the M-CHAT, scoring instructions, and follow-up interview are available at Dr. Robins's website: http://www2.gsu.edu/~wwwpsy/faculty/robins.htm

screenings is to make sure that none of the children with ASDs slips by the screener before their behaviors become sufficiently abnormal to allow detection. The screening tests are intended for all children even if the parent does not express any concerns. If a PCP, parent, or other person familiar with the child is worried that a child might have an ASD, use of an ASD-specific screening test appropriate for the child's age is recommended. The PCP is free to choose the screening tool but it is likely that the M-CHAT will be the main test used between sixteen and thirty months because of the research supporting its use and the fact that the test has been made available free of charge.

M-CHAT

The autism-specific screening test currently used most commonly to screen young children is the M-CHAT, developed by Drs. Diana Robins, Deborah Fein, and Marianne Barton. The researchers developed the M-CHAT by modifying a 1992 test developed in the United Kingdom by Simon Baron-Cohen and colleagues, called "The Checklist for Autism in Toddlers" (CHAT). The CHAT was not sensitive enough for use as a screening tool for autism (meaning that it failed to identify too many children who really did have ASDs). The modified CHAT has a much higher sensitivity (the M-CHAT and complete scoring instructions can be downloaded for free from the First Signs website).

The M-CHAT was designed to be completed by parents in the waiting room at a child's routine twenty-four-month checkup as a universal screen (for all twenty-four month olds whether or not the parents had any suspicion that their child might have an ASD). The questionnaire contains twenty-three questions to be answered in a yes/no format based on parental observations. Behaviors seen in TD children are scored as a passing response, whereas behaviors associated with ASDs are scored as failing responses (a key is provided with the M-CHAT). Six items are designated as "critical items" because they statistically differentiate between TD children and children with ASDs. If a child fails two or more critical items or a combination of any three items, the child is considered to have failed the checklist. When the M-CHAT is failed, additional evaluation is recommended.

The M-CHAT has been shown to be a very good test for use in children ages sixteen to thirty months (it has been validated in statistical terms). It is important to note that the M-CHAT, like any screening test, can yield many false-positive results (a false positive means that the child fails the M-CHAT but does not actually have an ASD).

To try to reduce the false-positive rate, the researchers added a follow-up interview for each child who failed the M-CHAT. During the interview, all the failed items were reviewed. An easy-to-follow flow sheet allowed interviewers with minimal or no specific training in ASDs to determine whether the reported behaviors were the kinds of behaviors seen in ASDs or not. If the new information obtained did not support the original answer, the item was rescored as a pass.

The addition of the follow-up interview to clarify the questions more fully resulted in a significant reduction in the number of false-positive screens without a significant lowering of the sensitivity. The result was that far fewer children who did not have an ASD were given referrals for a comprehensive ASD evaluation (although the downside was that a few children with ASDs were wrongly screened out).

The problem the developers of the M-CHAT were trying to address by adding in a follow-up interview is the same problem every screening test faces. If the screening test is adjusted to reduce the number of incorrect referrals (also called "over-referrals" or false positives). The improved PPV is often obtained at the cost of decreased sensitivity.

When a follow-up interview was conducted for each failed M-CHAT, the PPV increased from 36 to 74 percent. In other words, the follow-up interview decreased the number of referrals for comprehensive ASD evaluation by almost 40 percent (without a significant change in sensitivity). That is a significant difference in the number of ASD evaluations that have to be done, which is an important consideration, given the huge demand for initial ASD evaluations with limited numbers of appropriately trained clinicians to do them.

The most likely reason that the follow-up interview improved the test performance so greatly is that it is extremely difficult to capture the complexity of the ASDs in simple yes or no questions. It is easy for well-intended parents to misconstrue the meaning of the questions when reading through them without additional explanation.

Parents do not always overreport abnormalities on screening tests; sometimes they underreport, perceiving their child's behavior to be typical when it is not. The answers given depend entirely on the perspective of the person filling out the questionnaire, and different people have different interpretations about what they observe. For this reason, the authors of the M-CHAT caution that a passing score on the M-CHAT should not be interpreted to mean that a child definitely does not have an ASD. If the parents or PCP remain concerned, a referral should be made for a comprehensive ASD evaluation.

The 2007 AAP guidelines recommend using the M-CHAT at both the eighteen- and twenty-four-month visits to detect ASDs. Eighteen months is the well-check closest to the earliest age that the M-CHAT has been approved for use (sixteen months). The second administration is intended to avoid missing children who regress between eighteen and twenty-four months.

The guidelines were developed before the information about the follow-up interview was available. As a result, the use of the M-CHAT as recommended by the AAP will result in a high percentage of comprehensive evaluations that do not show an ASD. Some professionals consider these excess evaluations to be a waste of resources. In truth, the situation is analogous to what happens when general screening tests identify children who do not turn out to have severe developmental delays. The children who fail screening tests may not have the problems the tests were designed to detect but, more often than not, they have developmental issues that will benefit from recognition and intervention.

SCQ

The Social Communication Questionnaire (SCQ) is a screening test that was adapted by Michael Rutter, Anthony Bailey, and Catherine Lord from a lengthy interview called the "Autism Diagnostic Interview (ADI)—more about the newer version of the ADI (ADI-R) later in Chapter 4. The SCQ was introduced as the Autism Screening Questionnaire (ASQ) but has since been renamed. The SCQ was developed using children, adolescents, and adults. The lowest age range for the SCQ is forty-eight months, leaving a gap between the upper age range of the M-CHAT (thirty months) and the lowest age for the SCQ. Like the M-CHAT, the SCQ is formatted as yes/no questions, with a total of forty questions on the test. There are two versions of the SCQ available: a "Current" form designed to assess short-term behavioral changes and a "Lifetime" form that includes questions about the individual's complete developmental history. Many of the questions in the Lifetime form focus on the time period between the ages of four and five, when many of the features of ASDs are most prominent. Referral for a comprehensive ASD evaluation is recommended for anyone who scores at or above fifteen on the Lifetime form of the SCQ. Scores between fifteen and twenty-one correlate with the diagnosis of PDD-NOS, while scores of twenty-two or greater are suggestive of a diagnosis of autism. When the suggested cutoff is used, the correct hit rate for the SCQ is 65 percent (meaning that two out of every three children who fail the SCQ will turn out to have an ASD). Other researchers have suggested that the cutoff should be lowered for children less than eight years of age because they can be missed if the standard cutoffs are used.

Screening Tests for AS

Asperger's disorder is the most controversial and the least well defined of all of the ASDs. Because of the inconsistency in how examiners perceive AS, it should come as no surprise that the available screening tests are the least valid and reliable of all the screening tests for the ASDs. Screening for AS is not specifically addressed in the 2007 AAP guidelines (see the next section for details on the guidelines).

Most individuals with AS are identified at a later age than children with autism or PDD-NOS because their oddities of language and deficits in social skills are not as obvious when they are younger. Studies have shown that the commonly used screening tests for ASDs tend to miss more children with higher IQ and milder symptoms, the group most likely to contain individuals with AS or HFA.

A 2005 analysis of the available AS screening tests, conducted by Sally Ozonoff, Ph.D., and colleagues, revealed multiple problems with the available screening tests, most notably the lack of standardization and the inability of the screening tests to distinguish between AS and HFA. A broad screening test for ASDs is recommended over a test that claims to identify AS.

What Conclusions Can Be Drawn from Screening Test Results?

Sorting through the statistics on the sensitivity, specificity, and PPV for screening tests is a tedious but necessary process to drive home the point that screening tests are not designed to provide a diagnosis. Screeners are meant to make the first rough cut between individuals with a high or low risk for a specified condition. A failed screening test confirms that it is reasonable to proceed with further evaluation but a passing score on a screening test does not guarantee that the condition is absent. Anytime there is a strong suspicion that an individual has an ASD, they should receive a comprehensive ASD evaluation to definitively answer the question.

Of equal importance is the understanding that a positive screening test should never be interpreted as proof that the individual has an ASD. Screening tools are designed to be more inclusive than diagnostic tests. Roughly one third of the individuals who screen as being at risk for ASDs on the M-CHAT and SCQ do not have an ASD. The significance of screening tests for ASDs must be adequately understood by PCPs, teachers, and other professionals so they can relay the appropriate information to parents who want to know what the screening results mean for their child.

SCREENING FOR ASDS IN CHILDREN LESS THAN EIGHTEEN MONTHS OF AGE: CURRENT RESEARCH

For children younger than sixteen months, there are currently no proven autism-specific screening tests. There is tantalizing evidence coming from a number of different sources that screening for children at twelve months of age may soon be possible (perhaps even as young as six to nine months of age).

Video Studies

Red flag lists are an effort to fill the void in standardized screening tests for younger children. The development of the red flag lists would not have been possible without the groundbreaking research on the early signs of ASDs gleaned from early childhood videos. Researchers came up with the ingenious idea of studying family videos of children later diagnosed with ASDs to find clues about the earliest signs of ASDs. Using videotapes taken during first birthday parties, investigators were able to detect four main differences in the social behaviors demonstrated by children who went on to be diagnosed with an ASD compared with TD children. The social behaviors that were reduced in frequency consistently across the various studies were eye contact, pointing to objects of interest, showing objects of interest, and responding to name. Subsequently, researchers studying earlier videos found that these social deficits were present as early as eight to ten months of age. Additional studies revealed that only two of the four behaviors differentiated children with ASDs from children with other DDs; children with ASDs looked at faces less and oriented to name less frequently.

In 2004, Amy Wetherby and colleagues studied videotapes of children ages twelve to twenty-four months taken during the behavior sample portion of a language test called the Communication and Symbolic Behavior Scale (CSBS). Three groups were included in the study: children with ASDs, TD children, and children with other developmental disabilities (DDs). Thirteen observable behavioral patterns were statistically proven to differentiate children with ASDs from TD children (see Table 9). Four of the thirteen behavioral features that differentiated children with ASDs from TD children failed to differentiate children with DDs from children with ASDs (see Table 4). This study should help clinicians who conduct ASD evaluations and other professionals faced with the extremely difficult task of separating behaviors commonly seen in individuals with to all DDs from those that are more likely to indicate the presence of an ASD.

Infant Sibling Studies

Current research directed toward refining the ability to detect the earliest indicators of ASDs is largely focused on prospective, longitudinal studies of babies who have one or more siblings with an ASD. Siblings of children with ASDs have a much higher chance of developing autism than other children (see Chapter 5 for more detailed statistics). The higher risk in siblings

Table 9
Differentiating between ASDs and Other DDs in Children Twelve to Twenty-Four Months of Age: Nine Research-Based Red Flags

---

ABSENCE OF EXPECTED BEHAVIORS (observed more frequently in children with ASDs compared with TD and DD children):

(1) lack of appropriate gaze
(2) lack of warm, joyful expressions with gaze
(3) lack of sharing enjoyment or interest
(4) lack of response to name
(5) lack of coordination of gaze, facial expression, gesture, and sound
(6) lack of showing

PRESENCE OF UNEXPECTED BEHAVIORS (observed more frequently in children with ASDs compared with TD and DD children):

(7) unusual prosody
(8) repetitive movements or posturing of body, arms, hands or fingers
(9) repetitive movements with objects.

ABSENCE OF EXPECTED BEHAVIORS (observed with equal frequency in ASDs and DDs)

(1) lack of response to contextual cues (e.g., the request "Give it to me" accompanied by an open-handed reach)
(2) lack of pointing
(3) lack of vocalizations with consonants
(4) lack of playing with a variety of toys conventionally (i.e., failure to play with toys the way they were intended to be played with).

Adapted from Wetherby, A., Woods, J., Allen, L., Cleary, J., Dickinson, H., and Lord, C. Early indicators of autism spectrum disorders in the second year of life. *Journal of Autism and Developmental Disorders*, (2004) 34: 473–93. Used with permission from Dr. Amy Wetherby.

translates to more of the study participants developing an ASDs, which gives the researchers more information to work with. The baby siblings are enrolled in the studies as early as possible (some studies are even asking pregnant mothers to enroll their infants so that blood tests can be done on the mother during the pregnancy to look for hints as to the causes of ASDs). The infants are carefully followed for any sign that they may be developing an ASD. As the study progresses, the children with signs of a possible ASD are diagnosed as soon as it is clear that they have an ASD. Leads that may be useful for the early identification of ASDs are starting to come out of these sibling studies.

In the infant sibling study ongoing at the UCD M.I.N.D. Institute under the direction of Sally Ozonoff, careful observations of the infants through six months of age failed to reveal any detectable differences between the babies who went on to develop autism and those who did not. Between nine and fifteen months of age, the babies who eventually were diagnosed with an ASD showed a diminishing interest in social engagement, decreased joint attention, and less social use of eye contact. Over the same time period, the infants with autism showed diminishing vocalizations with slowing of receptive and expressive language development. In some but not all of the children, unusual patterns of looking at and manipulating objects were apparent by 12 months. None of the children with autism showed a sudden regression. Other infant sibling studies are yielding similar basic observations. Research is now ongoing to follow up on the preliminary findings in an attempt to determine which behaviors can be used as the basis for an early identification test.

Response to Name at Twelve Months of Age as a Possible Early Sign of ASDs

As part of the ongoing infant sibling study at the University of California, Davis M.I.N.D. Institute, researchers asked if failure to respond to name at twelve months (one of the signs of an ASD noted in the video analyses of first-year birthday parties) could be used as a simple screening test for ASDs. What they discovered was that failure to respond to name predicts the presence of an underlying developmental problem, but the finding is not specific to ASDs.

Seventy-five percent of the children who failed the test were diagnosed with autism, general developmental delays, behavioral problems, or social-communication problems at twenty-four months of age. The test did not turn out to be very sensitive for ASDs, detecting only half of the children who were later diagnosed with an ASD. The test had poor specificity. About one-third of the children who were eventually diagnosed with an ASD passed the test at age twelve months, indicating that caution should be taken to ensure that the possibility of an ASD is not discarded just because a child responds to her name.

Early Eye-Gaze Abnormalities

Using a sophisticated technique to track exactly where children are looking, Ami Klin and colleagues at the Yale Child Developmental Center showed that children are more interested in viewing movement than they are in viewing scenes that have social meaning as early as fifteen months of age (see the discussion of eye contact in Chapter 4 for more complete details about the Yale University eye-gaze studies).

In 2007, a study done by researchers at the M.I.N.D. Institute found that approximately one-third of children at high risk for an ASD have abnormalities of eye-to-eye gaze at six months of age. These infants focused more on the mother's mouth, missing the opportunity to interpret her social facial expressions. Many professionals feel that the failure to view the other parts of the face that provide important social information leads to "missed opportunities to learn," resulting in the poor understanding of facial expressions seen in individuals with ASDs.

Infant-Toddler Checklist as an Early Screen for ASDs

Amy Wetherby and Barry Prizant, both experts in speech and language issues for children with ASDs, developed a language test for children ages six to twenty-four months called the Communication and Symbolic Behavior Scales—Developmental Profile (CSBS-DP). The test is designed to detect the presence of language delays and identify children who are at a high risk for developing language delays. One of the components of the CSBS-DP is the infant-toddler language checklist, a brief form that takes parents about ten minutes to complete (available free of charge at http://www.firstsigns.org). Although this test is not specifically a screen for ASDs, research shows the test had a very high sensitivity for ASDs when used during the second year of life (94.4 percent).

AAP 2007 GUIDELINES FOR SCREENING AND IDENTIFICATION OF ASDS

The 2007 AAP guidelines for screening of ASDs use a complex flow chart to direct the PCP through the universal screening process and the proper use of ASD-specific screening tests. The AAP recommends that practitioners use a screening test that is specific for ASDs for all children at eighteen- and twenty-four-month visits and any other time a concern is raised. A variety of screening tests are listed in the AAP recommendations as having adequate sensitivity and specificity, but the statistical performance on the approved tests is not equal. For example, the CHAT—the precursor to the M-CHAT—is listed as an option, but the test fails to detect a large number of children with ASDs (unacceptable sensitivity). PCPs should choose their screening test carefully to avoid missing children with ASDs.

Will Healthcare Providers Follow the 2007 Screening Guidelines from the AAP?

The new AAP guidelines hold promise for the future, if only healthcare providers will follow them. The guidelines are an extremely well-thought-out road map for practitioners grappling with the issues surrounding early identification of ASDs, but busy clinicians often acknowledge guidelines and then return to their old habits.

As guidelines proliferate, many, if not most, fail to make an impact on clinical practice, a state of affairs that experts who labor over guidelines have had to contend with. To complicate the situation further, each type of healthcare professional has its own guiding organizations. Pediatricians have the AAP, family practitioners have the American Academy of Family Practice, and nurse practitioners have their own organizations, as do physician's assistants and school psychologists. Many pediatricians will not follow the AAP guidelines to the letter, but most will at least consider the information. But what about all of the PCPs who are not pediatricians? Will they change their practice habits? It is too early to say how many PCPs will follow the 2007 AAP guidelines, but most big changes in clinical practice take time to become the status quo. Parental awareness and concern about ASDs will undoubtedly speed the process.

To try to force adherence to the ASD screening guidelines, there is a movement afoot in several states to tie reimbursement for health-care services to the successful completion of screening for ASDs. However, there are limitations to how much the legislature can strong-arm PCPs. The legislature only has the power to issue healthcare directives for programs that receive state and federal funds (e.g., state health departments, Medicaid, or other government-subsidized healthcare plans for children). Legislation alone will probably not change the habits of the average healthcare provider, but an increased awareness of why the traditional approaches to screening fail children with ASDs may motivate PCPs to change their habits.

3

Diagnostic Evaluation for ASDs Part 1: Getting Started

Many paths can lead to the point where an ASD evaluation is sought out. Once the decision to obtain a comprehensive diagnostic evaluation for an ASD is made, the long and often frustrating process of finding a way to obtain a high-quality evaluation begins.

SOURCES FOR COMPREHENSIVE ASD DIAGNOSTIC ASSESSMENTS

There are four main options available for persons seeking comprehensive ASD evaluations: government-funded evaluations available through EI programs or other service systems for individuals with DDs, evaluations from a university-based specialty clinic, and evaluations from psychologists or developmental pediatricians in private practice; and evaluations through the public schools system. The cost to the family varies dramatically depending on the system selected.

EI Programs and Support for Other DDs

The most economical option to obtain a comprehensive evaluation is to take advantage of the free developmental services offered locally through a combination of state and federal funding. The passage of two important legislative acts in 1990 created the current developmental service system: the Americans with Disabilities Act of 1990 and Public Law 105–17, the Individuals with Disabilities Education Act Amendments of 1997. All states are mandated to provide EI services for children with developmental delays (from birth through thirty-five months) and a free appropriate public education for eligible children with disabilities from the age of thirty-six months through a state-determined age cutoff (usually at age twenty-two). A developmental services system (separate from the schools) must also be provided for persons with substantially handicapping DDs from age three throughout the life span.

If an individual is suspected of having an ASD before age three, the EI system provides the assessment. If the suspicion of autism does not arise until after three, the state system for developmental disabilities provides an appropriate evaluation without cost. Each state has a different way of fulfilling the federal mandates through various state agencies (including agencies specifically designated to serve persons with DDs, special education services, mental health services, and a host of other state agencies working in cooperation, although the cooperation part is sometimes more of a concept than it is a reality). All that is needed to access an assessment through EI or government-funded agencies for individuals with ASDs is a request for evaluation from a concerned parent. Many parents are not aware that they do not have to wait for a referral from the PCP to access an evaluation.

University-Based Clinics, Private Practice Developmental Pediatricians, and Private Practice Clinical Psychologists

For families or individuals who do not wish to go through one of the government-funded programs, evaluations for ASDs can be obtained through specialty clinics affiliated with university hospitals and other large healthcare systems, or from properly trained developmental pediatricians, and psychologists in the community. Some psychiatrists conduct diagnostic evaluations for ASDs, but most psychiatrists in private practice do not follow the procedures generally considered to be necessary for comprehensive best-practice evaluation. For most people, the available options are limited by insurance coverage. Private pay is always an option but not a realistic one for many people who cannot afford the high cost of an ASD evaluation (roughly $800 to $2000 or more). For the majority of people dealing with private insurance, accessing a timely evaluation for an ASD is not a simple task for a variety of reasons.

ASDs were once considered psychiatric disorders but are now recognized as neurodevelopmental disorders. Unfortunately, the health insurance system is lagging behind in recognizing that ASDs fit better into the category of medical conditions than they do in the psychiatric category. As a result of the failure to make this adjustment, evaluations for ASDs are often not covered by a family's medical health insurance. Change in this area has been slow to come, primarily because the health insurance agencies have no incentive to modify their antiquated systems: they do not want to pay for these costly evaluations. In fact, many health insurances have exclusionary clauses stating specifically that services related to autism will not be covered.

Spurred on by grassroots activists and major advocacy organizations, more and more states are passing legislation to ensure that health insurance companies cover diagnostic and treatments services for individuals with ASDs, a process that will ultimately result in increased access to treatment (at least for those individuals lucky enough to have private insurance). The cost to the healthcare system is not inconsequential and will likely lead to further increases in premiums.

Public School ASD Evaluations

Autism was added as a separate eligibility category for special education in 1990 under the IDEA. Before 1990, most children with ASDs were eligible for special education under speech and language impairment or MR. Data was not kept on ASDs—the main reason that school statistics cannot be used to track changes in the rate of ASDs). For special education purposes, autism was defined in the IDEA (P.L. 101–476) as follows: "A developmental disability significantly affecting verbal and nonverbal communication and social interaction, generally evident before age 3, that adversely affects a child's educational performance. Other characteristics often associated with autism are engagement in repetitive activities and stereotyped movements, resistance to environmental change or change in daily routines, and unusual responses to sensory experiences." The explosion of children with ASDs carried in the school system has led to school psychologists increasingly becoming involved in ASD evaluations. School psychologists are not typically trained to use the DSM for diagnosis, relying instead on the IDEA criteria to determine eligibility for special education services. Although some school psychologists and interdisciplinary team members have taken it upon themselves to achieve competency using diagnostic tests recommended for comprehensive diagnostic evaluations, most school evaluations do not give a specific ASD diagnosis based on the *DSM-IV* criteria. To differentiate between autism, PDD-NOS, and AS, a second evaluation by a developmental pediatrician or psychologist is usually required. The need for an additional evaluation to satisfy other agencies with different eligibility criteria can be very frustrating for parents, especially if there is a difference of opinion between the evaluators. To improve the situation, more and more school districts are collaborating with other agencies to perform joint evaluations, to process that greatly improves communication for all involved.

COMPONENTS OF A COMPREHENSIVE ASD EVALUATION

Consensus guidelines detailing the necessary and sufficient components of comprehensive ASD evaluation have been published by many different sources over the years. Dr. Pauline Fillipek, a pediatric neurologist at University of California, Irvine, was the lead author of a widely endorsed consensus guideline published in 1999 (Fillipek, 1999). Since then, many states have published their own "Best Practice Guidelines" based on independent reviews of the evidence by expert panels. An excellent example is the comprehensive 184-page document produced by the state of California entitled *Autism Spectrum Disorders: Best Practice Guidelines for Screening, Diagnosis and Assessment* (available online at http://www.ddhealthinfo.org/documents/ASD_Best_Practice.pdf). Other countries, including the United Kingdom and Canada, have also produced similar guidelines based on recommendations from expert panels.

A 2005 paper by Sally Ozonoff and colleagues entitled "Evidence-Based Assessment of Autism Spectrum Disorders in Children and Adolescents" reviews the evidence supporting the various tests used for screening and diagnosis and puts forth recommendations for the core components and supplemental evaluations that should be completed as part of a comprehensive ASD assessment (Ozonoff, 2005). The most up-to-date guidelines were rolled out by the AAP in November 2007, accompanied by wide media coverage (available at http://www.pediatrics.org/cgi/content/full/120/5/1183). All of the guidelines are in agreement that a high-quality diagnostic evaluation for an ASD should include the following components: (1) a comprehensive review of the individual's medical and developmental history, (2) use of the current *DSM* (or *ICD*) diagnostic criteria for ASDs, and (3) use of a standardized observation instrument. The final diagnosis is based on review of all of the available information by an experienced clinician (or teams of clinicians). The synthesis of the information necessary to come up with the best-fit diagnosis for the individual is the part of the process that is most dependent on the experience of the examiner.

Assessment of many other pertinent areas is strongly recommended (e.g., physical exam, appropriate laboratory testing, a standardized speech and language evaluation, IQ testing, and assessment of adaptive behaviors). These assessments are absolutely necessary for planning purposes, but a clinician can gather enough information to make an accurate diagnosis through an interview with the parents and observation of the individual even if some of the supplementary evaluations are not yet available.

MEDICAL HISTORY

The core areas covered in the medical history are birth history (including exposure to any medications, drugs, or alcohol the mother may have used during pregnancy), delivery, complications in the newborn period, significant illnesses or medical conditions, mental health history, medication use, and family history.

If the person being evaluated for an ASD has a medically significant birth history or significant illness as a baby, it is possible for the child's development to be affected. Parents commonly wonder if birth-related occurrences could be the cause of their child's developmental problems, particularly if the labor was lengthy, forceps were used, the infant's heart rate was down temporarily, the cord was wrapped around the infant's neck, the infant did not initially breathe well on its own, or the infant developed jaundice. Although all of these developments are scary for parents, none of these situations are medically significant complications. The types of medical problems that can affect development are the life-threatening problems that result in prolonged hospitalizations with evidence that there is a problem with the infant's neurologic status during the hospitalization. For example, if an infant has enough oxygen deprivation to cause serious problems, the baby is usually limp and unresponsive for a lengthy period of time (ranging from several hours to days). During the hospitalization, the infant may have seizures or the EEG may show slowing of brain activity. Other major medical complications at birth include a complicated course due to prematurity or infection. Fortunately, not all infants who suffer these complications will have lasting developmental problems—many will recover completely. The point to remember is that it takes a serious medical complication in the newborn period to cause long-lasting developmental problems. The medical history gives the evaluator clues about possible causes of the individual's developmental problems but the medical details do not influence the final diagnosis. A child who meets the diagnostic criteria for an ASD will receive that diagnosis independent of the presence or absence of any significant medical issues. Many clinicians in the ASD field feel that there is a substantive difference between children with ASDs who have GDD related to medical conditions and children without any obvious medical problems whose delays are restricted to communication and social behaviors (Benaron, 2004). Perhaps medical issues will one day be used to divide the autistic spectrum into subtypes but that is not the current practice (see the discussion of subtyping the autistic spectrum by medical features in Chapter 4 for more information).

When obtaining information on family history for an ASD evaluation, it is important to determine if any family members have ASDs or are suspected of having an undiagnosed ASD. Other relevant conditions include speech delays, learning disabilities, ID, mental health disorders (including schizophrenia, bipolar disorder, depression, anxiety, OCD, and ADHD), or any known genetic syndromes. Family history is extremely important in ASDs because of the strong evidence pointing to a wide variety of genetic causes of ASDs. The presence of another child with an ASD in the immediate family strongly increases the chance that others in the same family will have an ASD or a related condition (see the section on recurrence rates for ASDs in Chapter 6 for more information).

IMPORTANT MEDICAL CONDITIONS ASSOCIATED WITH ASDS

Epilepsy

Seizure disorders (also referred to as "epilepsy") occur in some, but not all, individuals with ASDs. The most commonly quoted statistic is that 20–25 percent of all individuals with ASDs will develop epilepsy during their lifetime. However, that statistic does not tell the whole story. All individuals with ASDs do not have the same risk of developing a seizure disorder. Some individuals with ASDs have a relatively small chance of developing epilepsy, whereas others have a substantial risk.

A 2004 study looked at the risk of developing epilepsy in subgroups of individuals with ASDs. For the group that had no complicating medical factors (referred to as the "idiopathic" or "primary autism" group), the overall chance of developing epilepsy was 7.4 percent. The degree of MR influenced the epilepsy rate, with higher rates of epilepsy seen in the individuals with severe ID (15 percent) compared with those with moderate ID (3 percent). The risk of epilepsy was much higher in the group with a known medical cause of their epilepsy (referred to as the "secondary autism" group), in which 55 percent had epilepsy. The authors concluded that it was not autism itself that is associated with epilepsy but the associated underlying brain dysfunction and level of impairment.

Landau-Kleffner Syndrome

A condition that bears mentioning during any discussion of seizures and ASDs is Landau-Kleffner syndrome (LKS), not because it is common but because it is frequently brought up as a possible alternative diagnosis when children are evaluated for an ASD. LKS is a seizure disorder that starts in childhood (usually between ages three and seven) and results first in the inability to understand language, followed by loss of the ability to speak. LKS is also called "acquired aphasia with epilepsy" ("aphasia" means absence of speech). All of the children who have developed LKS were developing perfectly normally before the onset of symptoms, with well-developed expressive speech. Children with LKS do not look similar to children with ASDs to an experienced examiner. These children usually demonstrate a strong desire to communicate using nonverbal communication (NVC), whereas children with ASDs do not make extensive use of gestures, facial expressions, and body language in an attempt to communicate.

Every so often, LKS is the subject of dramatic news stories, articles, or weekly TV shows that focus on doctors failing to assess for LKS, missing the diagnosis and condemning children to a wordless world until a smart doctor finally makes the diagnosis and the child recovers with antiseizure medication. Although the possibility of LKS is frequently brought up, particularly when a child with an ASD has a seizure disorder, LKS is very rare. According to the National Institutes of Health, just over 160 cases of LKS were reported during the interval between the first description of the syndrome in 1957 up through 1990. It is likely that some cases are being missed, but it is not likely that many individuals with LKS are thrown into the ASD group by experienced examiners.

Expert neurologists do not feel that the chance of discovering a case of LKS is high enough to justify obtaining electroencephalograms (EEGs) in every child with an ASD. Many studies have been done to look at which tests might be useful in the medical workup for ASDs, and none have found unsuspected cases of LKS. Fortunately, an EEG (a study of brain wave patterns) can be used to reliably diagnose or exclude LKS whenever needed. The EEG is always abnormal during sleep in children with LKS. If concerns arise, an EEG during sleep can be done to give a definitive answer.

Gastrointestinal Problems

Gastrointestinal (GI) problems are widely reported to be exceedingly common in children with ASD. Many parents think that the gut is directly involved in the process that causes the ASD. For a discussion of the controversy over the claim that there is an intestinal disease that is unique to ASDs, see the section on Dr. Wakefield and the measles, mumps, and rubella (MMR) vaccine in Chapter 7.

Estimates of the frequency of GI conditions in ASD vary greatly. Specialists who evaluate children with ASDs report rates for chronic constipation or diarrhea ranging from 46 to 85 percent. However, their estimates may be higher than the actual rates of GI issues because specialists only see children referred to them because someone has already noticed symptoms of a gut problem (in statistics, this is called a "referral bias").

Studies that have looked at randomly selected children with ASDs have yielded lower estimates (ranging from 9 to 24 percent), with rates often similar to those of TD children. A 2006 study tells a different story. The authors asked whether or not individuals with ASDs had significant GI problems at any time in their life (defined as an abnormal stool pattern, frequent constipation, frequent vomiting, or frequent abdominal pain). The researchers found that 70 percent of the ASD population had GI issues, much higher than the rate in TD children (28 percent) or children with other DDs (42 percent). Diarrhea was the most common symptom reported, but constipation was also seen frequently. Taken together, it appears that children with ASDs do have a higher frequency of GI problems. Still, it is not clear what conclusions can be drawn from the data. For one thing, the causes of the different GI symptoms reported (i.e., chronic diarrhea, chronic constipation, vomiting, and abdominal pain) are not necessarily the same. An additional complication in the interpretation of the data is the possibility that the public focus on GI disorders in ASDs may have influenced the parental responses.

Regardless of whether or not the gut problems are a clue to the cause of ASDs, parents and healthcare providers should always consider GI issues as a possible explanation for any unexplained changes in behavior or periods of distress that cannot be explained. Many children with ASDs (and other developmental delays) have gastroesophageal reflux (heartburn) or irritation of the stomach (gastritis) that can easily go undiagnosed. Treatment of these hidden GI problems can make a world of difference in the comfort level for any child. If GI problems are suspected, a referral to a gastroenterologist should be made.

Sleep Disturbance

Sleep problems occur in approximately 30 percent of TD children in the preschool and early childhood years but are far more common in individuals with DDs. A major difference between sleep problems in ASDs and other DDs is that the severity increases with increasing levels of ID whereas sleep disturbances in ASDs are not correlated with IQ. Estimates of the rates of sleep disturbances in ASDs compared with other DDs vary from study to study, with the overall pattern indicating that sleep disturbances occur at least as frequently and likely more commonly in ASDs. A survey of available studies on sleep in ASDs demonstrates that somewhere around 90 percent of individuals with ASDs will experience some form of sleep disturbance that often persists lifelong, albeit with lessening severity as the children age (Richdale, 1999). Children learn to sleep on a regular cycle as part of typical development, cued by light-dark cycles and routines. Children with ASDs have difficulties at multiple different points in the sleep cycle, including initiation of sleep, maintenance of sleep during the night, and achieving adequate sleep. The children usually do not adhere to a recognizable sleep pattern, staying up until they become so tired that they will often sleep wherever they drop. Nighttime awakenings are common, sometimes accompanied by unex-plained inconsolable crying and screaming, while other nights the child is con-tent to babble unintelligibly, pace in the crib, or otherwise self-entertain. When children reach the age where they are able to get out of their rooms by them-selves, they often choose to wander the house pursuing their own interests, accessing their parents only when they have the need for something. Irregular sleep cycles are exhausting for families, and are consistently rated amongst the most stressful issues for parents of children with ASDs. Following general rules to improve sleep (termed "sleep hygiene" in medical parlance) such as avoiding caf-feine-containing sodas, not allowing television viewing in the bedroom, and establishing strict bedtime schedules and routines can ameliorate the sleep diffi-culties. The use of natural or prescription medications can also help some chil-dren (see Chapter 8 for more details).

Self-Imposed Dietary Restrictions

In Kanner's original description of autism, he noted a variety of issues sur-rounding eating, including refusal of food for extended periods of time. Indi-viduals with ASDs tend to stick to a small selection of highly favored foods, shunning most new foods. They may have unusual food preferences (e.g., eat-ing uncooked Top Ramen noodles straight from the package or drinking salad dressing out of the bottle). They may go on food jags, eating only one food (e.g., cereal) for breakfast, lunch, and dinner for days or weeks on end, then suddenly changing to a different preferred food for no obvious reason. Most young children with ASDs will not sit at the table to eat, preferring to forage for food when they want something to eat. Chips and other snack foods, espe-cially fast foods, are popular choices. Some children seem to make food choices based on textures, disdaining soft foods such as yogurt or pudding, whereas others may show a preference or aversion to foods of a specific color or some other characteristic that is not usually influential in food selection. Many children with ASDs refuse to take vitamins or antibiotics and are highly sensitive to any attempt to sneak supplements or medications into their food. As the children grow older, they often expand their dietary repertoire.

It is not clear to what extent these eating patterns (often devoid of roughage, fruits, or vegetables) may be a direct cause of the frequent constipation and di-arrhea seen in children with ASDs. The possibility that individuals with ASDs are not getting their daily requirement of vitamins is high for many of the pick-iest of eaters. A 2007 study showed that boys with ASDs had thinner bones than TD boys. The researchers were not able to recruit enough girls with ASDs for the study, but the finding is likely to apply to girls as well. Boys on milk-free diets had the thinnest bones. The researchers proposed several possible explanations, including possible deficiencies of vitamin D and calcium, interference with calcium absorption attributable to GI problems, or decreased exercise. The study results need to be confirmed, but a consultation with a dietician is recommended for any child with an ASD on a restricted diet.

DEVELOPMENTAL HISTORY

The developmental history should include key information about motor development, speech and language, vision, hearing, social-emotional development and intellectual abilities. Understanding when a child's delays started and how the child has progressed over time is key to the diagnosis of ASDs (remember that ASDs are neurodevelopmental disorders that must be apparent before age three). Although much of the information obtained in a comprehensive developmental history does not directly relate to the *DSM-IV-TR* criteria for any of the PDDs, there are behaviors and issues that are common in the PDDs that contribute to the clinician's general impression about whether the individual being evaluated is or is not similar to other individuals with ASDs. All of the information obtained in the developmental history plays a part in the seasoned clinician's ultimate diagnostic opinion, although there is no formula for how the information is incorporated in the decision-making process.

Review of Previous Evaluations

The importance of obtaining and reviewing previous developmental evaluation cannot be overemphasized (e.g., EI assessments, school records, developmental and cognitive test results, speech and language evaluations, and documentation of early childhood milestones in healthcare records), especially for older individuals seeking an ASD evaluation. Because the symptoms of ASDs must start before age three, records documenting the child's early behaviors are indispensable. Evaluation of older individuals is usually more difficult because adequate records concerning early development are often not available. For adolescents and adults who are suspected of having an ASD, there is almost always a long and complex trail of psychiatric diagnoses and treatment that also needs to be sorted through.

Motor Development

"Motor development" refers to the person's ability to perform age-appropriate movements in a coordinated manner using large and small muscle groups. "Gross motor" skills involve the large muscle groups used for walking, lifting, and other activities that require strength. "Fine motor" skills involve the small muscle group used to perform precise movements with the hands. In Kanner's and Asperger's original papers, none of the children had significant motor delays (i.e., they sat, crawled, walked, and manipulated small objects at the normal ages). For a long period of time, it was commonly believed that motor skills were always a strength for children with ASDs. In the heterogeneous group of individuals with ASDs, the majority do not have a history of gross motor delays, but some do (usually those with complicated medical histories, underlying genetic syndromes, or ID).

Children with ID (with and without autism) tend to have delays in all areas of development. The first noticeable delay is in gross motor development. If significant delays in motor development are reported during the developmental history, the clinician is alerted to look for an underlying medical problem or ID (or both) to explain the gross motor delays.

Over time, it has become clear that children with ASDs often have subtle problems with their fine motor skills, called dyspraxia (or apraxia). Dyspraxia is a term used which mean that the individual has impaired abilities to perform skilled gestures, such as imitation tasks, self-feeding, drawing, or writing in a smooth, coordinated way. Many experts feel that motor dyspraxia involving the muscles used for speech is responsible for at least a part of the speech and language problems seen in ASDs. Dyspraxia is so common in ASDs that some researchers feel that it should be one of the core features used to diagnose ASDs. Recent research has implicated problems with the mirror neuron system as a potential cause of dyspraxia in ASDs (see the section on the motor neuron system in Chapter 6).

Although a few studies have suggested that gross mirror skill development was sufficiently abnormal in infants with ASDs to use motor skill analysis to select children at risk for ASDs, subsequent studies have not confirmed those findings.

Speech and Language

Speech and language level is one of the two major prognostic indicators for children with ASDs (the other is IQ). The starting point for every child with an ASD is a comprehensive speech and language evaluation. Most children with ASDs have expressive language delays that are easily recognized by parents by comparing the child's spontaneous language to developmental charts or to other similar aged children. Receptive language is more difficult to assess but is usually delayed to some extent in ASDs, although it is often difficult to separate inattention to language from true difficulty with understanding. The presence of highly characteristic language features (e.g., gibberish with odd intonation that is often described as a foreign language, or parroting and use of words with no clear meaning) is often the signal that first raises concerns about ASDs. However, the more subtle language problems in verbal children with ASDs can go unnoticed without the assistance of a speech therapist. Problems with starting and maintaining conversations (pragmatics), conversational skill, overly repetitive language, and understanding of complex language are common in ASDs.

Speech and language pathologists (SLPs) use a combination of standardized speech and language tests and their clinical observations to produce a report that contains invaluable information about the child's language level and social communication strategies. Language tests that specifically assess social language skills are increasingly being utilized in speech evaluations for ASDs. There are multiple language tests available for every age and language level, including tests that give levels based on parent report and observations by the SLP that are helpful for children who are difficult to test. A discussion of the array of available speech and language tests and interpretation is beyond the scope of this book, but a knowledgeable SLP will choose the appropriate tests to assess the individual's communication abilities to the fullest extent possible. The importance of working with an SLP who is skilled in the evaluation and treatment of children with ASDs cannot be overemphasized. In many ways, an observant SLP is in the best position to differentiate between children with ASDs and other causes of speech and language impairment (SLI)—a distinction that can be extremely difficult to make (see the section on synthesis and differential diagnosis in Chapter 4 for further information).

Intellectual Assessment

IQ is one of the two best predictors of how a child with an ASD will function in the future (the other predictor is language abilities). For this reason, it is very helpful to know the child's IQ. Professionals working with children who have ASDs are frequently surprised at how well some of the children perform on academic tasks.

There are a few generalities that can be made about cognitive test results in ASDs—recognizing that there will be many exceptions due to the heterogeneous nature of ASDs. Individuals with ASDs tend to demonstrate an uneven IQ profile, with relative strengths in scattered areas often hidden amongst areas of substantial delays. Most IQ tests are divided into two separate scores: "verbal" IQ and "nonverbal" or "performance IQ." A variety of tasks assessing different skills are measured in test sections called "subtests." Subtests that require the child to demonstrate understanding and use of language are summed together to come up with a verbal IQ score. Subtests that assess reasoning and ability to problem solve with a minimal requirement for language are used to calculate the nonverbal IQ.

Most individuals with ASDs perform at a substantially higher level on subtests measuring nonverbal IQ. It is not particularly surprising that individuals with language limitations perform less well on the verbal subtests. Interestingly, individuals with ASDs who start out with language delays but progress to the point where they have age-appropriate language continue to score lower on verbal IQ tests compared to individuals with ASDs who never had substantial language delays.

The subtests that assess the ability to reason using visually derived information (referred to as "visual-spatial skills") are frequently areas of strength in ASD IQ test results. However, these strengths are relative to the deficits seen in other areas and do not typically exceed the skills shown by TD individuals. When an individual with an ASD has skills in an isolated area that vastly exceeds the skill levels of TD individuals, they are said to have "savant skills."

Tasks that require more complex thinking (e.g., comprehension subtests on IQ tests) tend to be areas of weakness in ASDs. The ability to pull together pieces into a cohesive whole is the foundation of complex reasoning. Weakness in tasks that require synthesizing information by using higher-order thinking is a hallmark of most ASDs, with strengths typically seen in areas that require rote memorization, ordering and systematizing. "Weak central coherence" is a theoretical attempt to account for the pattern of strengths and weaknesses seen in ASDs. While most individuals find greater meaning in pieces of information that are integrated into a bigger picture (i.e., meaning is linked to the ability to form separate pieces of information into a central uniting concept), individuals with ASDs see the parts clearly without the usual need for the whole to provide context. An interesting experimental test of the weak central coherence theory revealed that individuals with ASDs were easily able to pick out geometric figures embedded in a picture with an overriding contextual theme, whereas TD individuals had more difficulty seeing the parts for the whole (referred to as "embedded figure" tests). Is the ability to bypass the whole and see the parts a skill that leads to genius? Potential associations between genius and ASDs are extremely intriguing to the general public, particularly when celebrities or persons of historical significance are concerned. ASDs in individuals of historical importance (see the sidebar entitled "Genius and AS").

The primary cause of the mismatch between demonstrated abilities and scores on standard IQ tests seen in children with ASDs is that the test often underestimates the child's true abilities. Even in TD children under age five, it can be difficult to obtain a reliable measure of intelligence.

Genius and AS: Speculations on Bill Gates and Other Famous Eccentrics

Speculation about famous people who seem to fit the HFA/AS profile has become a popular theme for writers and bloggers. In 1994, Bill Gates, the founder of Microsoft, was the first contemporary celebrity to be analyzed publicly for a possible ASD, when *Time* magazine ran an article entitled "Diagnosing Bill Gates." Since then, many articles have delved into whether or not Gates fits the profile of a person with an HFA/AS.

What is it about Bill Gates that brings HFA/AS to mind? For starters, it is hard not to notice when he engages in his repetitive rocking. There is nothing subtle about it: his entire upper torso sways in a back-and-forth-high amplitude motion. See it for yourself on a YouTube video entitled "Bill Gates Rain Man," taken during the 1998 Microsoft Hearings at http://www.youtube.com/watch? v=0qNVe024RvI. Gates' behavior would meet criterion B3 for Asperger's disorder—repetitive motor mannerisms (see Table 5 for the *DSM-IV* criteria for Asperger's disorder). Okay, so he rocks; this does not prove that he has an ASD.

What about his NVC and social awareness? In October 2005, journalist Walter Isaacson wrote a piece entitled "In Search of the Real Bill Gates." He commented on Bill Gates' poor use of NVC, including his eye contact and lack of awareness of appropriate voice volume: "He did not look at me very often but either looked down as he was talking or lifted his eyes above my head to look out the window." At a trendy New York restaurant, Gates' voice was so loud that an anonymous diner left his seat and asked the unrecognized Gates to speak more softly. (Gates appears to meet *DSM-IV* criteria A1—deficit in eye contact and other nonverbal behaviors).

In an article in *The New Yorker* entitled, "E-mail from Bill Gates," John Seabrook comments on Gates' lack of interest in other people's lives. "Broad discussions bore him, he shows little curiosity about other people, and he becomes disengaged when people use small talk to try to establish personal rapport. Even after spending a lot of time with him, you get the feeling that he knows much about your thinking but nothing about such things as where you live or if you have a family. Or that he cares." (Gates appears to meet *DSM-IV* criteria A4—deficits in social reciprocity). Seabrook's article is available on the web at http://www.booknoise.net/johnseabrook/stories/technology/email/index.html. Gates' all-consuming interest in technology most likely fulfills the requirement for an "encompassing preoccupation" (Gates appears to meet criteria B1).

Based on the above information, it seems highly likely that Gates would be given a diagnosis of AS if he were to seek out an evaluation (he appears to meet more than the three required criteria for AS: A1, A4, B1, and B3).

Famous historical figures selected by speculators for posthumous ASD evaluations include Sir Isaac Newton, Thomas Jefferson, Albert Einstein, Alan Turing, and Glenn Gould. *Diagnosing Jefferson* by Norm Ledgin is just one example of the many available books written to make the author's case.

Is it helpful to associate AS with genius? The jury is out, with some individuals with HFA/AS saying yes and others saying no. The upside of claiming Gates and an assortment of historical geniuses as members of the HFA/AS fold is to instill a sense of pride and potential in others with ASDs, emphasizing that differences in thinking styles can be advantageous. The downside is that public expectations for individuals with HFA/AS are set unrealistically high. Successful geniuses amongst individuals with HFA/AS are the exception, not the rule. The vast majority of individuals with HFA/AS struggle mightily against the challenges created by being different in a world that rewards conformity.

Children with ASDs are not likely to put forth their best effort during testing because they are more interested in pursuing their own interests than they are in pleasing the examiner. Giving a good effort to please an adult examiner is a social response that is usually present in TD children but sorely lacking in children with ASDs. Add in the fact that language delays depress IQ scores on most standard IQ tests and it becomes clear that children with ASDs are likely to perform poorly on early test of intelligence. Even with all the limitations, efforts should still be made to obtain an estimate of cognitive abilities. The score serves as a starting point for the continual process of reevaluation that should be a part of the child's educational course. The important point to remember is that cognitive test results in children with autism represent the minimal estimate of the child's abilities. The results should be interpreted to mean that the child can function at the level indicated by the score or higher. It is common for measured IQ scores to increase with age in ASDs.

For young children, there are many tests available that provide an estimate of intelligence. Which standardized test is used to assess cognitive abilities for young children depends on the child's age and language level and on the examiner's preference. Suitable tests for verbal children include the Bailey Scales of Infant Development—III (one to forty-two months), Mullen Scales of Early Learning (birth through sixty-eight months), Kaufman Assessment Battery for Children—II (ages three to eighteen), Merrill-Palmer Scales of Mental Tests (measures primarily nonverbal skills in children ages eighteen months to four years of age), Wechsler Preschool and Primary Scales of Intelligence, Revised (ages four to six and a half), and the Stanford-Binet, 4th edition (ages two to twenty-three).

Because verbal skills are still required for many of the subtests in the nonverbal sections (directions are given verbally and verbal answers are required for some of the sections), many individuals with ASDs will score even better on tests that are designed to reduce the language requirement to the greatest extent possible. The Leiter International Performance Scale, Test of Non-Verbal

Intelligence, and Raven's Progressive Matrices Test (RPM) are both examples of nonverbal IQ tests.

A 2007 study by Geraldine Dawson and colleagues compared IQ scores on the RPM with scores on a standard IQ test that uses both verbal and performance skills to estimate IQ (Wechsler Intelligence Scale for Children [WISC-IV]). Whereas none of the individuals with ASDs scored in the normal range on the WISC-IV, one-third were able to score in the normal range when given the RPM. The TD children achieved scores that were essentially the same on both tests. Tests of nonverbal intelligence can be useful to realize the cognitive potential in a child before their language develops to the point at which they can demonstrate their intelligence on standard IQ tests.

Children with lower-functioning autism (IQ in the range consistent with ID) and children with PDD-NOS tend to have lower verbal IQs and higher performance IQs. Although it is commonly thought that particular patterns of strengths and weaknesses can differentiate AS from HFA, the bulk of studies do not show a reliable difference in IQ profiles. Individuals with AS and HFA have verbal IQs that are statistically equivalent, with the verbal IQs usually higher than performance IQs in both groups. Despite countless studies looking at IQ tests in the ASDs, there is no pattern of strengths and weaknesses that can be used to confirm or reject a diagnosis of autism, PDD-NOS, or AS.

In years past, it was estimated that 75 percent of children with autistic disorder were retarded, but it is now recognized that the true proportion of children with MR is much lower (between 25 and 50 percent). Based on the studies of nonverbal IQ tests, it is possible that even less than 25 percent of individuals with ASDs have full-scale IQs less than 70.

Adaptive Behavior

Tests of adaptive behavior often tell a tale that is even more informative than IQ. Adaptive behavior tests measure everyday skills that are needed to get along in the world (e.g., the abilities to get dressed without help, cook, eat, handle money, get around, make day-to-day decisions, and keep safe). Even if an individual with HFA has a normal IQ, they often cannot perform many of the daily activities necessary to live independently. In contrast, if the adaptive behavior levels exceed the measured IQ, it is likely that the IQ tests have underestimated the child's cognitive level. Adaptive skills that determine the capacity to function independently, not the highest level achieved in a splinter skill area.

Medical Evaluation

Although guidelines for ASD evaluations include a strong recommendation for a medical evaluation as part of a comprehensive ASD evaluation, a medical examination is not required for diagnosis. The vast majority of ASD evaluations are done by psychologists who are not trained in medicine. ASDs diagnoses are based entirely on observed behaviors.

There are three main reasons to include a medical evaluation in a comprehensive ASD evaluation. The first reason is that individuals with ASDs often have coexisting medical conditions such as epilepsy that need to be recognized and managed appropriately. The second reason is that individuals with some genetic syndromes can be identified based on their dysmorphic appearance or other clues identified on the physical exam. The word "dysmorphic" comes from the Latin root "dys" for abnormal or diseased and "morphia" for form, meaning that the individual has physical features that appear unusual to the carefully trained eye. If a genetic problem is suspected, tests can be obtained to try to diagnose the condition. If the parents are planning on having another child, many parents, but by no means all, will want to have the opportunity to assess whether a genetic syndrome is present. The third reason for a medical evaluation is to make sure a treatable medical condition is not missed. Assessment for neurologic abnormalities that are not expected in ASDs is a key component of the medical evaluation that can lead to the discovery of a previously unsuspected medical condition (e.g., identifying Rett syndrome or an underlying metabolic problem).

Useful supplementary information can also be obtained during the physical exam. For example, the majority of children with ASDs (but not all) will experience accelerated head growth starting during the first year of life, resulting in a large head size (termed "macrocephaly"). Measurement of head size that reveal macrocephaly serve as a subtle confirmatory finding that might push an examiner slightly in the direction of giving an ASD diagnosis, although children may have abnormally rapid head growth and not have an ASD (see Chapter 6 for information about the significance of increased head circumference in ASDs). The finding of a smaller than normal head circumference (called "microcephaly," from the prefix *micro* for very small and *cephaly* for a condition affecting the head) is an important predictor of a poor outcome because it is associated with many genetic syndromes and catastrophic medical complications.

Recommended Genetic Testing in ASDs

A pediatrician who specializes in the evaluation and treatment of genetic conditions (a subspecialist called a geneticist) is best qualified to determine whether it is likely that a child with an ASD has a genetic syndrome and what types of testing should be done to find a cause for the ASD. It can be difficult to get an appointment with a geneticist because the specialty is in short supply and they often work only at large hospitals that are affiliated with medical schools. Because of the difficulty accessing a geneticist, it is recommended that the genetic workup be done in sequential steps, with first-tier testing done before more complex testing. To facilitate the process, most guidelines recommend that the PCP order the first-tier tests including a blood test to look closely at the chromosomes (called a high-resolution "karyotype") and a blood test to see whether the child has fragile X syndrome, a syndrome that is the underlying cause in 3–7 percent of boys with ASDs. If the first-tier tests do not produce an answer, a referral to a geneticist is recommended.

It is important for the parents to know that a normal chromosome test and a negative test for fragile X do not mean that the child is free from any genetic abnormalities, just as a normal amniocentesis does not mean that a baby will turn out normally. Karyotypes can only show very large abnormalities in the chromosomes; subtle abnormalities will not show up. The majority of genetic abnormalities found to date in children with ASDs are very small changes in the DNA that will not show up on a standard chromosome test. A new test is now available that detects many of these tiny changes in the genes (the test goes by the long name "microarray-based comparative genomic hybridization" [aCGH]). The aCGH test is expensive, and geneticists are divided as to whether it is worth the cost to have the test done for every child with "idiopathic" autism ("idiopathic" is a term used frequently in medicine to refer to any disease or condition with an unknown cause).

In general, if a child is not mentally retarded and does not have any of the characteristic findings that make his primary care doctor suspect a genetic syndrome, it is much less likely that a genetic cause will be found even if all the available tests are done. When children with ASDs are tested using a standard genetic workup for ASDs, an etiology (cause) is found in only 6–15 percent of individuals with ASDs. When geneticists add in a wide variety of specialized tests, including head magnetic resonance imaging (MRI) and an aCGH, a cause can be detected in up to 40 percent (Schaefer and Mendelsohn 2008). Because of the very high costs associated with a complete workup (around $8,000), geneticists are widely split as to whether the high cost of the comprehensive workup is a good use of funds given that the treatment recommendations do not vary based on whether or not a genetic defect is found.

Some geneticists recommend obtaining a brain MRI to see whether there are any obvious abnormalities of brain development, whereas others do not feel that the yield of the test is high enough. The vast majority of time, individuals with ASDs do not have brain abnormalities that can be seen on an MRI unless they have a medical condition associated with an ASD (e.g., tuberous sclerosis or neurofibromatosis). However, if the MRI shows that there is evidence of problems with brain development before birth, it can help reassure parents that nothing they did after the child's birth caused the ASD.

OTHER PERTINENT AREAS TO ASSESS DURING THE DIAGNOSTIC EVALUATION

Although the diagnosis of the ASDs is technically determined by the *DSM-IV-TR* criteria, some behaviors are so common in ASDs that their presence or absence subtly shifts the clinician toward or away from an ASD diagnosis.

Tantrums

The issue that is most likely to draw parents of children with ASDs to first seek advice is their child's erratic and unpredictable tantrums, referred to by many parents as "meltdowns." There are several features of these extreme displays of unhappiness in children with ASDs that are strikingly different from the kinds of tantrums seen in TD children. People who are intimately familiar with ASDs can almost instantly make the distinction between the unruly child in the grocery store pitching a fit and the child with autism who has been cast into despondency. There is almost never a manipulative, pouty, or outwardly defiant quality to the tantrum; there is just unbridled despair, as if the child's whole world was collapsing.

A hallmark of the emotional disregulation seen in children with ASDs is that the child's level of distress almost always seems out of proportion to the situation. A seemingly minor frustration with a toy train that has fallen off the track, the sound of a particularly irritating song on the radio, or the simple action of a mother trying to shut an open door can precipitate a meltdown. The child with an ASD has to have things just so, and anything that disrupts the way things should be cannot be tolerated.

The second unusual feature of the meltdowns experienced by children with ASDs is that they can go as quickly as they came if the situation is set straight. Replacing the train on the track, turning off the radio, or re-opening the door leads to a sudden almost eerie sudden calm, as if nothing had happened at all. As soon as the problem is remedied, it is as if a switch has been thrown and the tears, crying, protest, and aggression cease. The rapid transition between distress and happiness is almost never seen in TD children, who usually require time to fully recover. With autistic children, the usual parental comforting strategies (e.g., speaking reassuringly, holding the child lovingly, and offering sympathy) seem to have little to no power to make the situation better. As you can imagine, it is very tempting for parents of autistic children to try as hard as possible to give the child whatever it is that brings her calm to avoid these volatile displays. The tendency for parents to cater to the highly specific needs of the child is one reason why children with ASDs often have difficulty transitioning to daycare or school, where they are expected to follow the structure that the other children follow without consideration for their idiosyncratic personal requirements.

Aggression and Self-Injurious Behavior

Children with ASDs, especially those with limited or no language, often push, hit, or slap at others when they are not getting their needs met and cannot communicate exactly what they want. At times, children with ASDs will hit or push another child or adult for seemingly no discernable reason, but the majority of the time there is reason for the action from the child's point of view, even if it is not apparent to the observer. For example, a child with an ASD, bothered by an adult's singing or another child sitting too close, may strike out as a protest. As the autistic child's language or alternative communication strategies improve, aggressive behaviors almost always decrease. If parents or teachers cannot figure out what is bothering the child with an ASD, a functional analysis from a trained behavioral specialist can be a very effective way to uncover the real cause of the meltdowns. Once the cause is known, a strategy can be put in place to reduce the tantrums or other undesirable behaviors.

Although TD children can also be aggressive, there is something distinctly different about the way autistic children lash out. Children with ASDs do not typically hold a grudge or go after another child because they are jealous or for other complicated emotional reasons. They almost never pull their fist back, make threatening facial expressions, furrow their brow, stomp their foot in defiance, or stare down their opponent, all the kinds of things that typical children do when they are mad and want to show it. Aggression in children with ASDs does not seem to come from an emotional angry place but instead seems to arise from extreme internal distress when something is amiss in their autistic world and they cannot set it right. Aggressive behavior in ASDs is almost always an attempt to communicate that the child is bothered by something, is frustrated at not getting a need met, does not want to do what is being asked, or wants something to stop. During most of these distressing situations, if the child gets what she needs or if whatever is bothering her ceases, the aggression will vanish as quickly as it came.

When children with ASDs are overwhelmed, they often engage in behaviors that hurt themselves, referred to as "self-injurious behavior" (SIB), such as hitting themselves in the face, banging their heads against the floor or the walls, or biting or scratching themselves. In individuals with ASDs, SIB is virtually never an attempt to get attention or to manipulate adults. Improving communication skills almost always decreases SIB. It is exceedingly important to identify the stressors that lead to these behaviors in order to decrease their frequency and severity of SIBs.

Inattention, Hyperactivity, and Impulsivity

Although some professionals will give an attention-deficit hyperactivity disorder (ADHD) diagnosis children with ASDs who have short attention spans, are constantly on the move, and act impulsively with attention-deficit hyperactivity disorder (ADHD), these children are not likely to have the same underlying brain dysfunction as TD children with ADHD. ADHD is generally attributed to problems with the activation of a part of the frontal lobes in the brain that act like a central command center, directing attention to the most important goings on at any particular point in time. ADHD has been linked to problems with the way this command center functions (referred to as "executive functioning"). Although there is evidence that executive functioning is impaired in children with ASDs, the underlying neurologic reason for the impairment is likely to be very different.

To acknowledge these underlying differences, the *DSM-IV* specifically states that ADHD should not be diagnosed in children with PDDs. Nonetheless, some professionals use ADHD as a shorthand to indicate that a particular child with an ASD flits from activity to activity with a very short attention span and high levels of motor activity and impulsivity.

Sensory Issues

Unusual reactions to sights, sounds, smells, tastes, textures, and movement have long been noted in children with ASDs. Between 44 and 88 percent of all individuals with ASDs display these sensitivities. Descriptions from high-functioning individuals with ASDs confirm that some everyday sensory encounters such as noise or touch can be uncomfortable or distressing, whereas other sensations are often calming.

Children who cover their ears and scream when the vacuum is turned on, experience extreme distress at the buzzing sound of electric shears at the barbershop, or are bothered by the hum of a fluorescent light, the sound of a parent singing, or a baby crying are showing unusually strong negative reactions to auditory input. Children who gag if forced to try a new food, cringe and withdraw from any food that has a soft consistency, or detect and reject foods with even the minutest amount of medications or vitamin supplements that parents have attempted to hide in juices or other foods are demonstrating strong sensory aversions in the taste arena. Children who scream when they walk on grass barefooted, reject all clothes that are not loose fitting and soft, push away from someone trying to pick them up or snuggle, or become distressed if another student accidentally bumps into them are demonstrating signs of a high sensitivity to experiences involving touch. Children with visual sensitivities might cringe when the light is bright or cover their eyes and whimper. Those who are excessively fearful of slides or swings are demonstrating unusually negative response to movement-related sensory input (often called "vestibular input"). All of these children are showing signs of intolerance to sensory experiences (sounds, taste, touch, visual, and movement) that would probably not be bothersome to most children. These children are referred to as "sensory defensive" or "sensory avoidant," meaning that these experiences are disturbing to the child.

Children who show a high pain tolerance, seem impervious to the cold, and can go for hours, even days, without eating are at the opposite end of the spectrum. Occupational therapists (OTs) refer to these children as displaying features of "low registration," meaning that they do not seem to notice or react to sensory input that would prompt a response in TD children (e.g., crying and distress with injury, or hunger with food avoidance).

Many children with ASDs show unusually pleasurable responses to certain stimuli: running their hands repeatedly through a stranger's hair, staring at the light as it filters through the window, swinging for hours, smelling or licking nonfood items, or crawling into tight spaces, are all grouped together as "sensory-seeking" behaviors. For these children, the desirable sensory input can either lead to excitement or have a calming effect. A well-known example of a calming sensory experience is the sensation of deep pressure (e.g., the pressure in a massage or a big bear hug). Temple Grandin, a frequently profiled adult with HFA, found that deep pressure helped so much with regulating her emotional state that she invented a "squeeze machine," modeled after the contraptions used to hold cows still for shots or other veterinary treatments. Whenever she needed to calm down and reorganize her thoughts and feelings, she would put herself into the squeeze machine for a brief period of time. Strong sensory preferences can be as disruptive to day-to-day living as the distressing sensory experiences because the child will not readily transition from an activity that is generating pleasure to whatever else is next on the daily agenda.

Individuals with ASDs often show a mixed pattern of aversion to certain sensory experiences, profound enjoyment of others, and unexpected failure to show any reaction to other types of sensory input. A child might cover his ears and run away when the toilet flushes but become exceedingly excited while putting his ear to a booming stereo speaker and not even seem to notice when an object clatters noisily to the floor just inches from where he is sitting. There often seems to be a push-pull response, with simultaneous fascination with and fear of a sensory experience.

Unusual responses to sensory experiences are not limited to children with ASDs. Because these responses are not specific to ASDs, atypical sensory responses are not included in the *DSM-IV-TR* criteria as a core feature of ASDs. However, the high rate of abnormal reactions to sensory input has long been noted by family members and those who work with children or adults with ASDs. Recognition of these sensory issues is of the utmost importance because a significant number of individuals with ASDs have trouble in the day-to-day world because of these hot-button areas. Many different names have been applied to describe these abnormal sensory responses, the most common being sensory integration disorder, a term coined in the sixties by Jean Ayres, an OT and Ph.D. educational psychologist who pioneered the treatment of sensory issues. With little to no research behind the sensory integration disorder concept and proposed treatments, the area was essentially ignored by experts in ASDs but not by the families who often found the treatments used to be helpful for their children. Sensory processing disorder (SPD) is a replacement term proposed by researchers to highlight evidence that the nervous system in children with SPDs processes sensory experiences differently from that of typical children.

To decrease the gap between the scientific-minded professionals working in the autism field and the hands-on occupational therapy proponents of treatment for these problematic sensory areas, research has been directed toward proving the existence of abnormal neurologic responses to various sensory experiences. For example, a study by Lucy Jane Miller, Ph.D., showed that children who were overresponsive to smells had higher levels of nervous system arousal (an adrenaline-like response) when exposed to a particular smell. With repeated exposure to the same smell, the children with SPDs continued to show the same high level of nervous system activation. In contrast, children who did not have SPDs reacted less strongly on the first exposure than the subjects with ASDs and had progressively less reaction to repeated exposure (i.e., they became desensitized to the smell and stopped responding). Overresponsive children with SPDs respond more vigorously to certain stimuli because their nervous system sends a louder alarm and continues to send the same high-intensity warning each time the sensory stimulus is repeated. Children with ASDs may not make the necessary adjustments to their nervous system to allow the sensory input to fade into the background.

In contrast, children who are underresponsive to sensory stimuli showed a lower level of nervous system arousal on the first exposure that rapidly dissipated. Underresponsive children respond less because their nervous system does not sound a very loud alarm and even the quiet alarm stops after a very brief period of time. Dr. Miller's research demonstrates that the actual processing of sensory information is the reason for the abnormal responses. For those with an interest in SPDs, Dr. Lucy Jane Miller's website is a good place to start (http://www.spdfoundation.net).

Elopement

Some children have a particularly strong desire to get outside or run off whenever the chance arises. Even the most attentive parent can lose track of a child with an ASD in the blink of an eye. All it takes is for the parent to be momentarily distracted or try to do something as simple as taking a few seconds to slip off to the bathroom. Parents resort to installing special locks in an attempt to prevent the child from sneaking off. However, even the most complex locks are often no match for a motivated child with an ASD. Children with ASDs are adept problem solvers when they want to get at something out of their reach. A stack of chairs or boxes combined with fearlessness and well-developed climbing skills can remove most obstacles in their way. Finding a child with an ASD who has wandered off is not easy because most children with ASDs will not respond to their name or return when called.

Often, individuals with ASDs will head straight to a favorite spot where knowing parents can locate them. Other times, all the parents find is a trail of clothes left in the road or sidewalk, peeled off as the child heads off to an unknown destination. Alarm systems with bracelets that cannot be removed can be useful to alert parents or caregivers when an individual with an ASD leaves the premises unexpectedly. GPS-enabled units are also available for individuals at high risk for elopement. Professionals refer to this wandering off or running away behavior as "elopement." Others refer to the children as "runners" or "escape artists." Whatever you call the behavior, it is a serious safety problem.

Elopement is probably the single most frightening aspect of ASDs for parents, and it should be. The most common cause of death in children with ASDs is drowning, followed by injuries sustained from cars that cannot stop in time to avoid the child who runs into the street suddenly without warning. If a child has a particular fascination with water and has ready access to a body of water, special care must be taken to protect the child (e.g., pool covers, gates that cannot be opened, and alarm systems).

4

Diagnostic Evaluation for ASDs Part 2: Appropriate Use of the *DSM-IV-TR* Criteria for Autistic Spectrum Disorders and Supplemental Tests Used in the Diagnostic Process

I n Chapter 1, Kanner's initial description of the core features of autism were summarized to provide a general picture of the classic types of behaviors observed in children with autism. The words used to translate the observed core features of autism into a listing of behavioral and developmental characteristics (referred to as diagnostic criteria) have evolved over time. Lorna Wing coined the phrase "the triad of impairments" to describe the areas of atypical behavior seen in persons with ASDs, and the *DSM* has continued to divide the criteria for autism and PDD-NOS into the same three components: deficits in social interaction, deficits in communication (including imaginative play), and narrow and repetitive patterns of behavior (see Table 3 for a listing of the diagnostic criteria for autism and Table 4 for PDD-NOS).

The *DSM-IV-TR* criteria for AS use the same criteria as autistic disorder for impairments in social interactions and repetitive patterns of behavior (the numbering system is different but the criteria are the same). All of the criteria for communication used for autism and PDD-NOS are deleted from the diagnostic criteria for Asperger's disorder (see Table 5 for the diagnostic criteria for Asperger's disorder).

INTERPRETING THE *DSM-IV-TR* CRITERIA FOR AUTISTIC DISORDER

Reading through the *DSM-IV-TR* criteria is the first step toward understanding how ASDs are currently diagnosed, but words are notoriously imprecise. The proper interpretation of a particular criterion may not be immediately apparent to someone who is not intimately acquainted with the ASDs. Developing a keen sense of the types of behaviors each of the criteria is trying to describe is the key to accurate diagnosis. No test can capture the essence of the core deficits of ASDs without the aid of an experienced clinician, which is why the "gold standard" for whether or not a child has an ASD continues to be the opinion of an experienced clinician.

It is important to recognize that each clinician interpreting the *DSM* criteria has different opinions about what level of impairment is needed to satisfy each of the criteria. The different thresholds used by each examiner are the main reason why the final diagnostic impressions vary from one professional to another. Professionals usually agree on whether or not an individual has an ASD but disagree to an alarming extent on which of the three PDD diagnoses (autism, AS, or PDD-NOS) is the best fit. To understand the root cause of these disagreements, it is important to know about a concept called "operationalization" of the *DSM* criteria. Although the word is daunting, the concept is not hard to grasp. Simply put, diagnostic tools have been introduced to replace the examiner's clinical judgment about whether or not a criterion is met. The tests attempt to "operationalize" or set uniform standards for deciding whether or not an individual has an ASD and, if so, which one. In many ways, the use of these operationalized criteria makes much more sense than allowing each clinician to act as a loose cannon. Whereas some clinicians have the clinical feel necessary to accurately diagnose ASD, others do not.

In this section, each of the twelve criteria used to diagnose ASDs are broken down to get to their core meanings. For an added understanding of the behaviors sought through the various *DSM* criteria, the video glossary at http://www.firstsigns.org is an invaluable resource that provides visual images indexed to the *DSM-IV*.

DSM-IV-TR CRITERIA FOR AUTISTIC DISORDER SECTION A: QUALITATIVE IMPAIRMENTS IN SOCIAL INTERACTION

The four criteria included under the section devoted to impairments in social interaction are designed to capture different aspects of social connectedness. These four areas form the backbone of skills needed to successfully engage in the social world. Criterion A1a looks at ways to engage socially that are independent of language. Criterion A1b looks at the degree of interest in and success with developing social relationships with peers. Criterion A1c looks at how much effort is devoted to trying to share interests for the purpose of having a social interaction. Criterion A1d looks at the ability to initiate and respond to social and emotional situations. Note that the focus is on the quality of these social interactions, not the quantity.

Criterion A1a: Eye Contact and Other Nonverbal Behaviors

Criterion A1a requires that the individual has a "marked impairment in the use of multiple nonverbal behaviors such as eye-to-eye gaze, facial expressions, body postures, and gestures to regulate social interaction." The word "marked" means that the impairments must be strikingly noticeable. The requirement for impairment in multiple nonverbal behaviors is meant to emphasize that individuals with ASDs have difficulty understanding and appropriately using a wide variety of nonverbal social communication strategies.

NVC, often referred to colloquially as "body language," plays a huge role in everyday social interactions. In fact, NVC provides more information than words because the true meaning of words often hinges on NVC. To gain a first-hand awareness of just how much social information can be transmitted and received by a person with limited language, all one has to do is engage with a typical one year old. Even with very limited language skills, young toddlers manage to communicate their needs, desires, and interests, along with an impressive range of emotions using eye contact, facial expressions, and communicative gestures (e.g., pointing and reaching). By fifteen months of age, the typical toddler coordinates pointing with meaningful eye contact. In contrast, the natural and spontaneous use and understanding of eye contact and other NVC are impaired, to varying degrees, in persons with ASDs.

Use of Facial Expressions

There are many ways that facial expressions can differ from the norm in persons with ASDs. A person with an ASD may have distinctly unusual facial expressions that are hard to interpret. Facial expressions for emotions may seem exaggerated, unnatural, or out of place. The child's facial expression may not seem to bear any obvious relation to what is going on around them. A child might have an oddly somber expression with few spontaneous expressions of joy (often referred to as a "flat affect"). Parents can almost always tell when their child is happy, distressed, mad, or afraid by their facial expressions, even when the child has an ASD. However, children with ASDs often do not direct their facial expressions to others; there is an inwardly directed quality. Instead of turning to their mother with a quavering lip and a sad face, the child is more likely to continue to face the frustrating toy with an expression of extreme distress without even glancing at her mother to see if she has noticed her problem. Individuals with ASDs are more impaired in their use of the subtle facial expressions used to convey emotional experiences (e.g., indignation, mischievousness, or hurt feelings).

Expressions involving the eyes, eyebrows, and forehead are powerful ways to communicate that are not used effectively in individuals with ASDs. Rolling the eyes in disgust, lifting an eyebrow to express scepticism, opening the eyes wide in surprise, or narrowing the eyes to communicate anger are all nuances that are rarely seen in individuals with ASDs. Not only do persons with ASDs fail to use these types of NVC, but research has also demonstrated that they have problems interpreting facial expressions and other types of NVC. The lack of subtle expressiveness and difficulties interpreting facial expressions are undoubtedly related: if a young child does not attend to the facial expressions of others, the child does not learn the culturally accepted ways of expressing subtle emotions.

Gestures

Young children with ASDs often have trouble figuring out how to use gestures to get their needs met (most likely because they do not pay sufficient attention to common gestures used by others to gain a sense of the intended meaning). Whereas a TD child will point to a desired object with coordinated eye contact in an effort to obtain the object (referred to as "protoimperative pointing"), a child with an ASD may simply look in the direction of the object. Parents of nonverbal children with ASDs are forced to go through a litany of guesses because their child does not give them nonverbal cues to narrow the choices. Because of the difficulties they have in using NVC to make requests, children with ASDs often forgo efforts to communicate their desires, choosing instead to get the object themselves. The industriousness and relentless persistence of children with ASD who are determined to reach a desired object are impressive.

The earliest gestures children typically pick up are reaching, pointing, and waving "bye bye." Waving is a social gesture that does not come naturally to most children with ASDs. Even if they do wave, the gesture is characteristically used in an unusual manner, most commonly to indicate the desire to leave instead of a social way to acknowledge a person. The wave itself frequently looks unnatural.

Expressive gestures that are typically used to convey feelings and other states of mind are often lacking in individuals with ASDs. Many expressive gestures do not have obvious meaning in and of themselves (e.g., shrugging the shoulders to convey indifference, blowing kisses, and scratching the head to indicate the act of thinking). Understanding and using gestures require the child to have enough interest in the social world to figure out the meaning of a particular gesture and then incorporate it into his working nonverbal "vocabulary."

Body postures can also have social meaning. A child who reaches upward to indicate a desire to be picked up positions herself in front of a parent looking upward to indicate a desire to interact or approaches a person who is talking to her is demonstrating the desire to interact in a nonverbal way. A child who places her hands on her hips while scowling or stomps her foot and turns away with crossed arms when asked to do something she does not want to do is sending clear social messages. Persons with ASDs do not tend to use conventional body postures as a means of communicating social intent (unless the gestures have been taught in an intervention program).

Coordinating eye contact with other types of NVC is a powerful way to communicate and convey social meaning. To make requests, a child typically coordinates looking at the desired object with looking at the person he wants help from in a back-and-forth manner. To share enjoyment, eye contact is essential. The use of eye contact to regulate social interactions is impaired in children with ASDs and continues to be problematic for most older individuals with ASDs.

Unusual Eye Contact in ASDs

The atypical quality of eye contact, even more than the decreased quantity, is a hallmark of ASDs. It is often said that individuals with ASDs seem to look past or through others. Recent advances have shed light on the basis for abnormal eye contact in ASDs.

Many verbal persons with HFA report that they avoid making eye contact because it makes them uncomfortable or anxious. Avoidance of eye contact is referred to as "gaze aversion" or gaze avoidance because individuals consciously turn their eyes away from the gaze of another person, choosing instead to make furtive glances to keep track of what is going on. Studies have demonstrated that some persons with ASDs experience a physiologic activation response (i.e., similar to a fight-or-flight response) to direct eye contact. A 2005 study out of the University of Wisconsin–Madison used a technology called functional magnetic resonance imaging (fMRI) to show that the part of the brain that processes fear and other emotional responses (the amygdala) is strikingly more active in individuals with ASDs compared with TD individuals when they gaze directly at an image of a face. The authors suggested that the threat signal generated by gazing at faces is the basis for the abnormal facial processing seen in children with ASDs. The theory is that the fear response reduces the amount of time that individuals with ASDs spend regarding faces. As a result of decreased experience examining faces, the individuals do not learn to interpret facial expressions.

There is another possibility. Not all persons with ASDs seem to feel threatened by direct eye contact. In fact, it is not at all uncommon for a child with an ASD to grab an adult's face and stare into their eyes in an overly intense manner. Rather than actively avoiding the processing of faces, it is possible that some children with ASDs do not spend a great deal of time looking at faces because they do not find faces particularly informative in the first place. A study by a University of California, Los Angeles (UCLA) neuropsychologist named Susan Bookbinder used fMRI technology to investigate the responses of individuals with ASDs and TD persons to pictures of faces with eyes directed straight at the subject or eyes averted. The subjects with ASDs did not respond to the expressions shown by either of the faces. In contrast, the TD subjects showed a response to the faces with direct gaze but not to averted gaze. Could it be that some individuals with ASDs avoid eye contact because they feel threatened by direct gaze, whereas others simply do not register the gaze and facial expressions of others?

In a series of brilliantly engineered studies, researchers at the Yale Child Study Center have greatly expanded our understanding of what captures the attention of individuals with ASDs and how eyegaze influences what individuals with ASDs take away from social interactions.

The Yale Eye-Tracking Studies

Ami Klin, working closely with Warren Jones, Fred Volkmar, and colleagues at Yale, developed a sophisticated apparatus to track eye movements, allowing them to pinpoint exactly where their subjects were looking at any point in time (Klin 2002). They found that the typical viewer observing a social interaction between two individuals scanned back and forth between the eyes of the two characters to gain information. In contrast, the viewers with autism concentrated their vision completely on the area around the mouth of the character who was speaking, ignoring the nonspeaker and missing any information they might have gained from that character's reaction. Individuals with ASDs seemed to view the moving mouth as the driver of the situation.

Similarly, when two characters were involved in a heated discussion while a third character looked on in silence, the viewer with autism focused only on the mouths of the two speaking characters, entirely oblivious to the reaction of the background character. In contrast, the TD viewer scanned between all three characters, a process that provided the TD viewer with vastly more information about the social impact of the exchange on all involved.

In other experiments, the Yale group demonstrated that individuals with ASDs spent more time looking at extraneous objects in the room than the TD subjects, preferring objects to social interactions. Whether their preference for objects is because it is disquieting for them to look at faces or just uninformative is not completely clear; however, the Yale eye-tracking experiments support the theory that persons with autism are simply more interested in objects.

The Yale eye-tracking experiments provide information that fits seamlessly with what is already known about eye contact in ASDs. Previous studies have shown that TD individuals use the eye and eyebrow region to identify pictures of people, whereas those with ASD use the mouth area. Not only is face recognition impeded by the gaze habits of individuals with ASDs, but so too is any chance of picking up on the nuances that control social interactions.

Eye Contact Abnormalities Not Attributable to ASDs

Armed with an understanding of eye-gaze in individuals with ASDs, it becomes easier to differentiate decreased eye contact attributable to an ASD from decreased eye contact attributable to another issue. For example, a child in constant motion with a short attention span may not make eye contact when a parent tries to convince him to take a bath or perform an unwanted activity. He may not make to use eye contact when he is engrossed in an activity that he loves, but he will make appropriate eye contact when he is snuggled in bed with his mother or pleading with his parents to buy him a BB gun. His eye contact deficits are attributable to attention issues. The ability to make meaningful eye contact is in children with attentional issues is not always used, but it is present.

A very shy child who does not make eye contact when first approached but makes better and better eye contact as she gets to know a person does not have the types of eye contact abnormalities that are seen in ASDs.

Children who say "No!" to every request, cross their arms, and pout without looking at their parents may make less eye contact than other children. These children are often described as oppositional and defiant. They make less eye contact by choice. They do not have the widespread deficits in NVC seen in children with ASDs. There are many other children who make less eye contact than expected, including children with depression and those who have been neglected or abused. None of these children have qualitative deficits in eye contact that are similar to those seen in children with ASDs, nor do they demonstrate life-long deficits in the use of other nonverbal behaviors. The take-home message is that the deficits in nonverbal behaviors seen in children with ASDs have a unique quality that makes these individuals stand apart.

Criterion A1b: Failure to Develop Peer Relations Appropriate to Developmental Level

The importance of considering developmental level is specifically spelled out in criterion A1b. Developmental level is considered with regard to peer relationships because there is an orderly progression of social play that occurs over the first few years of a child's life that is highly dependent on mental age and language level. For example, at twelve months of age, toddlers should not be expected to engage in complex back-and-forth play because they are not developmentally ready, but there are many subtle ways of showing interest in peers that should be present in toddlers.

Starting during the first year of life, infants show an interest in other children by looking, smiling, vocalizing, gesturing, reaching out, and touching one another. Typical toddlers are aware of and interested in other children. They spend a lot of time observing peers and make simple, brief, playful social approaches by offering and accepting toys, imitating each other, and mutually manipulating toys. They show the ability to recognize familiar peers. They may follow a preferred peer into the sandbox or smile at them when they come in to daycare in the morning. Children with ASDs demonstrate their disinterest in social interactions with peers in a variety of ways. They may be completely oblivious to the presence of other children, be bothered by the intrusion of other children into their isolated play, or observe other children but make no attempt to initiate or respond to social opportunities. Toddlers who do not show adequate interest in their peers meet criteria 1b.

By the time TD children reach preschool age, they show an increasing desire and ability to coordinate social activity, often actively seeking out other children for companionship and play partners. In contrast, children with ASDs tend to isolate themselves from peer group activities, preferring their own self-directed exploration to anything interactive.

What constitutes a typical peer relationship changes over time. Although some children with ASDs remain aloof as they get older, most start to show an interest in interacting with peers as they grow up. The problem is that they missed out on the early opportunities to practice social skills so they do not know the conventions that govern the process of making and maintaining friendships. They often approach others in odd ways that alienate the other children. For example, they may start talking about a subject of great personal interest without checking to see whether it is interesting to the other child or they may join a game in progress and unintentionally ruin the game for all by insisting that everyone play by their own convoluted rules.

Older individuals with ASDs often report that they have friends, but their idea of friendship is very limited. They might list all of the individuals in their class, church group, or workplace as friends, although they never see any of the people outside those venues, nor do they have the type of close relationship that most people mean when they use the word "friend." A reported "best friend" may turn out to be an acquaintance from the distant past who has not been heard from in several years or just someone who was nice to them once. Friendships are often built entirely on shared interests, with no interpersonal connection. When the child with an ASD has a "friend" come over, it is not unusual for them to sit in the same room, each separately playing their Game Boy without interacting.

Adults are much more flexible about adjusting their expectations for children with ASDs. As a result, adults may be fooled into thinking that the child with an ASD has good social skills. Because peers are more sensitive to social quirkiness than adults, criterion A1b specifies that there must be a deficit in the ability to develop *peer* relations. To fully assess an individual's peer relationships, it is very helpful to have information from an outside source (e.g., daycares, schools, or the workplace).

Temple Grandin, an adult with HFA, inferred that there is an advantage to hiring individuals with ASDs, stemming from their lack of interest in the social milieu of the workplace. In her frequent talks at autism conferences, Temple commonly points out that "We aren't the ones standing around the water coolers." The desire to participate in lighthearted small talk, share personal information, and hear about another person's interests and experiences are all crucial skills for starting up work-related and other casual friendships that do not come naturally to people with ASDs.

Criterion A1c: Lack of Spontaneous Seeking to Share Enjoyment, Interests, or Achievements

Children go out of their way to draw an adult's attention to items of interest purely for the chance to initiate a social interaction. They want to get Mommy's attention and will do whatever they can to accomplish their goal. There are three main ways a child can call another person's attention to something: pointing, bringing, and showing.

Pointing is an extremely effective way to start a social interaction or gain information. A great deal of language is learned by a toddler pointing to an object, saying "Dat?" and looking to the parent for a response. Toddlers spend a significant portion of the day pointing to objects while parents respond with enthusiasm (e.g., "Yes, I see the kitty!"; "That's the moon."). The social interaction around these shared interests provide the foundation on which the child learns language and shared emotions. Pointing to share interest has a specific name: protodeclaritive pointing. The absence or reduced use of protodeclerative pointing is a very common early sign of an ASD.

Bringing objects to adults is another effective strategy to gain the parent's attention. Parents of TD children find themselves receiving a variety of objects in a seemingly continuous stream from toddlers seeking attention. A penny from the floor, a wooden block, or a prized stuffed animal are all examples of objects brought to parents purely for the purpose of having the parent respond (e.g., "Oh, thank you!"). With TD children, an enthusiastic response leads the child to go out and find something else to bring back. In contrast, children with ASDs bring objects to parents for very different purposes. Instead of trying to engage with the parent in a social manner, they mainly bring objects to receive assistance with a task they cannot accomplish by themselves (e.g., opening a container, fixing a toy with a dead battery, or bringing a DVD so the parent will put it on for them). Parents of children with ASDs often report that their child brings objects to share, but, on closer examination, it becomes clear that the child is using the parent as part of a preoccupation without any true sharing going on. For example, the child may use the adult like a bench or a table. A pile of cars might be placed on the parent's lap or in their hand, manipulated by the child, and then moved without any attempt to engage with the parent. Although the child brought the cars to the parent spontaneously, there was no social intention in the action.

"Showing" refers to the strategy of orienting an object so another person will notice it. A child may hold up a prized stuffed animal or pick up an object that is unfamiliar and hold it up with a quizzical expression as a way to ask for input. Showing behavior is done purely for the purpose of engaging another person in a social interaction. The desired response is for the observer to comment or engage in an interaction with the child around the object.

Because the typical social drive to share enjoyment is not as pressing in most individuals with ASDs, they tend to keep their interests to themselves during their early years. If a child with an ASD loves trucks, he is very likely to stare at trucks when they go by, collect trucks, or perhaps say "truck" when he sees one on TV or in a book, but he is not likely to try to get his parents to look at the truck. He seems completely satisfied to experience the truck by himself. He does not point to the truck when he sees it because it does not matter to him whether his parents see the truck or not. He does not feel a need to share his joy or appreciation of the truck with others; it is enough for him to have his own personal experience with the truck.

All of the strategies used to share an experience (pointing, bringing, showing, and giving) create a common focus referred to as "joint attention" (JA). JA is the essential building block for all learning. Failure to develop JA is arguably the central deficit underlying the behaviors seen in ASDs. Encouraging children with ASDs to engage in JA is the fundamental concept underlying all of the available intervention programs for ASDs (see Chapter 8 on treatment of ASDs).

There are seeming exceptions to the autistic person's lack of interest in sharing, but closer observation reveals that these behaviors are actually examples of unusual ways of relating in ASDs. Higher-functioning individuals with ASDs may talk incessantly about their particular, focused interest. They may want a parent to listen to everything there is to know about their favorite video game, but they do not want the parent to play with them (unless two players are required). The person with an ASD who brings an object of intense interest to another individual does not bringing the object for the express purpose of sharing the joy of the experience but is instead indulging their obsessive interest.

The degree to which an individual can be expected to spontaneously share his interests varies depending on the stage of development. For example, most TD children do not come home from school and start to recount the day. Almost all parents have had the experience of asking how school went that day only to be met with a monosyllabic "fine." Remember that ASDs have to be present before age three, so the early history of bringing, pointing, and showing must be elicited, even when the person being evaluated is an adolescent or adult.

Criterion A1d: Lack of Social or Emotional Reciprocity

If there is one diagnostic criterion that encapsulates the heart of ASDs, it is this one. Social reciprocity refers to the back-and-forth social interactions that most people seek and respond to willingly. For ease of understanding, problems with social reciprocity can be broken up into three main areas: initiation problems, responding to problems, and lack of awareness of social conventions.

To have a social interaction, someone has to attempt to start the social interaction, perhaps by saying "Hello," asking another child to play, or offering to share a snack. These efforts to engage socially are called "social initiations." Children with ASDs do not initiate social contact to the same extent as TD children. Aloof children may seem oblivious to those around them. Other children with ASDs are aware of others but show a strong preference for isolated play. When they do approach others, there is often a nonsocial reason for the approach. For example, a child who is fascinated by her mother's hair may climb on to her lap to play with her hair. No attempt to make a social connection is made; the child plays with the hair as if it was separate from her mother, because it is the hair that interests her, not the social interaction. A child may involve an adult in an interaction only as a means to an end, using their hand as a tool or mechanical aid to gain necessary assistance, without making eye contact or any other attempt to interact with the person attached to the hand. A person with an ASD may be inappropriately intrusive with others when they initiate an interaction, virtually guaranteeing an unsuccessful social initiation.

Children with ASDs may respond to social approaches from others in an atypical manner. The arrival of Mom, Dad, or Grandmother, with arms outstretched for a welcoming hug, does not engender the expected degree of joyful response. The child is likely to continue to do whatever he was doing before they showed up. If the adult becomes more insistent, the child may shrug off any advances or turn his back. The child may not respond to his name when someone is trying to get his attention to see something interesting. Children with ASDs may passively go along with what is asked of them, coming to circle time or sitting in a chair for snack, but there may be no back-and-forth interpersonal interactions at snack time. Instead of smiling at the preschool teacher doling out the pretzels, the child sits mechanically eating the snack while gazing around the room with a faraway look. When the toddler seated next to him taps him on the forearm, he may look at the spot where his arm was touched but fail to show any interest in the child who tapped him. Often, an autistic child chooses to abandon a toy if another child shows interest, so that he will not be bothered anymore. The common thread in all of these examples is that the child with an ASD usually does not respond enthusiastically the vast majority of times when another person tries to start a social interaction, with the exception that rough-housing, tickling, and chasing are almost always enjoyed.

Lack of awareness of social conventions is another way that social reciprocity is atypical in ASDs. Adherence to the rules that govern expected social behaviors is how children learn to fit in. Turn-taking and flexibility in play are requirements for successful social interactions in childhood, but individuals with ASDs have great difficulty noticing and understanding the subtle social rules. Even when they are aware of the social conventions, they may not feel motivated to follow them. They prefer to keep desired objects to themselves instead of sharing. Instead of learning to "go with the flow" in social interactions, individuals with ASDs are frequently very rigid and insistent that the group follow their rules, resulting in social rejection. As the individual with an ASD grows older, social conventions become increasingly complex and baffling.

Emotional reciprocity is also compromised in ASDs. The mood of a person with an ASD is not influenced by the mood of others around him to the same extent as with a TD individual. Emotional reciprocity involves appreciating the emotional state of another person and responding appropriately. Individuals with

ASDs often have limitations in their ability to express empathy, most likely because they do not understand the emotional displays of other persons. When a baby expresses distress by crying, a child with an ASD may respond with irritation instead of concern. A parent in tears may puzzle the child with an ASD, but that is likely to be the extent of the interaction. A child with an ASD is not likely to laugh at a funny face or other non-physical attempts to engender mirth.

Children with ASDs often have emotional responses for reasons that are not clear to those around them. They may laugh as if something hilarious has just happened for no apparent reason that others can discern. Their emotional world is frequently insulated from the social environment around them. An adult's attempts to amuse a child with jokes are likely to fall flat if the child has an ASD, although simple humor such as funny sounds and slapstick is frequently enjoyed by children with ASDs. Humor that depends on social understanding is often lost on individuals with ASDs. Contrary to popular dogma, many persons with HFA/AS do demonstrate a sense of humor. Intellectual humor is most common, based on linguistics and logical principles that are often related to their preoccupations. The usual social and emotional reciprocity that motivates most TD individuals to tell jokes or funny stories is lacking. Humor is expressed primarily for their own personal enjoyment (Lyons and Fitzgerald 2004).

DSM-IV-TR CRITERIA FOR AUTISTIC DISORDER SECTION A2: QUALITATIVE IMPAIRMENTS IN COMMUNICATION

Criterion A2a: Language Delays

Many children with ASDs have language delays. In the early years of autism awareness, it was commonly thought that less than 50 percent or less of individuals with autism would go on to develop the ability to talk. More recently, it has been estimated that 75 percent of children with ASDs will develop expressive language skills; the improvement is attributed to earlier recognition and better intervention techniques.

The ability to use words to communicate is called "expressive" language, and the ability to understand speech is called "receptive" language. Delays in expressive and receptive language are the main focus of this criterion, but there are other types of problems with language that also need to be considered. Persistent errors in syntax (word arrangement in sentences) and grammar (tenses, plurals, etc.) are examples of delayed language acquisition. Problems with the use of language for social purposes, referred to as pragmatics, are often present. Specialized speech and language testing is needed to detect problems with pragmatics. An important point to remember about this criterion is that a child with language delays who makes every effort to communicate with gestures, mime, and other types of NVC is not considered to meet this criterion (these children are felt to have a specific language impairment [SLI]).

Criterion A2b: Marked Impairment in the Ability to Initiate or Sustain a Conversation

This criterion is only assessed if the individual has adequate speech to have a conversation. Clinicians differ in how much speech they feel a child should have before this criterion can be judge. This is a difficult criterion to assess because the child's language level, age, and intellectual abilities all play a part in determining what level of conversation should be expected from an individual.

Impairment in conversational abilities can result from problems initiating conversations, responding to another person's attempt to start a conversation, or maintaining the conversational interchange. Children with significant expressive and receptive language delays have problems conversing because of their limited vocabulary and decreased understanding of language.

For individuals with more developed language skills, the problems with conversation are more directly linked to deficits in pragmatic language skills, the skills needed in social conversation. When a person with an ASD initiates a conversation, they often jump right in without giving their partner enough preparatory information to make sense of what they are saying. The topic of conversation tends to revolve around the individual's special interests and they talk about that interest incessantly without any awareness of or concern for the interests of their conversational partner (often referred to as "one-sided conversations" or "monologues"). Excessive or irrelevant detail is often provided. Most of the time, the person with an ASD does not really care if their partner is following along or not. The "conversation" seems to be more for their own benefit than it is for the listener, who often cannot get a word in edgewise. Lack of interest in the social aspects of humor, difficulty comprehending irony, and a tendency to take things literally are all common in individuals with ASDs, and all of these deficits can be conversation killers.

Criterion A2c: Stereotypic, Repetitive, and Idiosyncratic Language

The types of language impairments noted in individuals with ASDs are highly characteristic. For this reason, speech therapists are often the first persons to suggest that a child needs additional evaluation for a possible ASD.

Voice Quality

The tone of voice, rhythm, volume, intonation, pitch, and stress are all features that control the flow of language. Individuals with ASDs may speak in unusually loud or quiet voices, place an emphasis (stress) on the wrong syllables of words, vocalize in an unusually high-pitched manner, or utter words in an odd cadence. All of these components of voice quality contribute to the natural flow of language—the rhythm or melody of speech—referred to as "prosody." Prosody is almost always unusual to some degree in persons with ASDs.

Monotone or robotic speech and "sing-song" rhythms are two common manifestations of abnormal prosody. Repetitive sounds uttered over and over with the same odd intonation patterns are very common in ASDs. Children with ASDs who are nonverbal often produce unusual sounds that are not directed at anyone and seem to function as self-talk. The atypical quality of voice made by many children with ASDs are so distinctive that it is often possible for a person familiar with ASDs to hear a brief snippet of vocalization from the waiting room and recognize instantly that the person behind the voice is probably someone with an ASD.

Jargon

Jargon is a term used to describe the unintelligible, meaningless talk that is often one of the early signs of an ASD. Jargon is synonymous with gibberish. Parents of children with ASDs often report that their child has his "own language" or that the child is speaking "a foreign language." Jargon differs from normal baby babbling. When babies vocalize, they go through a fairly standard progression of cooing sounds or other vocalizations that express their emotional state to repetition of single consonant sounds (e.g., ba-ba-ba-ba, da-da-da-da). Babies try to respond to vocalizations directed toward them with babbling. Babbling then progresses to include variation in intonation in a manner similar to adult speech (although no real words are used). The infants then progress to single words. By the age of fifteen months, most children have three words (e.g., mama, dada, and bye bye). It is normal for TD children to intersperse some jargon with words as they develop their language abilities, but the jargon fades out as language abilities increase. Children with ASDs often continue with jargon for extended periods of time. The jargon used in ASDs does not have any communicative intent or reciprocal component and almost always sounds unnatural or odd.

Echolalia

Echolalia is the best-known form of unusual speech in ASDs. There are two main forms of echolalia: immediate and delayed. Immediate echolalia consists of parroting a word or phrase shortly after hearing it. Immediate echolalia can be present briefly in normal children as they pass through the phase in which their language is developing rapidly, but persistence of immediate echolalia is abnormal. Immediate echolalia can be taken from nondirected language that is overheard or from language directed to the child. An announcer on the radio may say the word "groceries" and the child will parrot the word for no obvious reason. Pushing a button on an electronic toy may result in a recorded voice saying, "The cow says moo," resulting in the child saying, "The cow says moo." A mother saying, "Olivia, come here" may prompt Olivia to repeat, "Olivia, come here." Frequently, there does not seem to be any intention to communicate on the child's part, but researchers believe that echolalia is sometimes by individuals with ASD as an attempt to communicate.

Delayed echolalia refers to repetition of words or phrases that were heard at a prior time. Most of the time, the delayed echolalia does not obviously relate to what is going on at the time the child utters it. Often the words or phrases are from familiar electronic toys, videos, or TV shows. A child sitting in a car who suddenly says, "A ... A ... A is for apple" without any obvious reason is demonstrating delayed echolalia. Repetition of movie or TV show dialog verbatim is considered delayed echolalia. At times, delayed echolalia is used for a purpose. Both immediate and delayed echolalia are more common when children have limited language, and both tend to resolve when the child has adequate language to communicate him intentions.

Other Characteristic Types of Speech in ASDs

Scripted speech refers to the use of phrases the child has learned word for word. For example, a child might say, "I'm going to tickle you," to a parent as a request to be tickled because that is how the parents routinely start an enjoyable tickling session. Or a child might say, "You are okay, sweetie" in a sympathetic voice to soothe herself after she falls because that is how her parents offer comfort.

Another unusual language feature used by some, but certainly not all, persons with ASDs is the incorrect use of personal pronouns when referring to themselves. For example, a boy named Eric might say, "Eric is tired" or "You are tired" to convey that he is tired. The child hears others refer to him as "you" or "Eric" and fails to adjust the personal pronoun to the first person form when speaking about himself. Like the other language features seen in ASDs, children with other language disorders and TD children can make similar pronoun errors. The differentiating factor is that SLI and TD children quickly adjust their speech to use the first person pronouns appropriately, whereas children with ASDs can take much longer to understand the need to adjust their speech.

Another common language anomaly in individuals with ASDs is the use of "pop-up" words: the frequent repeating of a particular word for no apparent reason. The word is often used for a brief period of time before being discarded. An example of a pop-up word is the repetition of the word "yellow" over and over with no clear relationship to anything yellow.

Many individuals with ASDs learn phrases in chunks, as if the phrase was one long word. "Whatisthat?" "Timetogo," and "Morejuiceplease" are all examples of phrases that the child may have learned as a chunk because that was how the language was taught to them. Some speech specialists refer to these chunks as "giant words."

Neologisms are words that a child has made up for something that they steadfastly refuse to change, although they have enough language skills to change to the correct word. A child who refers to all dogs as "dee-bo-dees" is using a neologism (for it to be a true neologism, the child's word should not bear any obvious resemblance to the correct word for "dog," nor should it relate to the name of any dog he might know).

Metaphoric language is language that can be understood by people who know the child but not by others. It has been suggested that the reason children with ASDs use metaphorical language is that they may not be paying attention to the same object that the parent is when the word is supplied to them. An example of metaphorical language is a child who uses the word "daycare" to request to play on a slide because the first slide he saw was at daycare. This type of language abnormality may be a direct effect of deficits in JA.

Rote use of language is common. The child who starts each request with the exact sequence of words he was taught in his developmental program can seem like he has well-developed language until the repetitive, invariant nature of the phrases becomes apparent. The child who turns the pages in a picture book on colors and says, "I see blue. I see green. I see yellow. I see orange" is using rote language. So is the child who says "Wow!" in exactly the same way whenever anything is interesting or surprising or puzzling. Rote language is much better than no language. The hope is that the child will be able to use language in a more flexible way over time.

Even in the individuals with higher language skills (HFA and AS), unusual language features are frequently present. Word choices are often odd or more formal sounding than expected from a young child. For example, the two year old who shuns the word "No" in favor of "I would not prefer that" is using overly formal language, as is the three year old who refers to the "chance of precipitation." Part of the impression of formality lies in the fact that individuals with HFA/AS tend to not use slang or common expressions. Their tendency to interpret language very literally makes slang and other types of informal language difficult for them to understand. An intelligent child who uses a few big words does not necessarily have overly formal language. The quality of the formal language has to be distinctly unusual to meet this criterion. For more information about language abnormalities common in ASDs, see the section on semantic-pragmatic language disorders.

Criterion A2d: Lack of Varied Make-Believe Play and Social Imitative Play

Although it may at first seem odd that play skills are included in the same grouping as language deficits, there is a strong relationship between the intellectual skills required to develop varied make-believe play, the ability to imitate in a social manner, and the development of language skills. The need to assess the criteria with respect to developmental level is emphasized in the *DSM-IV-TR*. Both children with significant language delays and children with IDs develop play skills later than expected.

Lorna Wing included deficits in imagination in her initial triad of impairment; criterion A2d is where the ability to have flexible imaginary abilities is assessed in the *DSM-IV-TR*. Children with ASDs tend to have limited or absent imaginary play when young. Social role-playing does not hold their interests. Instead, children with ASDs usually prefer to interact with objects in a mechanical way, such as stacking, lining up, or organizing. A child with an ASD is more likely to separate his collection of plastic animals into farm animals and jungle animals than he is to pretend that two of the plastic animals are making friends. Unlike TD children, who are willing to pretend a branch is a sword, a child with an ASD will steadfastly maintain that the branch is a branch, not a sword (i.e., literal interpretation of word meaning). When children with ASDs do participate in imaginary play, they often act out scenarios they have seen previously in an inflexible, rigid, unchanging way (sometimes referred to as "playlalia," a term meant to convey "echoing" of play). The child is easily upset if an adult or other child tries to modify the play theme.

As children get older, deficits in imagination show up in other ways. Although an individual with HFA may have no trouble writing a report on Emperor penguins, she may draw a blank when asked to compose an original story about penguins. Imagination is constrained in children with ASDs.

Criterion A2d also includes interest in social imitation. Social imitative play requires a child to want to be like other people. When most little boys watch their daddy mow the lawn, they want to push their plastic lawn mower around, pretending to be like their fathers. When they watch mommy cook, they want to pretend to cook in their play kitchens. This type of imitation is referred to as "spontaneous imitation" to distinguish it from the type of imitation that occurs when a child is asked to imitate something. Although children with ASDs may have problems with both types of imitation, the primary deficit is in spontaneous social imitation (a finding that may be explained by problems with the mirror neuron system in the brain).

When parents approach their children to play simple imitative games like pat-a-cake, most children join in for the sheer joy of the social experience. Children with ASDs are not interested in the common imitation games enjoyed by other toddlers, at least not in the typical way. For example, some children with ASDs do like pat-a-cake, but they do not want to go through the hand motions themselves; they prefer to watch the parent go through the routine unaccompanied over and over again. The desire for inclusion and belongingness is not strong in children with ASDs. Children on the spectrum do not tend to spontaneously imitate those around them or show a strong interest in group activities. In the preschool setting, "circle time" group activities that require an interest in being a part of a social group (e.g., learning the hand motions that accompany a song, sharing, and turn-taking games) do not appeal to children with ASDs.

DSM-IV-TR CRITERIA FOR AUTISTIC DISORDER SECTION A3: RESTRICTED REPETITIVE AND STEREOTYPED PATTERNS OF BEHAVIOR, INTERESTS, AND ACTIVITIES

Kanner's observations of monotonous repetition, "anxiously obsessive desire for the maintenance of sameness," and "dread of change and incompleteness"; Lorna Wing's "narrow and repetitive patterns of behavior"; and Michael Rutter's "unusual behaviors including, but not limited to, resistance to change, unusual responses to the environment, and motor mannerisms" form the basis of this section of the *DSM-IV* criteria for autistic disorder.

Different words have been used to summarize these features, but the substance has not changed since Kanner's earliest description. The word "perseverative" (meaning to repeat or get stuck on something) has replaced Kanner's "monotonous repetition." "Restricted" has replaced Wing's "narrow," and "stereotyped" has been added to Wing's "repetitive patterns of behavior" to convey the unvarying quality that makes these behaviors distinctly unusual.

Criterion A3a: Encompassing Preoccupations with Stereotyped and Restricted Patterns of Interest

Children with ASDs occupy themselves in ways that are distinctly different from TD children. Over the course of their lives, individuals with ASDs often move through a succession of intense, all-consuming interests. These highly preferred interests are often referred to as "fascinations" or "obsessions." Examples of common fascinations seen in young children with ASDs include repetitive activities such as manipulating buttons and switches, stacking or lining up objects in a precise manner, and putting things into containers and taking them back out (e.g., toy cars, blocks, and plastic figurines). Although none of these activities are distinctly odd, it is the intensity of the interest and the perseverative quality that make these pastimes atypical. Left to their own devices, children with ASDs would quietly engage in the same monotonous, repetitive play in an unvarying form for much longer periods of time than would be expected from a TD child.

Children with ASDs can be fascinated by toys that are commonly interesting to TD children, but there is almost always a distinctly unusual feature to their play with standard toys. Many children love bubbles, but very few stand rigidly still, staring at the bubbles until the last one pops. Balls are popular with many children, but most TD children do not throw the ball repeatedly in the air and watch it drop with an expression of ecstasy. Miniature cars are favorites with young children, but TD children do not pile them up and repeatedly move the pile or line them up by color. Most children enjoy water play, but they do not pat the water and watch the ripples with intense concentration, nor do they take baths multiple times a day so that they can run their hand back and forth as the water flows from the bathtub spigot, ignoring the rubber duckies and sail boats their parents bought for their bath-time entertainment. Almost all children enjoy TV programs such as *Dora the Explorer* or *Blues Clues*, but only children with ASD will choose the TV guide station or the financial report as their favorite show. Colorful children's books may hold the interest of a child with an ASD as they flip slowly through the pages, but so do phone books, their parent's college textbooks, technical manuals, and advertising fliers—all of which are examined with an intensity that is distinctly unusual.

Objects that have no more than passing interest to TD children often fascinate children with ASDs. Pieces of string, shoes, spatulas, clothes hangers, DVD cases, street signs, logos, lawn mowers, air conditioners, escalators, street lamps, fans, automatic sliding glass doors, leaves that can be torn to bits, animal fur that can be thrown up in the air, geometric figures, or anything straight and narrow that can be waved back and forth (e.g., pencils, the antenna from a remote control car, sticks, or straws) is vastly preferred over army men, cute plastic farms complete with all the usual animals, pretend kitchens, dress-up trunks, baseball gloves, or stuffed animals.

In this day and age of Game Boys, Xboxes, and computer games, many children are obsessed with playing electronic games, making it difficult to sort out the obsessive interests that are seen in the TD population from those that might indicate an underlying ASD. Similarly, it is difficult to discern if a child who has focused interests in dinosaurs, Pokemon, trucks, trains, or Power Rangers is showing behavior that is unusual. With careful questioning, oddities will almost always emerge if the fascination is a result of an ASD. For example, the child who insists on having every Power Ranger figurine so that he can set up creative scenarios with the characters is not likely to have an ASD, whereas the child who repetitively stacks the unopened containers is likely to be on the spectrum.

Recent research has suggested that the types of intense, all-encompassing interests seen in ASDs vary depending on the individual's intelligence and age. Higher-functioning individuals with ASDs tending to amass facts about their focused interests (e.g., the classifications of insect species, astronomy, or sports statistics). Memorization of facts such as train timetables, historical dates, radio station call letters, airport abbreviations, or other feats of rote memory related to unusual interests can be seen in older, higher-functioning individuals with ASD. Lower-functioning and young children with ASDs tending to engage in repetitive mechanical activities.

Criterion A3b: Inflexible Adherence to Nonfunctional Routines and Rituals

The two keywords in criterion A3b are "inflexible" and "nonfunctional." Almost all children find rituals and routines comforting and stabilizing—that's why families develop bedtime routines and other predictable routines. Individuals with ASDs construct their own routines and rituals that do not seem to serve a purpose. Observant family members figure out the routines, but that doesn't mean they understand what drives an individual with an ASD to follow the routine or ritual at all costs. Nonfunctional routines and rituals (NFRR) can appear out of nowhere and last for varying periods of time before they fade out gradually or disappear as suddenly as they came. A child who predictably becomes distraught every time his mother drives in the slow lane on the freeway, stops holding his own drink and insists that an adult stand behind him and bring the glass to his lips, or repeatedly takes his mother's purse off the coat rack hanger and moves it to a specific place on the rug are all demonstrating the unusual kinds of NFRR that are the hallmarks of ASDs. Other routines and rituals that are seen frequently in individuals with ASDs include repeatedly walking a path that is selected by the individual for no clear reason (e.g., back and forth in a hallway, a lap through various rooms in the house, or the periphery at the park), returning objects that have been moved to their proper places, making it a priority to close any door that is open, refusing to drink unless a specific cup is offered, wearing a heavy coat without any consideration of the outside temperature, refusing to eat a sandwich if it is not cut in exactly the same way that it was cut the first time it was served, becoming distressed when a parent takes a different route to get to a familiar place, and heading to a preferred area immediately upon arriving at a known destination (e.g., to the coffee table to flip through the book on ducks at Grandpa's house or to the marble lion in the front hall at Grandma's house). NFRR are easily differentiated from typical childhood routines.

Each child has their own unique NFRR: the uniting feature is the extreme distress that ensues if the system is violated. Kanner's description of a child's reaction to a breach in his orderly world captures the essence of NFRR: "The absence of a block or the presence of a supernumerary block was noticed immediately, and there was an imperative demand for the restoration of the missing piece. If someone removed a block, the child struggled to get it back, going into a panic tantrum until he regained it, and then promptly and with sudden calm after the storm, returned to the design and replaced the block" (Kanner, 1943, p. 245). The rapid transition from extreme distress to calm is a striking feature of ASDs that is not seen in TD children or children with other DDs. The inability to predict each and every occurrence that may disrupt a child's NFRR and send them into a tailspin is one of the main stressors for families coping with ASDs.

Criterion A3c: Stereotyped and Repetitive Motor Mannerisms

When children flap their hands while jumping up and down in an oddly repetitive way or tense their body with closed fists in seeming ecstasy, the movement patterns have an easily discernable atypical appearance. The word "stereotyped" is used to indicate that the movements have a fixed and unvarying quality. The stereotypic movements are also referred to as "stereotypes" (pronounced steri-ah-toe-peas). These types of movement patterns are also called repetitive motor mannerisms (RMMs) or restricted and repetitive motor mannerisms (RRMMs). The most commonly recognized RMM involves rapidly shaking the hands at the wrists, referred to as called "hand flapping," but there are many other movements of the hands and body that are seen frequently in ASDs. Rotating the hands back and forth, and holding the hands in front or to the side of the face while wiggling the fingers are all seen frequently. Complex whole-body movements are also common in ASDs (e.g., jumping up and down in an excited manner in a kind of "happy dance," body rocking, foot-to-foot rocking, body swaying, and spinning in circles). Other body motions that can be included under this criterion include facial grimacing, repetitive squinting, daytime teeth grinding, and unusual body postures.

The public understanding of autism includes the incorrect assumption that hand flapping means autism. Many different children, including TD children and children with ID or other types of developmental delays, engage in RMMs. The presence of RMMs is not one of the hallmark features selected for use on the gold-standard test for ASDs, the Autism Diagnostic Observation Schedule (ADOS) because the presence or absence of RMMs does not statistically differentiate between ASDs, DDs, and other nonspectrum individuals. However, the presence of RMMs has been shown to have some utility in differentiating between children with isolated language disorders (termed SLI) and children with ASDs (RMMs are more common in ASDs). On a positive note, because of the association of hand flapping with ASDs, children who engage in these unusual movements are usually diagnosed at a much earlier age than children who do not exhibit RMMs.

Criterion 3C includes toe walking as an example of an RMM. Toe walking is seen frequently in TD children and children with a wide variety of neurologic issues. Many clinicians would be hesitant to consider this criterion to be satisfied if toe walking was the only example of an RMM unless there was something distinctly odd about the toe walking (e.g., it only occurred in times of intense excitement).

Not all children with ASDs will demonstrate RMMs. In many children with ASDs, RMM are not present in the first two years of life, with an increase noted toward the end of the third year of life. The appearance of RMMs at a later age highlights yet another problem with the current separation between PDD-NOS and autistic disorder. A clinician seeing a child at age two may give a diagnosis of PDD-NOS instead of autism because the child does not meet enough criteria for a diagnosis of autism, only to change the diagnosis to autistic disorder when the child returns at age three demonstrating hand flapping.

Although there are many different types of RMMs seen in individuals with ASDs, all of the movement patterns have some features in common. The most likely time to see RMMs is when the child is ecstatic about something or when the child is very upset, both situations with extreme emotions. Frequently the situations that inspire RMMs do not seem very exciting to the observer, but each child has highly preferred activities that brings out RMMs. Tearing leaves apart and watching them fall to the ground, watching a spinning top, watching bubbles, and gazing at light streaming through a window are all situations that commonly bring out RMMs.

The tendency for these stereotypic motor mannerisms to come out in times of great joy is the main feature that separates these movements from other RMMs such as anxious hand wringing or a motor tic. Tics are involuntary movements, usually involving eye blinking, grimacing, shoulder movements, or other complex body movements, that occur quite randomly.

No one knows why children with ASDs engage in RMM, but there is no shortage of theories. RMMs are often considered to be "self-stimulating behaviors" ("stims" for short). Self-stimulating behaviors are thought to be pleasurable or calming in and of themselves. Repetitive rocking, spinning endlessly, and examining a hand held to the side of the face while flicking fingers fit the profile of self-soothing behaviors. In contrast, hand flapping and happy dances that spill out as a sign of intense happiness—the most characteristic RMMs that are seen in individuals on the autistic spectrum—seem fundamentally different in that the occur as an outward manifestation of extreme emotions, rather than an activity chosen by the individual.

In the past, intervention programs worked to stop these RMMs because they were viewed as abnormal and the goal of intervention was to reduce all undesirable behaviors. Current intervention programs do not focus specifically on reducing or eliminating RMMs. Instead, the child is allowed to engage in RMMs unless the movements are distracting the child from engaging with the people around them. If the child gets a faraway look while engaging in an RMM, attempts are made to motivate the child to engage without specifically targeting the RMMs for intervention.

Criterion A3d: Persistent Preoccupation with Parts of Objects

Children with ASDs interact with objects in atypical ways that involve focusing on parts of objects rather than the whole. A toy truck is not interesting as a truck per se but rather for the wheels that can be spun repetitively. Bicycles are less interesting for riding than they are for the opportunity to turn them over to access yet another wheel to spin. The main attraction of a toy may be the battery compartment or the metal plate on the bottom that identifies the manufacturer instead of the intended function of the toy. Doors are interesting for their hinges and toy planes for their propellers. A specific color may be the source of the attraction. For example, any orange item might attract a child; orange foods such as macaroni and cheese and orange juice, or orange clothes or crayons are all preferred over other choices. Objects that are round may be particularly appealing such as buttons, the face of a watch, or a bead on a necklace. Certain textures may be sought out in a variety of forms: the smooth feel of glass, a countertop, or a mirror. A child may be fascinated with noses or feet or hair, approaching complete strangers without so much as a glance before launching into an investigation of the object of interest whenever the urge strikes.

Close visual inspection of objects is a common phenomenon that is grouped with the other behaviors that fulfill this *DSM-IV* criterion A3d. Objects are carefully examined from every possible angle with an intensity and focus that seem excessive. Children with ASDs frequently lay their head on the ground, cheek pressed to the floor, watching intently as they push a car back and forth. It is not the car but the motion that fascinates the child. Similarly, the motion of a spinning fan or top is a favorite attraction. Describing Donald T., the child profiled in the first vignette in the introduction to this book, Kanner wrote, "He spun with great pleasure anything he could seize upon to spin" (Kanner, 1943, p. 219). It was not the object itself, but the spinning, that pleased the child.

COUNTING THE DSM CRITERIA: DIFFICULT DECISIONS

Once the core focus of each of the *DSM* criteria is understood, the most subjective and difficult part of the evaluation begins: using the acquired information to decide which criteria are met. If the child is classically autistic, it is usually quite clear that he meets the minimum of six or more diagnostic criteria required to qualify for a diagnosis of autism. When a social child with language delays but no behaviors suggestive of an ASD is evaluated, it is immediately obvious that an ASD is not the right diagnosis. However, there are many times when the situation is neither black nor white but gray, with many of the described behaviors not quite odd enough for autism but not undeniably normal either.

Subjectivity in Determining Which Criteria Are Fulfilled

Deciding whether or not a child behaves in a way that is consistent with a particular *DSM-IV* criteria is not a simple task. There are no exact rules that tell the clinician specifically how much of a deficit is enough to say that a criteria is satisfied. It is up to the clinician to make a judgment between three options: counting the criterion as fully satisfied, considering the behavior to be similar to those that fulfill the criterion but present to a lesser degree (the *DSM* refers to the criterion as being met at a "subthreshold" level), or counting the criterion as not fulfilled.

The more information that is available about the person being assessed, the better the chance that the examiner will be able to formulate an accurate opinion about whether or not an ASD diagnosis is appropriate. An unstructured play session with the child is one way to gather valuable information, as is the use of a test that allows the examiner to directly interact with the child in a semistructured way (e.g., Autism Diagnostic Observation Schedule [ADOS]). The ADOS is not designed to provide information to assess the *DSM* criteria (that is the job of an interview tool called the ADI-R), but the ADOS allows the examiner to gain an important feel for the child's use of eye gaze, social and emotional reciprocity, and many of the other behaviors relevant to the *DSM-IV* criteria for ASDs. An accurate *DSM-IV*-based diagnosis cannot be given on the basis of an interview alone, no matter how accurate the parents are in their reporting.

Deciding on the Appropriate *DSM-IV* Diagnosis

The *DSM-IV-TR* rules for diagnosing autistic disorder, PDD-NOS, and AS are fairly straightforward once the examiner has determined which *DSM* criteria are fully met, met at a subthreshold level, or not met. For a diagnosis of autistic disorder, a total of six criteria must be met. To emphasize that the essential core of autism is the unusual ways of relating socially, two of the six criteria must come from the social category (a1a, a1b, a1c, and a1d). To acknowledge that autism is composed of a triad of impairments, at least one criterion must come from the language section and one from the restricted and repetitive behavior section. The other two can come from any of the sections, but the total must equal six or more to get a diagnosis of autistic disorder. These thresholds were set based on the data gathered in the field trial that preceeded the release of the *DSM-IV*.

For a diagnosis of PDD-NOS, there still must be unusual ways of relating socially, but it is not necessary for six criteria to be fully satisfied. If some criteria are only partially met or the total is less than six, then a PDD-NOS diagnosis is given. PDD-NOS is also given if the child has behaviors consistent with autism but there is some part of the story that does not fit with the typical course of autism. For example, if the child did not show signs of atypical social interactiveness until after age three, then PDD-NOS would be given instead of autistic disorder because of the late age of onset.

For AS, the numbering system changes (see Table 5), but the same criteria are used for the social deficits and the restricted and repetitive behaviors (the communication criteria are left out altogether). For a diagnosis of AS, only two criteria need to be met under social deficits, and only one criterion is required under repetitive and restricted interests and behaviors. A crucial part of evaluating for AS is to make sure to review the communication criteria from the autistic disorder criteria. The reason is that at least one-third of individuals who are diagnosed with AS actually meet the criteria for HFA (some researchers say as many as 80 to one hundred percent are more appropriately diagnosed with AS). Unless the full criteria for autistic disorder are reviewed, it is possible to misclassify HFA as AS.

For AS to be diagnosed, there must not be a history of significant language delays (although the definition used for no significant language delay is very loose, with single words delayed until age two and phrase speech delayed until age three) and the individual's IQ has to be over 70 (70 is the cutoff for MR). Additionally, the individual cannot have a history of delays in the development of "age-appropriate self-help skills, adaptive behavior, and curiosity about the environment in childhood." Although individuals with AS do not have significant delays in developing language, that does not mean that their language is completely normal.

If the time is taken to look carefully, most individuals with HFA or AS have semantic-pragmatic language disorders that satisfy criteria 2b. Their choice of words is often overly formal or odd, and they tend to interpret language literally, often showing intolerance if another person uses language incorrectly. Conversations do not flow in a reciprocal fashion.

Individuals with AS also tend to have trouble with creative, imaginary activities (criteria 2d in the autistic disorder diagnostic criteria). They prefer logical, systematic pursuits. Hence, most individuals with AS will meet two criteria for autistic disorder under communication (2b and 2c) if that information is sought, which often qualifies them for a diagnosis of autistic disorder. The *DSM-IV-TR* requires that a diagnosis of autistic disorder be given if six or more criteria are met. The diagnosis of autism trumps the diagnosis of AS as long as six criteria are fulfilled. A shorthand way to express that an individual diagnosed with autistic disorder has fluent verbal abilities and an IQ in the normal range is to add in the words "high-functioning" before the autism to make HFA. HFA is not an official *DSM-IV-TR* diagnosis, but the label has become an accepted way to quickly indicate that there is a significant difference in functional level compared with a person with classic autism.

Whether or not AS is a useful diagnostic label is the subject of continuing debate, with more and more experts coming to the conclusion that there is no substantive difference between individuals given the label of HFA and those classified as AS. A 2003 review of twenty-six studies comparing AS with HFA did not reveal obvious differences in rates of social, emotional, or psychiatric problems; current behavior profiles; or motor or neuropsychological cognitive profiles (Howlin 2003). Nonetheless, the categories still exist as of this writing (with no chance of change until the *DSM-V* is released in 2011–2012). The important take-home message is that anyone with suspected AS needs a full evaluation for autistic disorder. It is not appropriate to jump to a diagnosis of AS simply because the individual has apparently normal language skills and IQ. A systematic consideration of an HFA diagnosis must be completed.

Why is it important to be so careful about distinguishing between HFA and AS? Because, illogical as it may be, the services available to people with AS are often less comprehensive than services for individuals with autistic disorders. To act responsibly toward each person coming in for a diagnostic evaluation, examiners must be vigilant about looking for autism in individuals referred for an AS evaluation.

Tests Used to Assess the *DSM-IV* Criteria for Autistic Spectrum Disorders: ADI-R

Many clinicians, particularly at the major university clinics, have done away with efforts to pick their way through the inexact process of deciding which of the *DSM* criteria are fulfilled. Instead, they make use of a diagnostic tool that standardizes the information collected and uses a statistically validated process to assess the core *DSM-IV* criteria. This process is referred to as operationalizing the *DSM-IV* criteria. The ADI-R developed by Catherine Lord, Michael Rutter, and Ann LeCouteur in 1999 provides a format for a thorough interview covering areas relevant to ASDs. The items are scored, and the scores are tabulated to arrive at total scores for communication and reciprocal interaction. The restricted and repetitive behavior section did not statistically aid the diagnostic process; therefore, it isnot included in the ADI-R. The scores are compared to cutoffs that yield a diagnostic classification of autism, ASD, or not on the autistic spectrum. The test takes between one and a half to three hours to administer and requires extensive training to ensure that the examiner is scoring the test according to conventions (inaccurate scoring provides inaccurate classifications). The results are not intended to provide a definitive diagnosis but are meant to be combined with other information available to the examiner to assist in coming to a final diagnosis.

In an attempt to standardize the information coming out of research studies on ASDs, most clinical studies now require that scores on the ADI-R and the ADOS (see below) must both fall in the range consistent with an ASD for the subject to be included in any study. To administer these tests in a research study, the examiner must undergo rigorous training with the requirement to achieve "reliability" (proving that the scores the examiner gives are sufficiently close to the scores given by the developers of the test). Using uniform ways of diagnosing the ASDs allows for better comparison of results from study to study.

Observational Instruments to Supplement the Diagnostic Process: CARS and ADOS

The first widely used test for autism that required the examiner to directly observe the child was the Childhood Autism Rating Scale (CARS) developed by Eric Schopler and colleagues in 1988. The CARS is appropriate for children twenty-four months and up. An experienced observer rates behaviors representative of the three core features of autism from typical to severely deviant. The scores are used to arrive at a numerical score that is consistent with typical behavior, mild-moderate autism, or severe autism. If the examiner pays attention to the instructions and takes the time to complete the test accurately (around thirty minutes), this test continues to be a fairly good observational test for ASDs. The CARs is invalid if it is completed solely on the basis of interviews.

The most widely used supplemental test for ASDs is called the Autism Diagnostic Observation Schedule (ADOS), developed by Catherine Lord, Ph.D., and colleagues in 2000. The test is designed to give the examiner a chance to observe firsthand the ways that the individual communicates and interacts socially. Because many children with language delays are referred for ASD evaluations, the ADOS was designed so that language impairments would not influence the test results (i.e., individuals with language delays in combination with normal NVC and social skills would not be identified as having an ASD). To accomplish this task, the ADOS is divided into four separate modules based on language level. Module 1 is for children who do not yet speak ("preverbal") or use only single words, module 2 is for children who can put words together into short phrases, module 3 is for children and adolescents with fluent speech, and module 4 is for fluent adolescents and adults. The ADOS can be used for children as young as 12 months of age all the way through the life span (as long as the individual's NVIQ is at least equivalent to a 12 month old).

Each module has different components. Module 1 is designed to be appealing to young children. A wide variety of play opportunities are offered with typical age-appropriate toys (balls, blocks, toy phone, pop-up toy, cars, bubbles, balloon, doll, and pretend birthday party). During the play, the examiner takes notes on the child's communication strategies, social interactions, and the extent to which the child integrates speech, facial expressions, eye contact, and other NVC to facilitate social interactions. After the test is done, the examiner goes through a list of questions about communication and social interactions and selects the score that best describes the child's behavior during the ADOS. The items are scored from zero to three, with the lower scores given for typical behavior and the higher scores given for behaviors that fit the ASD profile. For example, if the child takes the examiner's hand and moves it to a toy as a way of asking for help, a score of two would be given because that behavior is highly specific for ASDs (typical individuals and those with other DDs do not use an adults hand as a tool to accomplish a desired task).

Different activities are included in modules 2 through 4 that take advantage of the increased language skills. Module 2 provides opportunities for more advanced imaginary play and conversation. There is progressively less play and more questions about emotions, relationships, and feelings in modules 3 and 4.

When the authors studied each module, they discovered that some of the scored items did not effectively separate children with ASDs from non-ASD children. Only the statistically proven indicators were selected for the scoring algorithm used to arrive at the final ADOS classification. Because the presence of perseverative interests and RMMs during the ADOS did not function adequately as a way to discriminate ASDs from non-ASDs, the ADOS makes use of scores for communication and social behaviors but does not include a score for restricted or repetitive behaviors on the part of the test that is used to determine the diagnostic classification.

Scores on the key statistically significant items are combined to produce three separate scores communication, social and total score. Statistical tests were used to set cutoffs that separated the bulk of the individuals with autism from the non-autism ASDs and non-ASD diagnoses. There are five important points to remember about the ADOS. First, it is of the utmost importance to realize that the ADOS was never intended to provide a definitive dividing line between autism and PDD-NOS because the groups overlap significantly. Final decisions about diagnosis should never be based solely on the ADOS classification. Second, individuals with AS were not studied specifically when the cutoffs were developed; it is not clear what pattern of ADOS scores would support an AS diagnosis. Some clinicians use the social score cutoffs as a guide, but that is not a validated practice. Third, an ADOS score that yields an autism or ASD classification does not necessarily mean that the individual has an ASD. Many mental health conditions can elevate the score into the autism or ASD range even though the individual does not have an ASD. Fourth, in very young children, the ADOS cutoffs are not as reliable. To address this issue, a toddler module (ADOS-T) is being developed (preliminary data presented at the International Meeting for Autism Research in 2008 demonstrated 95 percent sensitivity and specificity for children ages twelve to thirty months). Fifth, examiners using the ADOS must be trained appropriately and then work diligently to maintain their reliability. Incorrect administration or scoring can result in an incorrect classification. The bottomline is that the ADOS classification is an extremely useful piece of information, but it is not a diagnosis.

Synthesis: The Crux of the Diagnostic Evaluation

By far the hardest part of an evaluation for an ASD is the process of combining all of the available information into a final diagnosis. There is no formula that helps the clinician combine the classification from the CARS or ADOS with the results from the ADI-R classification or review of the *DSM-IV* criteria for autistic disorder or AS and clinical experience to arrive at a diagnostic decision. Experienced examiners have a high rate of agreement (i.e., come to the same conclusion separately), but the process can be fraught with uncertainty even for the most seasoned clinician.

In the end, all the clinician can do is make the best decision they can at the time (referred to as the "best-fit" or "best estimate" diagnosis). Every child has here own developmental trajectory, and a child who receives one diagnosis when young may be better described by another diagnosis later on. Every examiner who is thoughtful will admit that the diagnostic system is imperfect, and any examiner can come to a conclusion that later proves to be wrong. The best test of the correctness of an ASD diagnosis is time.

ATTEMPTS TO IMPROVE THE CLASSIFICATION SYSTEM: SUBTYPING THE ASDS

Over the years, researchers have proposed a wide variety of systems to try to divide the ASDs into more homogeneous subgroups, commonly referred to as subtypes. The current dividing lines provide these subgroups (AD, PDD-NOS, AS) that are still extremely heterogeneous. The autism group contains very low-functioning and very high-functioning individuals and everything in between. The PDD-NOS group is even more heterogeneous. All individuals with AS are similar with regard to level of language and IQ greater than 70, but there is still immense variability in how each individuals functions. Is there a better way to divide the spectrum? The idea behind subtyping the ASDs is to create a system that divides individuals in ways that might be more meaningful than autism, PDD-NOS, and AS.

Wing's Behavioral Subtypes

Lorna Wing was one of the first to suggest a way to subdivide the autistic spectrum. She proposed division into three groups based on observed behavioral styles: aloof, passive, and active but odd. Children with classic autism are almost always aloof (noninteractive). Children with the passive subtype tend to be flexible enough to go with the flow of day-to day-activities without complaint but do not actively seek social interactions. Children with the active but odd subtype make social approaches but often do so in an intrusive, inappropriate way.

Subtyping by Medical Features: Essential versus Complex Autism

A geneticist named Judith Miles proposed a classification scheme that divides the autistic spectrum into "essential" and "complex" subtypes. Miles used two easily ascertained features to make the first division: the presence of microcephaly (head size smaller than the third percentile) and the presence of physical features that were identifiable as or suspicious for a genetic syndrome (referred to as "dysmorphic features" in medical terminology).

Individuals with microcephaly or dysmorphic features were placed in the complex autism group. Individuals without either finding were grouped together in the essential autism group (also referred to as "idiopathic autism," meaning without obvious cause). Of 260 patients, 5 percent had microcephaly and 16 percent had significant dysmorphic physical features; together, they comprised 20 percent of the study population (essential autism accounted for the other 80 percent).

The simple division into essential and complex autism had profound implications for the individuals in the two groups. The complex autism group had a higher incidence of seizures, lower IQ, and more brain abnormalities on MRI. Although this division might give parents a better idea about the future, subtyping into essential or complex has not been adopted for mainstream use.

Subtyping by Behavioral Profile

Other investigators have tried to separate individuals with ASDs by specific behavioral features (called behavioral "phenotypes"). Examples of behavioral phenotypes include RMMs or an obsessive desire to maintain sameness. The researchers are looking for genes that govern each specific behavior. To date, the attempts to develop distinct behavioral subtypes have not been particularly successful, mostly likely because behaviors in ASDs are usually displayed in a continuum.

Subtyping by Intellectual Level

Dividing the autistic spectrum by intellectual level has been found to separate the ASDs into meaningful subgroups. Individuals with autism with ID have a very different future ahead of them compared with individuals with autism with cognitive abilities in the average to above-average ranges. The difficulty with using this subtyping strategy is that it is often very hard to accurately determine IQ in young children with ASDs.

Early-Onset Subtype versus Late-Onset (Regressive) Subtype

It is now clear that there are two distinctly different courses that children with ASDs can follow. Some children show clear evidence of developmental abnormalities consistent with autism from the very first few months of life, termed "early-onset" autism. The "late-onset" or "regressive" subtype is characterized by typical speech and social skills during the first ten months of age, followed by gradual or sudden loss of the language and normal social responsiveness (typically between twelve and eighteen months of age). Early evidence suggests that regression is a poor prognostic indicator (meaning that the children with regression fare worse over the long haul).

Subtyping by Biologic Markers

A biomarker is a measurable biologic feature that can be used to identify the presence of a condition. There are currently no biomarkers that reliably distinguish different subtypes of ASDs, but there are some tantalizing clues that biomarkers for ASDs may be close at hand.

A 2001 study from California made use of stored samples of blood collected from the heels of newborn babies in the first few days of life that are used to screen for harmful conditions, such as phenylketonuria (PKU) and hyperthyroidism. The researchers looked to see whether there were any hormones that were present at abnormal levels in children who went on to develop autism, MR, or cerebral palsy (CP). In children who developed autism or MR, the researchers identified elevations in many neural growth factors that are known to influence the development of the brain. None of the TD children or children who went on to develop CP had elevations in the brain-related growth factors. Research is currently ongoing to see whether newborn testing for brain-related growth hormones can lead to early identification of a subgroup of children with ASDs.

Abnormal Brain Growth in the First Year of Life as a Possible Biomarker

Evidence from studies of early brain growth in ASDs have shown that a large percentage of children with ASDs show a pattern of accelerated brain growth during the first year of life. MRI studies have demonstrated an increase in the amount of brain white matter that accounts for the accelerated growth (see Chapter 6 for details). Excessive early brain growth might be a potential way to subtype the ASDs. Studies by Judith Miles and others have suggested that large head size (called macrocephaly—literally, big head) and rapid head growth in the first year of life are poor prognostic indicators.

**Failure to Separate the ASDs into Subgroups Interferes with
Attempts to Determine the Underlying Causes of ASDs**

All researchers agree that sorting out the causes of ASDs is hampered by
the diversity of individuals lumped together under the ASD umbrella. Until
the ASDs are subtyped into more homogeneous groups, progress toward
uncovering the causes of ASDs will be hindered.

5

What Can Statistics Tell Us about ASDs?

IS THERE AN AUTISM EPIDEMIC?

In Kanner's classic 1943 paper, he wrote, "These characteristics form a unique 'syndrome,' not heretofore reported, which seems to be rare enough, yet is probably more frequent than is indicated by the paucity of observed cases." Kanner was right.

The CDC estimates that there are at least 560,000 people under the age of twenty-one with autism in the United States. The most recent CDC estimate for the frequency of ASDs is one case for every 150 children (written as 1:150). Autism is certainly not rare; that is not up for debate. What is at the center of the firestorm is the question of whether or not ASDs are becoming increasingly more common.

The media is chock full of reports on the "autism epidemic." The adamant belief that an autism epidemic is occurring in the United States and other developed countries is so widely held among the general public and families affected by ASDs that it seems like a foregone conclusion. Epidemiologists, statisticians trained to look at health-related issues, have been more circumspect.

How do we determine whether we are in the midst of an autism epidemic? First, it is helpful to know what is meant by the term "epidemic." An epidemic exists when more than the expected cases of a condition or disease occurs in a region during a given time period. Epidemics often involve a sudden severe outbreak (e.g., severe acute respiratory syndrome) but can unfold over a longer period of time (e.g., human immunodeficiency virus/acquired immunodeficiency syndrome). The word "epidemic" comes from the Greek *epi-*, which means upon, and *demos*, which means people or population. ASDs represent an epidemic if the number of cases exceeds the expected number. But how is that determined? To get to the bottom of the epidemic controversy, we need to know whether there are more new cases of autism than expected. That sounds like a simple question, but finding an answer has been complicated by a variety of statistical problems that will be reviewed in this chapter.

After intensive study and careful examination of the issue, the epidemiologists are starting to split into two distinct camps. A small minority of epidemiologists are starting to voice their opinion that the mounting evidence supports a true increase in ASDs, although the exact magnitude of the true increase is not completely clear. The rest of the experts continue to maintain that the available information is still insufficient to determine whether there has been a true increase in new cases of autism or ASDs. How can there be such differences of opinion on an issue of such importance? That is what we will try to understand in this chapter as we take a look at what we know, what we do not know, and what we need to know to solve the mystery.

KEY STATISTICAL TERMS

There is a reason that statisticians go to school for many years to learn their trade; understanding what numbers can and cannot tell us is a tricky business. Although it may seem that the numbers collected on ASDs are telling a clear story of increasingly more new cases of ASDs over the past fifteen to twenty years, careful interpretation is necessary to understand where the numbers come from and why there are no exact numbers to definitively answer the epidemic question. Every effort has been made to minimize the need for specialized knowledge about statistics in this section, but there are two key terms that have to be understood to follow the controversy. The two main statistical terms that are used to monitor health-related conditions are prevalence and incidence.

Prevalence tells how common a condition is in a selected population. For example, the number of eight-year-old children in the state of New Jersey with an ASD compared with all the eight-year-old children in New Jersey is a prevalence proportion (frequently referred to as a "prevalence rate," although the use of the term "rate" here is not technically accurate). Prevalence proportions are usually written as fractions like 67/10,000 or they can be written as a ratio (1:150). Most of the time, the numbers reported in press releases are ratios because it is easier to get a feel for what it means when we say that there is one eight-year-old child with an ASD for every 150 eight-year-old children in the sample population. Whether you prefer to look at fractions or ratios is up to you.

Incidence rates tell us the number of *new* cases that occur over a set period of time in all individuals who are at risk for the condition. To be "at risk" for a condition means that the individual started the time period free from the condition but had a chance of developing the condition over a specific time period. For example, a meaningful incidence statistic would be the number of new cases of ASDs in the United States by the year 2015 out of all the births in the United States in 2007. If the incidence rate for any given year was known, then we could compare the incidence rates over successive years to see if the incidence is increasing, decreasing, or staying at a stable rate. When looking at prevalence proportions and incidence rates, make sure to compare apples with apples and oranges with oranges. Do not try to compare incidence rates with prevalence rates or statistics for autism with those for all ASDs (autism, PDD-NOS, and AS).

Incidence rates for autism are hard to determine for a variety of statistical reasons, so epidemiologists have mostly collected prevalence statistics about autism and ASDs over the years. Because prevalence statistics alone cannot be used to determine whether there is an autism epidemic, many epidemiologists continue to maintain that we still cannot tell for certain what is happening with the incidence of ASDs.

The distinction between incidence and prevalence may sound obscure, but it is one of the issues at the heart of the current controversy about ASDs. Evidence of increasing prevalence for ASDs is now undeniable, but prevalence will differ depending on the age range examined and can be affected by a change in the age at diagnosis or other changes in the population. The optimal way to determine whether the risk of developing an ASD is or is not increasing is to examine the true incidence of ASDs with data collected up to an age when most cases of ASDs will have been identified (e.g., eight to ten years of age). A look at how the autism epidemic controversy unfolded will make the issues more clear.

THE FIRST WAKE-UP CALL: THE CALIFORNIA AUTISM DATA

California has twenty-one state-funded agencies called regional centers that provide services for individuals with autism and three specific DDs (MR, CP, and epilepsy). The number of individuals receiving services in each category is tracked on a quarterly basis and reported to a central system maintained by the California Department of Developmental Services (DDS).

Starting in the early nineties, a disturbing trend was seen in the DDS data: the number of individuals receiving services for autism was increasing at a much higher rate than for the other developmental disabilities. Apprised of the situation by the DDS, the state legislature requested more information. In 1999, a report authored by Dr. Ron Huff that was released to the California legislature caught the nation's attention.

Based on the data from the California DDS, the number of individuals in the system with a diagnosis of autism increased by 273 percent over the ten-year period between 1987 and 1998. Over the same period, the number of individuals with the other eligible DDs (MR, epilepsy, and CP) also increased but by a much smaller amount (ranging from 30 to 50 percent). No simple explanation such as an increase in the California population or a general increase in the usage of the regional center system could explain away the results.

The information was like fuel on a fire for the already growing concerns expressed by many parents of children with autism that there was an undetected autism epidemic in progress. Epidemiologists responded with scholarly papers, citing numerous reasons that the number of cases in the regional center system could increase without a true increase in autism incidence, Most experts expressed their beliefs that the increase in autism cases at the regional center could be explained by broadened diagnostic criteria, more familiarity with autism driving more individuals to seek services, and diagnostic substitution (counting individuals under the autism category who had previously been counted under the MR category).

The DDS study of the California data made no claims to answer statistical questions about the incidence or prevalence of autism in California, but that was how the general public interpreted the report. The report has been heavily criticized by expert statisticians, who considered the study to be woefully inadequate to allow any conclusions to be drawn regarding a possible increase in ASDs. The only conclusion drawn from the study that was not in dispute was that California needed to expand regional center services for individuals with autism. The aftermath of the 1999 DDS report led epidemiologists to reexamine existing studies on autism prevalence, examine trends, and gather more data in California and elsewhere to try to determine if there is evidence for a true increase in autism incidence. The California legislature quickly appropriated $1 million to look at these confounding issues in a systematic way.

2002: More California Data Suggesting a True Increase in Autism Prevalence

Robert Byrd, an epidemiologist at the M.I.N.D. Institute at the University of California, Davis was put in charge of the epidemiologic study designed to clarify the situation. In 2002, Dr. Byrd reported to the California legislature on a follow-up study called *The Epidemiology of Autism in California Study*. The author concluded that there was no evidence that broader diagnostic criteria, misdiagnosis, or diagnostic substitution could explain the increasing numbers of individuals with autism in the California regional center system. The possibility that the increase was a result of more public awareness of autism still remained. Byrd's conclusions have been challenged by other epidemiologists who feel that he may have overinterpreted the available data.

2008: The Trend Continues with No Sign of Easing

The most recent study using data from the California DDS database was published in January 2008 (Schechter 2008). The study looked at children between the ages of three and twelve and assessed the prevalence of autism in each age group during the successive years between 1989 and 2003. During the fourteen-year study period, the prevalence of autism rose in all age groups, with the most significant increases noted in the youngest age groups.

For example, the prevalence of ASDs in six year olds born in 1985 (measured in 1991) was 6/10,000 live births (1:1666), whereas the prevalence rate in six year olds born in 1994 (measured in 2000) was 45/10,000 (1:222). Although the DDS data cannot prove that there was a true increase in incidence, the progressive increases in prevalence rates over time suggest that there may be a true rise in the incidence of autism.

A useful way to look at the validity of the prevalence estimates drawn from the California DDS data is to ask how the numbers compare with statistics gathered in other studies using different methods. To do that, it is helpful to take a brief trip back in time to look at the earliest statistics on the prevalence of autism and how those estimates have changed over time.

Estimates of Prevalence: Past and Present

Victor Lotter (Lotter 1966) and Lorna Wing (Wing and Gould 1976) conducted the two largest early studies of autism prevalence, resulting in estimates that were quite similar: 4.1/10,000 for Lotter and 4.9/10,000 for Wing (between 1:2000 and 1:2500). Since then, a huge number of prevalence studies have been conducted in numerous countries. The studies differed significantly in the methods used to find cases of possible autism in the study population (referred to as "case-finding" or "case ascertainment"), which criteria were used to diagnose autism and how the accuracy of the diagnosis was confirmed. Better case finding produces higher estimates that are likely to be more accurate. The more inclusive the criteria used for diagnosis, the higher the numbers. The less vigilant the researchers are in making sure that school and medical records with a diagnosis of an ASD are correct, the higher the numbers will be for the prevalence in that study. The result of these methodologic variations was that the prevalence rates differed from study to study by three- to ten-fold, even when the studies were done in similar locations during the same time period.

Dr. Eric Fombonne, a noted epidemiologist who has conducted numerous investigations of autism prevalence, reviewed the sum total of the available epidemiologic data through 2001 (Fombonne, 2003). From 1966 to 1991, the average prevalence of autism was in line with the data from Lotter and Wing: 4.4/10,000. From 1992 to 2001, the average prevalence for autism rose to 12.7/10,000—an increase of almost 300 percent. Returning to the 1998 California DDS data (which are not prevalence data but do give a rough estimate of the relative increase in numbers of children with full syndrome autism), it is interesting to note that the increase of 272 percent over the ten-year period from 1987 to 1998 is strikingly similar to estimates from the studies reviewed by Fombonne.

What Do We Know about the Prevalence of PDD-NOS and AS Compared to Autism?

Although PDD-NOS was not incorporated into the DSM until 1987 and AS was not included until 1994, some of the earliest studies of prevalence include estimates for conditions similar to autism with less severe manifestations—a group that is very likely to be similar to the nonautism ASDs (PDD-NOS and AS). A study done by Victor Lotter in 1966 yielded a prevalence of 4.1/10,000 (~1:2500) for autism and 3.3/10,000 (~1:3000) for the less severe variants for a total prevalence of 1:1350 for all ASDs. Wing and Gould's study in 1976 found the prevalence of autism to be 4.9/10,000 (close to 1:2000, the number most frequently quoted for decades) with the prevalence for the milder condition reported as 16.3/10,000 (1:613) for a total of 21.2/10,000 or 1:472 for all ASDs. As you can see from these two early studies, there was poor agreement about the relative proportions of autism to the nonautism ASDs, with Lotter estimating that there were less children with the milder forms than there were children with autism and Wing and Gould estimating that there are three times more children with the milder forms than there are children with autism.

The discrepancies in the ratios between autism and the nonautism PDDs did not end with the Lotter and Wing's early studies. In fact, eight studies later, the estimates for the ratio of nonautism ASDs to autism still covered the same approximate ranges, with estimates of nonautism ASDs running from half as many cases as ASDs up to slightly more than three times the number of cases of autism. Fombonne decided to go with the average of all the studies, estimating that there were 1.5 children with the nonautism ASDs for every one child with autism (i.e., for every two children with autism, three have a milder form). Fombonne's estimate is by no means the final word.

Studies looking at the ratio of AS to autism are few and far between. The quality is limited by the low numbers of subjects in each study, resulting in estimates that are less reliable. Fombonne estimates that there is one individual with AS for every four with autism, but he acknowledged that the number could be even higher.

Although the relative proportions of autism, PDD-NOS, and AS vary from study to study to vary, the total prevalence rates for all of the ASDs added together have been remarkably consistent across recently published studies. For this reason, it makes much more sense to monitor the ASDs as a group rather than continuing efforts to parse out the statistics. As a result, the CDC uses the prevalance of all the ASD combined for the purpose of monitoring in the United States. Based on a summary of all the extant studies, Fombonne concluded in 2003 that the prevalence of any form of ASD (e.g., autism, PDD-NOS, and AS) is best estimated at sixty per 10,000 (1:167).

Monitoring the Prevalence of ASDs in the United States: The CDC Response

In 1997, the citizens of Brick Township in New Jersey became concerned about the alarming number of children in the area being diagnosed with ASDs. They worried that the seemingly localized increase represented a possible autism cluster (similar to the concept of a cancer cluster).

The uneasy townspeople contacted the New Jersey department of public health for help. The New Jersey congressional representative for Brick Township got into the act, requesting a full investigation. Public health personnel from the Agency for Toxic Substances and Disease Registry (ATSDR) were instructed to search for evidence of toxic exposures, and a team of epidemiologists from the CDC was dispatched to assess the prevalence of ASDs in Brick Township. The ATSDR investigation found multiple environmental contaminants in the groundwater and a local river but dismissed the toxicants as unlikely causes of ASDs (see the ATSDR website for specific information). The CDC results, released three years later in 2001, shocked the nation: 1:167 or 6.7/1000 of the children between three and ten years of age was diagnosed with an ASD. The townspeople were right that ASDs were common in their community. What they did not yet realize was that the prevalence of ASDs was equally high across the United States and other developed countries.

The Autism and Developmental Disabilities Monitoring Network

In response to the Brick Township Study, efforts began in earnest to gather the necessary information to better assess the prevalence of ASDs. The CDC responded to the call to action by creating the Autism and Developmental Disabilities Monitoring Network (ADDM) to monitor trends in the prevalence of ASDs across the United States. The results of the first two studies conducted in 2000 and 2002 were published in the February 9, 2007, issue of the *Morbidity and Mortality Weekly Report* (ADDM, 2007). In the year 2000, the prevalence of ASDs in eight year olds was calculated using data from six sites scattered across the United States. The rates in the selected states varied by about a factor of two, with the state of West Virginia showing the lowest prevalence (4.5/1000) and the state of New Jersey showing the highest prevalence (9.9 per 1000). The states with the lowest prevalence were the states that did not have ready access to educational records, increasing the chance that some children identified as having an ASD through the school system would go undetected by the CDC researchers, leading to an underestimation of the true prevalence in those states.

The CDC made the decision to use an average of the prevalence rates obtained at each of the six sites, resulting in a prevalence estimate of 6.7/1000 (1:150) in the year 2000. It is worthwhile to ask what the prevalence would have been if the CDC used the state with the highest prevalence as a yardstick, assuming that the better detection rate in that state meant that the case ascertainment was more complete. When New Jersey numbers are used, the rate for ASDs is very close to 1:100.

In 2002, data were collected from fourteen sites to get a better representation of the entire country. Once again, New Jersey had the highest prevalence at 10.6/1000 (1:94). The CDC again decided to use an average of the prevalence estimates, resulting in the 1:150 figure that is widely quoted as the most current prevalence estimate of ASDs in the United States. The average prevalence did not change between 2000 and 2002, but the CDC cautioned that two years was too short of a time span to make any definitive statements about trends in the prevalence rate for ASDs. There were two states that did show small increases: Georgia and New Jersey. The 1:94 statistic calculated from the New Jersey data circulated rapidly in the press and on the Internet as proof that the prevalence of ASDs is continuing to rise, but that conclusion is not statistically valid.

Role of Diagnostic Substitution in the Increasing Prevalence Rates for ASDs

Supporters of the theory that there is an increase in the incidence of ASDs of massive proportions frequently ask the rhetorical question, "If all of these children with ASDs were out there the whole time, where were they?" An attempt to respond to that query requires understanding of how a process called "diagnostic substitution" can influence prevalence statistics. Diagnostic substitution is the process of replacing one diagnosis with another with the result being that a person who was counted in a specific category of disability at one point is removed from the original category and placed in another. A possible explanation for at least part of the increasing prevalence rates for ASDs is that the children who are now counted in the ASD numbers were previously counted under a different category such as mental health, MR, language impairments, or learning disabilities. If diagnostic substitution is driving the increased prevalence of ASD, it should be possible to detect what categories the individuals were previously placed in to see if there is a corresponding decrease in those categories as the ASD diagnoses increase.

In the mental health area, there have been a variety of labels attached to children who would likely be diagnosed with ASDs in the current system of categorizing childhood neurobiologic conditions with behavioral manifestations. The most common categories used were childhood schizophrenia, schizoid personality disorder, and schizotypal personality disorder. Extensive chapters have been written in prominent autism reference texts that attempt to make the differentiation between schizoid and schizotypal personality disorder (defined as a mental health diagnosis applied to individuals with "a pervasive pattern of social and interpersonal deficits," leading to problems with forming close relationships and eccentric behavior) and ASDs, but it remains unclear how separable these conditions really are. Other individuals with ASDs have received mental health diagnoses as the primary explanation for their odd behaviors when it was likely that the mental health issues were comorbid with an underlying ASD that was not recognized. Most adolescents and adults with ASDs who are not recognized during childhood come to the initial ASD evaluation with a thick pile of records from previous psychiatric evaluations that often include diagnoses of ADHD, OCD, depression, and anxiety. The number of unrecognized cases of ASDs hidden behind mental health diagnoses is not known, but it is clear that many of the higher-functioning individuals with ASDs have long been lumped into the mental health category. ASDs are now better recognized, likely accounting for at least a part of the increased referrals for ASD evaluations in older individuals with normal IQ, a group that has substantially increased in recent years.

Numbers from the special education system are difficult to interpret because autism was not tracked by the schools until after the IDEA reauthorization was passed in 1990, making school data an unreliable source for long-term monitoring. Studies looking at the diagnostic substitution of an autism or

ASD diagnosis for MR have yielded mixed results, with some studies showing that decreases in the MR category are of the same magnitude as increases in autism and others failing to show a link.

It is likely that a significant percentage of children previously identified as having a developmental language disorder are now counted in the ASD category. Isabelle Rapin, a pediatric neurologist, proposed the term "semantic pragmatic disorder" to describe children with adequate language who nevertheless have difficulty with comprehension and tend to use language in odd ways, although they are perfectly capable of repeating language verbatim or reciting the dialogue to a favorite show. Rapin proposed that there is an overlap between language disorders without social abnormalities (called specific language impairments), semantic-pragmatic language disorders, and the PDDs that may indicate that they are all on the same spectrum. To try to estimate the number of missed ASD diagnoses in previous studies of language disorders, a group of researchers reevaluated thirty-eight children who participated in a study of language disorders that ran from 1986 to 2003. The subjects were between ages fifteen and thirty-one when they reevaluated. Their results, published in 2008, revealed that 25 percent of the individuals met the current diagnostic criteria for an ASD yet none had previously been diagnosed with an ASD. Unrecognized ASDs in children with language disorders are likely to account for a significant part of the increase in ASD prevalence.

Learning disabilities refers to cognitive areas that are disproportionately difficult for the individual to master compared to expected performance based on IQ. Since many individuals with ASDs have uneven profiles in verbal and nonverbal cognitive skill, it is likely that many have been and continue to be identified as individuals with learning disabilities without proper evaluation for the possibility of an ASD. In particular, individuals classified as having a "nonverbal learning disability" (NLD) have a high degree of overlap with AS. NLD is a category that is based on IQ profiles showing a verbal IQ score that is significantly higher than the performance IQ. Because the definition does not rely on behavioral features, individuals with NLD do not necessarily have significant social deficits. Social deficits are a core feature of approximately one-third of individuals with NLD who meet the criteria for HFA/AS. Comparisons of children with AS, HFA, and NLD have shown that the cognitive and behavioral profiles differed on only a few measures, providing a strong argument that they are all on the same spectrum.

A recent study of diagnostic substitution in the special education system estimated that one-third of the increase in the prevalence of ASDs can be attributed to diagnostic substitution from other special education categories. Taken together, the recognition of ASDs in individuals previously diagnosed with childhood schizophrenia, eccentric personality disorders, semantic-pragmatic language disorders, and learning disabilities (including NLD) is likely to account for at least one third of the increase in ASD prevalence.

CONCLUSIONS AND A LOOK TO THE FUTURE

What conclusions can be drawn from the available information? The prevalence of ASDs in the United States as of 2002 is between 1:94 and 1:150. The prevalence rate for all ASDs has increased between three- to tenfold since the early studies by Lotter and Wing, depending on which numbers are chosen for comparison (Fombonne's 60/10,000 for all ASDs is only a threefold increase over Wing's 20/10,000). Although the press often quotes figures as high as a hundredfold increase in ASD, those numbers are not supported by the bulk of the data. Despite all of this information, it still is not known for certain how much of the increase in prevalence can be attributed to diagnostic substitution, changes in the DSM criteria for ASDs, and wider public and professional awareness of ASDs leading to increased recognition of cases.

Some of the answers should soon be known. Changing diagnostic criteria should not influence the next several prevalence estimates from the CDC because the diagnostic criteria have been "operationalized" (specific rules have been laid out to decide whether or not the criteria are met that will stay stable from year to year for the ADDMN studies). The issue of increasing knowledge of ASDs leading to more referrals should level out as we reach a saturation point, with the vast majority of parents, PCPs, and teachers already thoroughly familiar with the ASDs. One caveat is that the 2007 AAP guidelines promoting better screening for ASDs might result in a spike in diagnoses (if the screening recommendations are followed by enough PCPs). Although the CDC data cannot provide firm data on incidence, the reliable information on prevalence trends should be close enough to answer the remaining questions.

Despite all the remaining unknowns, it is clear that ASDs are much more frequent than previously thought. The high numbers of children with ASDs requires a robust response from the state and federal agencies charged with providing appropriate intervention services. While we wait for the final verdict as to whether the true incidence of ASDs is increasing, it makes sense to make a tentative assumption that there is at least some percentage of the increase in ASDs that is attributable to a true increase. This assumption may or may not be proven in the end, but there is no downside to searching vigorously for clues that may help us understand why the incidence of ASDs may be rising and what can be done to reverse the trend. There are at least 1:150 children who deserve for ASDs to be treated as an urgent public health issue.

WHAT ELSE CAN STATISTICS TELL US ABOUT ASDS?

Sex Ratios

All ASDs are more common in boys. The most commonly quoted figure is four boys with autistic disorder for every girl (4:1), but that ratio does not really tell the whole story. In the HFA/AS group, there are as many as ten boys for every girl. In lower-functioning persons with autism (sometimes referred to as "autism with MR"), the numbers even out, with approximately equal numbers of males and females.

Intelligence in ASDs

In the past, it was commonly stated that 75 percent of individuals with autistic disorder had MR. The 75 percent statistic was included in the *DSM* as recently as 1994 but was deleted from the 2000 *DSM-IV-TR* because of increasing evidence that MR is not found as commonly in children with autism as it once was. The *DSM-IV-TR* continues to state that most cases of autistic disorder are associated with MR, ranging from mild to profound, but that statement is somewhat misleading. Chakrabarti and Fombonne found that 29.8 percent of children between ages four and six with an ASD had MR, with the percentage varying by the PDD subtype. In the autism group, 66.7 percent scored in the MR range, whereas only 12.0 percent in PDD-NOS showed MR.

The evolving statistics on the intellectual abilities in individuals with ASDs can be partly attributed to the increase in high-functioning individuals diagnosed with autistic disorder. It is also possible that more effective EI is resulting in better intellectual outcomes. A third contributing factor to the higher measured IQs may be the use of more appropriate tests that allow individuals with autism to show their cognitive strengths (which are often, but not always, better demonstrated in tests that require good visuospatial awareness, memory, and problem solving with no or minimal requirements for the use of language).

A topic of great interest to all is the highly developed abilities in isolated areas shown by some individuals with ASDs, many of whom function at a much lower level than their talents would suggest. To learn more about individuals with ASDs who possess astounding skills, see the sidebar entitled "Autistic Savants."

Loss of Language and Social Skills (Regression): How Common Is It?

In Kanner's 1943 paper, he wrote, "We must, then, assume that these children have come into the world with innate inability to form the usual, biologically provided affective contact with people, just as other children come into the world with innate physical or intellectual handicaps." The belief that all children with autism were developmentally atypical from the time of birth was prevalent for decades despite parental protestations that their child had been developmentally normal up until they lost language skills and withdrew into their own world, usually between twelve and eighteen months of age. Professionals remained

Autistic Savants

The term "idiot savant" has been used to describe individuals with limited intellectual abilities who possess highly developed skills in a particular area. The more accepted name for this condition is "savant syndrome," and individuals with certain highly developed skills are referred to simply as "savants." People with ASDs who have savant syndrome are often referred to as "autistic savants."

Just how many individuals with savant syndrome have ASDs is not known, with estimates varying from 50 to 100 percent. ASDs are common in individuals with savant syndrome, but the reverse is not true. Only 10 percent (or less) of individuals with ASDs have savant skills. Autistic individuals with savant syndrome span the range of IQ from very low to extremely high.

The range of talent areas is quite diverse. Many individuals with savant syndrome have excellent visual memory and artistic skills (Stephen Wiltshire is an autistic savant who drew a massive cityscape of Tokyo from memory, after a brief helicopter tour of Tokyo). Check out his intricate art on his gallery website (http://www.stephenwiltshire.co.uk), where you can buy an authorized print for a reasonable price.

Photographic memory for random facts and figures allows some autistic savants to rapidly and accurately memorize lengthy lists of data. Mathematical prowess is also common. Many autistic savants can perform complex mathematical calculations in a matter of seconds with astounding accuracy. "Calendrical calculators" have the ability to determine the day of the week for any date in the past or future in the blink of an eye.

Musical abilities are also common among autistic savants who often possess perfect pitch and can play a complicated tune after listening only once (Stephen Wiltshire has both artistic abilities and perfect pitch). Glenn Gould was a

Stephen draws Tokyo Skyline III 2005. © The Stephen Wiltshire Gallery. Used by permission.

virtuoso classical pianist who was probably an autistic savant (decide for yourself by watching the documentary *Glenn Gould: Life and Times*).

A window into the mind of a highly intelligent individual with AS is available in the fascinating book *Born on a Blue Day* by Daniel Tammet. Daniel has an unfathomable ability to memorize numbers and calculate with lightning-fast speed. In 2004, he memorized the mathematical number Pi to 22,514 decimal places, reciting all the numbers without a single error in a record-setting performance that lasted just over five hours. Daniel's abilities to work with numbers and words are tied to a rare phenomenon called "synesthesia," a brain response that links numbers and words to colors and shapes that have various textures and move in specific ways as he manipulates them to solve problems.

Daniel has used his skills to decode the systems underlying multiple foreign languages including Lithuanian, Spanish, Romanian, Welsh, Esperanto, and Icelandic. Tammet was profiled in a documentary made in the United Kingdom entitled *Brain Man* (a tip of the hat to Kim Peek, the real-life Rain Man immortalized in the Oscar-winning movie starring Dustin Hoffman and Tom Cruise). For the documentary, Tammet learned the exceedingly difficult Icelandic language to perfection in only one week.

How savants develop their skills is still a scientific mystery, despite people like Daniel who can describe in detail how his mind works and graciously volunteers his time for scientific research. Why individuals with ASDs have such a high rate of savant syndrome is not well understood. Clues might be found in their preference for focusing on details instead of the big picture or in neurology patients who have acquired savant skills after a stroke or brain injury has interrupted the usual connections to other parts of the brain.

skeptical, attributing the parental reports to failure to recognize the early signs of ASDs until home video studies of children developing normally proved beyond a doubt that regression does occur in a subset of children with ASDs.

A commonly quoted estimate for regression in ASDs is 30 percent, but studies have yielded estimates as low as 20 percent and as high as 50 percent. In an ongoing study at the M.I.N.D. Institute, thorough attempts were made to elicit any history of language loss or loss of previously acquired social skills. Fifteen percent (50 of 333) of the children with ASDs lost both language and social skills, whereas 41 percent (138 of 333) lost either language or social skills.

ASDS AROUND THE WORLD

Estimates of prevalence are available from a wide range of countries in the developed world, including the United States, the United Kingdom, Japan, Iceland, Finland, Australia, Canada, Sweden, and China. Most of the estimates fall in approximately the same range. Studies showing significantly lower rates that are likely to be attributable to differences in study design. All countries are reporting increases in prevalence rates. Estimates from developing countries are not available given the general lack of information on any DDs.

6

What Causes Autism?
Part 1: Basic Science

No topic in ASDs is as divisive as the question of causation. There is now universal agreement that the ASDs are a heterogeneous group of neurodevelopmental disorders with onset in early childhood (before age three) that are characterized by a recognizable pattern of behaviors. Experts and parents all agree that there are likely to be many different causes of ASDs.

To emphasize the multiplicity of causes leading to the ASDs and the wide variability in language, intellectual, and social skills displayed by individuals with ASDs, some experts have proposed a shift in terminology from the singular label of autism to a plural form: "the autisms." However, that is where the consensus ends and the contentious arguments begin. The exact causes of the abnormal brain function that leads to the behaviors that we call ASDs have yet to be definitively worked out. There are clear differences of opinions regarding which possible explanations are plausible and which are not. This chapter will review the important basic science studies that have added to our understanding of ASDs. In Chapter 7, alternative theories for autism causation are reviewed.

TERATOGENIC EXPOSURES DURING GESTATION

Exposure to a variety of different agents during gestation can cause something to go wrong with fetal development. These agents are referred to as "teratogens" in medical terminology. Infections during the mother's pregnancy caused by viruses (e.g., rubella or influenza), exposure to medications that harm the developing fetus (e.g., thalidomide or valproic acid), and exposure to toxic substances (e.g., alcohol) are all associated with higher than expected rates of ASDs. The types of brain injury that occur in response to each of these three different kinds of exposures are quite different, yet the end result is an increased risk for ASDs in all three groups.

Congenital rubella is a condition that is frequently included in lists of "causes" of ASDs. Congenital (a condition that exists at birth) rubella can occur when a mother gets sick with rubella during a critical time in gestation as the embryo is forming important organs (e.g., the brain, the lenses of the eyes, and the heart). Developing infants who become ill with a rubella infection during the first trimester of pregnancy stand a good chance of sustaining damage to their developing brain, resulting in a smaller than normal head (microcephaly) and ID. Damage to other developing organs result in cataracts and heart defects. The risk for developing autism in a series of children with congenital rubella (born during a rubella epidemic in the United States during the sixties) was 7 percent, almost twenty times higher than the estimated rates for autism at that time.

Additional studies showed a threefold to fourfold increase in risk for autism after maternal infection with rubella or influenza. It is likely that other viral infections during pregnancy can also interfere with brain development during gestation (e.g., a cytomegalovirus [CMV] has been implicated). The influenza connection is intriguing because influenza during pregnancy does not result in the devastating developmental syndromes detectable at birth in children with congenital rubella or a congenital CMV. There is no such thing as congenital influenza syndrome, yet influenza infection during pregnancy clearly affects the developing brain (an increased risk of schizophrenia has been definitively linked to maternal influenza during pregnancy).

A medication called thalidomide was frequently given to pregnant mothers for morning sickness before it was recognized that many exposed babies were born with short, disfigured limbs. When thalidomide was given during a specific time early in the pregnancy (between twenty to twenty-four days), the risk for an ASD was increased. If the medication was given earlier or later, it did not affect the brain in a way that led to an ASD. It is not known how thalidomide disrupts the normal process of brain development, but the fact that it happens tells us that a glitch in brain development during a very specific time window can be an underlying cause of what we now call ASDs.

Exposure to alcohol in the womb can cause varying degrees of neurodevelopmental disability attributable to a direct toxic effect of the alcohol on the developing fetal brain. The severely affected infants with fetal alcohol syndrome have smaller than normal brains, ID, and behavioral problems. Children who are less affected may look normal but have learning disabilities and behavioral problems to varying degrees. The risk for an ASD is higher in children exposed to alcohol in the womb ("in utero" exposure), but the vast majority of children exposed to alcohol do not have ASDs.

Babies exposed to these three different teratogens look and act differently from each other because their brain development was altered in very different ways. Still, there must be some commonality because a higher than expected percentage from each group were diagnosed with autism in a 1971 study by Dr. Stella Chess. Because we still do not know what the common factor is, it is probably best to avoid drawing specific conclusions about the causes of ASDs from studies of individuals with damaging exposures in utero. These types of brain injuries can produce conditions that resemble autism enough to receive the diagnosis but are not likely to be representative of the kinds of brain development problems seen in the majority of children with ASDs.

PREMATURITY AND ASDS

A 2005 study from the CDC showed that ASDs are 2.5 times more common in premature infants (infants born before thirty-five weeks gestation). The reason for the increased risk for ASDs in premature infants is not clear, but there are several possibilities. Something before or during preterm labor may affect the developing brain. The causes of preterm labor are not completely known, but infection and inflammation are thought to play a role in many cases. Premature infants often experience medical complications during the long neonatal intensive care hospitalizations that can result in injury to the infant's immature brain. Finally, ASDs are more common in any child with ID (below average IQ), and premature infants are at an increased risk for cognitive problems.

ENVIRONMENTAL FACTORS CAPABLE OF HARMING THE DEVELOPING BRAIN

Many environmental exposures are capable of causing direct toxicity to the developing brain, in utero or after birth. It is not yet known whether these environmental factors play a part in the increasing incidence of ASD, but studies from several centers studying the effects of environmental toxicants suggest that contamination from heavy metals (mercury, lead, and arsenic), pesticides, and chemicals used in the plastics industry such as polychlorinated biphenyls (PCBs) and phthalates are very likely to be contributing to the increase in ASDs and other neurodevelopmental disorders (see the Environmental Protection Agency [EPA] website at http://es.epa.gov/ncer/childrenscenters/autism.html for a comprehensive overview of ongoing investigations).

GENETIC CHANGES AS CAUSES OF ASDS

ASDs are highly heritable, more so than breast cancer, Alzheimer's dementia, or schizophrenia. The main thrust of scientific investigation into the causes of ASDs has long been focused on genetic studies, with at least 90 percent of all funding for ASDs directed toward genetic research. An enormous amount of headway has been made toward understanding the genetic mechanisms of ASDs, but there is far more that has yet to be clarified.

Twin Studies

Whenever geneticists want to determine whether inherited genes are the cause of a particular condition, they look at twins for clues. The chance of both twins developing a condition of interest is referred to as "concordance" for the condition. The rate of concordance in twins gives valuable information about how much of a role genetics plays in the development of the condition.

There are two kinds of twins: identical twins (also called "monozygotic twins" to indicate that both of the twins came from the same fertilized egg) and fraternal twins ("dizygotic twins" from two separate fertilized eggs). Identical twins have virtually identical genes, whereas fraternal twins have a random mix of similar and different genes.

If one twin has a disease or syndrome that is caused by a defective gene, the chance of the other twin having the same condition is different for identical and fraternal twins. If all that is needed for a condition to be inherited is for a gene to be passed down by one or the other parent, both of the identical twins should have the condition 100 percent of the time because they share the same genes. Fraternal twins have a much lower chance of concordance than identical twins because their genes are not identical (although their genes are more similar than two unrelated people).

In 1994, a study of twins in the United Kingdom led by Anthony Bailey, M.D., at Oxford University showed that there was a 60 percent chance that identical twins would both have autism, whereas autism in both twins did not occur in any of the fraternal twins. The chance for both identical twins to have any type of ASD was 92 percent, whereas fraternal twins both had ASDs only 10 percent of the time. Other researchers have repeated the study with results falling in approximately the same range. Because the concordance rate is so close to 100 percent in identical twins, there must be genetic factors that are highly influential in the etiology of ASDs. However, 92 percent is not quite

100 percent, and that difference leaves room for some other yet unknown factors to come into play (for additional details, see the section below on G×E effects, "Genetics Interacting with the Environment").

Recurrence Rates of ASDs in Families

Another method used to assess how much the inheritance of a condition is controlled by genes is to look at a statistic called "the recurrence rate." When ASDs occur more than once in the same family, the family is referred to as a "multiplex" family. If only one child has an ASD, then the family is referred to as a "simplex" or "singleton" family. The recurrence rate is the chance that a family who already has a child with an ASD will have a second child with an ASD. If the recurrence rate for family members is much higher than the rate that ASDs occur in the general population, then there must be something about that family's genes that accounts for the increased risk.

Many studies of multiplex families have been done with estimates for recurrence rates ranging from 2 to 10 percent depending on the study. The results show that the recurrence rates in families who already have a child with an ASD are anywhere from three to fifteen times higher than the current estimates for ASDs in the general population. If a family already has two children with ASDs, the recurrence rate for the third child increases to a daunting 25 percent. The high recurrence rate figures make a convincing argument for a strong genetic influence on the heritability of ASDs.

Surprisingly, the recurrence rate varies with the sex of the first child with an ASD diagnosis. If the family already has a female child with an ASD, the risk of having a second child with an ASD is 4 percent (at least six times the current estimated risk in the general population). If the first affected child is male, the recurrence rate increases to 7 to 14 percent (approximately ten to twenty times higher than the current risk in the general population).

The much higher risk of recurrence in families with at least one child with an ASD strongly supports a genetic cause for ASDs, at least in the multiplex families. It is likely that families with only one child with an ASD and no history of other family members with ASDs or other related developmental problems will turn out to have genetic changes that occur for the first time (de novo, for "from the beginning") in the affected child (see the sections on DNA mutations, deletions, duplications, and other acquired genetic changes). Children in families with multiple affected children are almost certainly inheriting the responsible genes from their parents. The take-home lesson is that there appear to be many different ways to arrive at the type of brain dysfunction that causes the behaviors that we recognize as ASDs.

Autistic Traits in Family Members: The BAP

If inherited genes cause ASDs, then the traits that are found in ASDs should be found in family members at a higher rate. The observable abnormalities in ASDs are deficits in social abilities, problems with communication, and a tendency to engage in restrictive and repetitive behaviors. The aggregated behaviors are referred to as "the autistic phenotype" (phenotype means the observable characteristics of an individual that are based on her genes).

Many researchers believe that ASDs are caused by a wide variety of separate genes, with specific genes causing each of the abnormal types of behavior. If behaviors can be linked directly to genes, then difficulties functioning in social situations, communication deficits, and restricted and repetitive behaviors should be seen at higher frequencies in the family members of children with ASDs. Researchers have succeeded in identifying a higher than expected rate of similar behaviors in family members, referred to as the BAP. A 1994 study showed that parents of children with ASDs, as a group, were more likely to be socially aloof and lack tact. In the extended family of children with ASDs, there are also higher than average rates of anxiety, shyness, psychiatric disorders (including depression and more serious conditions such as bipolar disorder and schizophrenia), slow language development, and learning disabilities, with 15–45 percent of family members having at least one of these social, communication, or cognitive problems. Interestingly, the rates of schizophrenia and bipolar disorders are also on the rise, and some genes associated with schizophrenia have also been found to play a part in increasing the risk of ASDs.

A 2005 study by the CDC showed that children born to parents with schizophrenia-like psychiatric disorders were 3.41 times more likely to develop autism than children born to parents who did not have any psychiatric issues. Children born to parents with depression were 2.91 times more likely to develop autism. Parental genes for major mood disorder are risk factors for ASDs in children. These findings suggest that ASDs might be caused by the aggregation of enough of these separate genes in an individual to create the behavioral profile that we call ASDs. It is very likely that the presence of the BAP in parents of children initially evaluated by Kanner led to his conclusion that lack of parental warmth was the cause of ASDs.

In 2008, researchers Joe Aven and Michael Spezia published a study on the ability to interpret emotion from pictures of faces in parents of children with ASDs compared with parents of TD children. They found that parents of children with ASDs, who possessed aloof social qualities, processed facial emotions in very similar ways to their children with ASDs, primarily relying on the region around the mouth to interpret emotions. Parents of TD children used the eyes to detect emotion, and nonaloof parents of children with ASDs fell somewhere in between.

Genetics and Uneven Sex Ratios

The uneven numbers of males and females with ASDs is another clue that genes might be involved. Genetic conditions that are attributable to a faulty gene on the X chromosome are much more common in boys. Because boys only have one X chromosome, they cannot make up for a damaged gene on their X chromosome, whereas girls can partially or completely compensate with the good gene on their other X chromosome. If some of the genes that cause ASDs are on the X chromosome, that could explain why more boys than girls have ASDs.

Not all researchers agree that the uneven sex ratio means that damaged genes on the X chromosome cause ASDs. British researcher Simon Baron-Cohen came up with a controversial theory that posits that ASDs are the result of "the extreme male brain." Baron-Cohen (first cousin of the comedic actor Sacha Baron-Cohen) attributes the higher number of males with autism to the fact that male brains are naturally programmed to focus on understanding and building systems (termed "systematizing), whereas female brains are oriented toward understanding and sharing emotions with others (termed "empathizing"). Baron-Cohen proposes that high levels of the male hormone testosterone in a pregnant mother can push the brain to develop more of the systematizing abilities and less of the empathizing tendencies. His theory is by no means universally accepted, but it is important to at least recognize that there may be reasons other than genetics for the much higher rate of autism in males. For those interested in Baron-Cohen's theory, check out his book *The Essential Difference— Male and Female Brains and The Truth about Autism* (Baron-Cohen 2003).

Genetic Syndromes Associated with ASDs

Genetic syndromes are conditions with recognizable patterns of developmental abnormalities that are so distinctive that they are eventually linked to a specific genetic defect. Many genetic syndromes have a much higher than expected rate of ASDs. If a genetic glitch causes the recognizable syndrome and ASDs are more frequent in these genetic syndromes, then it stands to reason that something about the gene change also makes it more likely that an ASD will result.

Once the cause of a genetic syndrome is discovered, it is often possible to see that there is great variability in how much the individual is affected by the genetic problem. Individuals with Down syndrome, for example, may be only mildly retarded with good social abilities or may suffer from such severe retardation that they never speak or interact. The variability in the degree to which a genetic glitch affects each individual with a similar genetic defect might help explain the wide range of variation in intelligence and language abilities in ASDs.

Syndromes that have been shown to have a higher than expected rate of ASDs include fragile X syndrome and tuberous sclerosis. The jury is out on Down syndrome, with some experts saying that the rate of ASDs is increased in Down syndrome, although others maintain that the rate of ASDs in Down syndrome is no higher than the rate of ASDs in other conditions that are associated with ID.

Are Genetic Syndromes Really Causes of ASDs?

Although fragile X, tuberous sclerosis, and other genetic syndromes are often listed as causes of ASDs, these conditions are better thought of as being "associated with" ASDs: some individuals with the malfunctioning genes have ASDs, whereas others do not. The list of known genetic syndromes that are associated with the ASDs now contains over fourteen different syndromes that are mostly far less common than fragile X or tuberous sclerosis. Should each child be tested for all fourteen syndromes? That is a question that geneticists are struggling to answer in a way that avoids missing the chance to make a correct diagnosis but does not encourage massive expenditures on tests that are not necessary for each child.

Inborn Errors of Metabolism Associated with ASDs

There are many different kinds of metabolic processes that must function properly for humans to stay healthy. If there is a genetic defect that prevents one of the pathways from working the way it is intended, the brain can be damaged by compounds that build up to toxic levels or by the absence of metabolic products that are needed for the human body to function optimally. ASDs occur more frequently than expected in some of the known metabolic disorders and are very likely to be linked to some as yet undiscovered metabolic pathway defects.

The metabolic disorder that was first associated with autism is the disease PKU. Phenylalanine is an amino acid that is normally broken down by the body. Individuals who have defects in genes that control the breakdown cycle suffer varying levels of progressive brain damage from the higher than normal levels of phenylalanine unless their PKU is discovered early and treated appropriately.

The metabolic defect in PKU was not discovered until 1961. When the first children were diagnosed with PKU, approximately 5 percent had previously been diagnosed previously with autism as an explanation for their developmental problems. Because almost all newborns in the United States and other developed countries are screened for PKU, this metabolic condition currently accounts for a vanishingly small number of cases of children with ASDs (unless they were born in a country that does not screen for PKU). Still, PKU is a useful model to help us remember that unrecognized metabolic defects might occur in a subset of children with ASDs and other DDs. Because it can be very difficult to diagnose a metabolic disorder, there is a very good chance that undiscovered metabolic disorders underlie some cases of ASDs. A massive effort to implement expanded newborn metabolic screening in the United States, largely completed over the last ten years, should lead to early detection of most serious metabolic defects affecting newborns.

ERRORS IN CHROMOSOME COPYING: MUTATIONS, DELETIONS, AND DUPLICATIONS

When chromosomes are copied in the developing embryo, three main kinds of errors can be made. When an accidental change is made in the DNA sequence of a gene during copying, the affected gene is said to have a "mutation." If a small piece is left out during the copying process, that is called a chromosomal "deletion." A "duplication" is the genetic term for an error in copying in which a piece of a chromosome is copied too many times. If a gene is altered in one of these ways, it usually cannot perform its intended function. If the altered or deleted gene is important in brain development, then an individual who does not have a functional copy of that gene has a good chance of having problems with how his brain works.

Recent work has shown that children with ASDs have many more mutations in their genes than their parents do (the same finding was also recently observed in schizophrenia). This discovery means that the mutations in the child's DNA were not passed down from either of the parents but instead occurred spontaneously during the chromosome-copying process (de novo). Mutations that are found in a child's DNA but are not found in the parent's DNA are called "spontaneous" or "sporadic" mutations. This finding could explain why it is often not possible to identify other family members with ASDs: the mutation causing the ASD is unique to the child. Many of the toxic chemicals that have been building up in the environment at an alarming rate since the forties are capable of causing mutations and deletions in DNA. Dietrich Stephan, a prominent geneticist involved in the hunt for the genes underlying ASDs, feels that environmental contaminants are very likely to explain the high de novo mutation rates seen in ASDs.

Deletions are the most common type of chromosomal abnormality seen in children with ASDs. Over the years, deletions in every single chromosome have been found in children with ASDs. Almost all of the deletions occur de novo (i.e., almost none of these deletions are present in the parental DNA). Deletions in specific areas on a handful of chromosomes are found more frequently than others (e.g., on chromosomes 2, 7, 15,16, 17, and 22). In some cases, autism results from having extra copies of a gene (called a duplication) instead of a deletion of the gene; either way the gene function is disrupted. For example, on chromosome 16 at a spot on the short arm of the chromosome identified as 16p11, either a deletion of the genes in that area or extra copies are seen in about 1 percent of individuals with ASDs.

Duplications and deletions are now commonly referred to as "copy number variants" (CNVs). Recent studies have shown that CNVs are very common in all humans, making us much less alike than was previously thought. CNVs probably account for the lion's share of our genetic diversity. Everyone will be hearing more and more about CNVs in the next decade (perhaps enough to make CNV as much of a household word as DNA).

Geneticists have looked carefully at the areas on the chromosomes with the most frequent deletions to see whether they can identify the actual gene defects that might cause ASDs. The process of identifying the exact gene that causes problems is extremely time consuming because the large areas covered by the deletions often involve more than one gene. The genes in the areas of the deletion are called "candidate genes" because they may or may not turn out to be important in the development of ASDs.

There are many other methods that geneticists have used to try to find the genes that are important in ASDs, but the methods are so complex that they cannot be adequately explained in a book of this length. Suffice it to say that geneticists have succeeded in identifying two main ways that genes can influence the possibility of developing an ASD: (1) single genes have been identified that are so crucial for the development of the brain that autism results if the gene does not function as intended; and (2) genes have been found that increase the risk of developing autism if they either are not able to function or do not function optimally.

To date, only three genes have been discovered that will result in an ASD if they are rendered nonfunctional. The remainder of the genes that have been described are all associated with ASDs; the risk is increased by a factor of two or three when these genes do not function appropriately, but the gene defect is not sufficient to cause an ASD.

SINGLE-GENE CAUSES OF ASDS

Between 2006 and 2008, the first four genes that are capable of causing ASDs when their function is disrupted were discovered: Neuroligin-3 and

Neuroligin-4, CNTNAP2 (conectin associated protein-like 2), and SHANK3 (SH3 and multiple ankyrin repeat domains 3). All four of the genes perform functions related to the functional and structural organization of neuronal synapses, the central location for neuron-to-neuron communications. The Neuroligin genes were found in two brothers (one with a diagnosis of autism and one with AS), but other researchers have not found either mutation to be a common cause of ASDs. In contrast, several research groups have confirmed the presence of mutations in the CNTNAP2 gene at a frequency of around 0.75 percent of cases of ASDs. Clearly the single gene mutations described to date explain only a very small percentage of cases of ASDs, but the importance of the discoveries lies in the fact that the mutations prove two extremely important points. First, that the typical behavioral syndrome that we call ASDs can be caused by isolated problems with brain development. Second, that a single gene mutation can cause autism in one brother and Asperger's in the other, clarifying that the two separate diagnostic categories are describing different manifestations of the same genetic defect.

EXAMPLES OF GENES THAT ARE ASSOCIATED WITH ASDS

MECP2

The MECP2 (methyl CpG binding protein 2) gene (pronounced Meck-pee-two) is located on the X chromosome. The gene provides instructions for making a protein (called MeCP2) that is essential for normal brain development and for the formation of synapses. The MECP2 gene also performs a variety of other functions, such as silencing other genes and splicing DNA.

Abnormal function of the MeCP2 protein is the cause of Rett syndrome, a condition that is included in the PDD category in the *DSM-IV* but differs from ASDs because of the loss of motor skills, characteristic hand-wringing behavior, and inevitable deterioration to severe MR. The MECP2 gene can be prevented from functioning by a wide variety of mutations and deletions or by epigenetic mechanisms (see the section below on epigenetic regulation of genes for details).

Mutations in the MECP2 gene are detected in girls with ASDs who do not have the syndrome and in boys with spasticity and autistic-like behaviors 3–13 percent of the time. How can a problem with the MECP2 gene cause Rett syndrome in one person and be associated with an ASD in another when the two conditions do not follow the same course? The answer is not known, but there are many examples of defects in a single gene causing different problems in different individuals. The MECP2 gene is known to be involved in several other brain-related disorders, including schizophrenia. A possible explanation is that different mutations in the gene may render the gene completely inactive or only partially incapacitated. It turns out that the extent of problems from mutations in the MECP2 gene is related directly to the amount of functional protein made from the altered gene. Too much of the MECP2 gene product causes too many synapses to form at the junction of the neurons; too little causes an insufficient number of synapses for optimal brain functioning. If the amount of synapses is not just right, the brain goes through changes to try to compensate.

The discovery that the MECP2 gene is involved in both Rett syndrome and ASDs supports the continued inclusion of Rett syndrome in the pervasive developmental delay category.

UBE3A

Angelman's syndrome is a developmental disability marked by ID, communication problems, and abnormal movements. The gene involved in Angelman's syndrome (UBE3A [ubiquitin protein ligase E3A]) may also be linked to ASDs. Duplication in chromosome 15 in the area in which the UBE3A gene is located have been found in about 1 percent of individuals with ASDs.

A twist in the UBE3A story is that ASDs are more common only if the duplication occurs in the mother's chromosome 15, a phenomenon known as "imprinting," which is under epigenetic control (see the section below on epigenetics). It should be apparent from this example that the genetic contributions to ASDs can be extremely complex and difficult to tease out.

PTEN Genes

A family of genes called PTEN (phosphatase and tensin homolog) function to regulate cellular life cycles. Mutations in PTEN genes occur in 2–3 percent of individuals with ASDs. PTEN mutations are seen at a much higher frequency (17 percent) in children with macrocephaly. PTEN is a particularly attractive candidate gene for ASDs because it is also involved in the regulation of GI function and the immune system, two systems that many parents, and an increasing number of researchers, believe to be affected in ASDs (see Chapter 7 for additional details).

MET Gene

The MET gene was discovered by studying families with more than one child with an ASD, which alerts genetic researchers that there is a heritable gene causing the children's ASDs in these families. The MET gene is located on chromosome 7 in an area that has long been suspected of being involved in ASDs (chromosome 7 is also important in language disorders). The MET gene makes a product that is important in the controls of cellular development in many areas of the body.

The MET gene story differs slightly from the other genes discussed so far because there are no deletions or mutations that render the gene unoperational. Instead, there are different forms of the normal gene that affect the chance of developing ASD. There are nine slightly different forms of the MET gene (termed "variants" or "polymorphisms") circulating in the normal gene pool. These variants are separated by tiny changes in the MET gene DNA sequence that can affect how well the MET gene makes the product it is designed to make. If a person makes too little of the MET gene product, trouble with the development of different types of cells may result.

The researchers found that individuals who receive two copies of a particularly ineffective form of the MET gene have about twice the risk of developing an ASD compared with an individual with two efficient forms of the MET gene. Individuals who have one copy of an inefficient form of the MET gene and one copy of a more functional variant have a 1.5-fold greater risk of developing an ASD. Having two of the less efficient MET gene products is not sufficient to cause an ASD; some other genetic or environmental factor must come into play before an ASD develops.

Other Genes Linked to ASDs

The list of genes that are linked to ASDs grows longer each day. Other genes that have been shown to increase the risk for autism (often referred to as "susceptibility" genes) include neurexin 1, DISC1 (disrupted in schizophrenia 1), and the clock genes. The point of all these examples is to provide a window into the astoundingly diverse types of genes that may play a part in causing an ASD in any one individual. Given the extreme genetic variation discovered so far in ASDs, it is no wonder that the spectrum is so diverse. Geneticists have long since abandoned the idea that a single gene defect would be found to explain the cause of ASDs in all, or even most, affected individuals. Geneticists have estimated that there are at least ten to fifteen different genes that play a part in the development of an ASD and it is likely that the number of genes will be significantly higher.

As genetic technology improves, more and more deletions, duplications, and mutations are being found that are associated with ASDs. Even so, it does not appear that damaged or deleted genes explain all of the cases of ASDs, particularly in cases in which it makes a difference if the gene is inherited from the mother or the father. What else could be going on with genes that might cause an increase in ASDs? The answer lies in an up and coming area of genetics called "epigenetics."

EPIGENETICS

In1886, a monk named Gregor Mendel published the results of his famous pea hybridization experiments that demonstrated that inherited traits could be explained on the basis of dominant and recessive genes. Mendelian genetics (named after Mendel) has formed the cornerstone for the understanding of human health and disease since that time. The problem is that Mendelian genetics alone cannot explain the inheritance patterns for many complex conditions, autism included. A breakthrough occurred in the late nineties with the discovery of another layer of genetic control that has come to be known as epigenetics (the greek prefix *epi* means "on, upon, or in addition"). Epigenetics is the study of how normal genes are turned on and off. Epigenetics is a control system for genes that acts on the gene but does not change the gene itself. Perfectly good genes can fail to function the way they are supposed to if they have been modified in a way that turns the gene off when it is supposed to be on or vice versa.

Neurologist and developmental biologists have long known that brain development is like a carefully choreographed dance, with genes turning on and off in a specified sequence that must be followed if brain development is to proceed normally. This process requires working genes that are recruited when they are needed and put to rest when their job is done. As the embryo develops, the orderly progression of brain development is partially controlled by a continuous flow of gene activation and suppression that is orchestrated by epigenetic mechanisms. Evidence that epigenetic changes play a part in causing ASDs has already been uncovered. Hopes are high that better understanding of epigenetics may even open a window for attempts to restore normal gene function.

The investigation of epigenetic control mechanisms in still in its infancy, but there will undoubtedly be more breakthroughs in this promising area. Recently the National Institutes of Health committed the first substantial block of grant funding to develop the necessary technology to take a closer look at epigenetics with specific attention to autism. Understanding the interplay between standard genetic changes (e.g., mutations, deletions, and duplications) and epigenetic regulation will undoubtedly bring us closer to understanding the complicated genetics of ASDs.

RISK FACTORS FOR ASDS THAT ARE LIKELY TO BE ATTRIBUTABLE TO A COMBINATION OF STANDARD GENETIC MECHANISMS AND EPIGENETIC CONTROL

Advanced Maternal and Paternal Age as Risk Factors for ASDs

A number of studies have shown that the risk of developing an ASD is higher for the offspring of older mothers and older fathers. This finding strongly argues for genetic mechanisms as causes of ASDs. All forms of DNA damage (e.g., mutations, deletions, and duplications) are more common as parents age. Epigenetic changes also increase with age and can be passed on from parent to child. It is likely that both direct damage to DNA and epigenetic changes increase the risk of having a child with an ASD as parents age. The same genetic mechanisms are linked to explain the increased risk for schizophrenia and bipolar disorder with increasing parental age.

Some parents of children with ASDs are not comfortable with these findings because they feel like they are being blamed for their child's autism. All parents pass on DNA to their children. Parents who pass on genes for disorders such as fragile X, muscular dystrophy, depression, or cancer do not do so intentionally. The intricacies of genetic transmission are useful to understand but not for the purpose of blame.

Environmental Causes of Gene Modification

Environmental exposures that can cause mutations in DNA are called "mutagens." Radiation is the clearest examples of an environmental mutagen. Interactions between environmental contaminants and genes are increasingly being studied. Some pesticides have been shown to cause DNA mutations and epigenetic changes that are heritable, and it is likely that other environmental exposures can do so as well. As of yet, there are no proven examples of mutations, deletions, or epigenetic changes associated with ASDs that have conclusively been linked to environmental exposures, but it is likely that supporting evidence will emerge in the future.

In 2007, a preliminary study conducted by the California Department of Public Health demonstrated a possible link between exposure to pesticides and autism. Mothers living within 500 meters of fields sprayed with an organochloride pesticide during their first trimester of pregnancy were six times more likely to give birth to a child with an ASD. The risk increased when a higher poundage of pesticides was used and decreased as distance from the fields increased. If the link is validated, the mechanism could be genetic or due to direct toxic effects.

Making Sense of the Scope of Possible Genetic Contributors to ASDs

How can we make sense of all of the available information on genetic contributors to ASDs? A geneticist named Huda Zoghbi from Baylor University proposed a framework to summarize the genetic possibilities in ASDs. Her theory is that ASDs are caused, to some extent, by every one of the available genetic mechanisms. She proposed a model that goes by the acronym "MEGDI" to account for ASDs and any other condition that has complex inheritance patterns.

MEGDI stands for "mixed epigenetic and genetic and mixed de novo and inherited model." Although it sounds complicated, the title explains it all. ASDs could be caused by the usual genetic mechanisms that we have already discussed that involve changes to the DNA sequence through mutations, deletions, duplications, and other rearrangements of the DNA. Epigenetic mechanisms are likely to play a part as well. Both the usual genetic mechanisms and the epigenetic changes can occur de novo (for the first time in the affected individual) or be passed down from affected family members. The occurrence of all of these different mechanisms is likely to account for a large part of the heterogeneity in the population that we call ASDs.

WHAT CLUES ARE AVAILABLE FROM THE STUDY OF BRAIN STRUCTURE?

Neuroanatomical Changes at the Cellular Level

Neuroanatomy is the study of normal and abnormal brain development. Sophisticated techniques are used to look at the cellular structure in different parts of the brain (frontal lobes, temporal lobes, parietal lobes, occipital lobe, cerebellum, and brainstem). Specific areas within the brain known to have specialized functions (e.g., emotional responses, memory, and recognition of faces) are examined closely for evidence of changes from the normal patterns that might give clues about the cause of neurodevelopmental disorders such as autism.

The first studies done on postmortem brain specimens (obtained after the death of individuals with autism of varying ages) were done in the seventies. Each new study compared their findings with the studies that had come before to see whether previous conclusions were upheld or contradicted. Each study was limited to a handful of cases of widely varying ages (mostly in older individuals) with developmental histories that were not uniform (e.g., some had early motor delays, whereas others did not) and inconsistent comorbid conditions (most were mentally retarded but some were not, and some had epilepsy but others did not). As you might imagine from what we already know about the heterogeneity of the ASDs, the researchers discovered a wide variety of findings. They focused on the features that seemed to be consistent between the different studies, reasoning that the similarities were likely a hint at the brain changes that account for the core features of ASDs.

One consistent finding was that there were areas in the brain that had less cells than expected, suggesting that these cells either did not develop properly or that the cells died for unknown reasons. Margaret Bauman, a respected neuropathologist, did not see any evidence of cell death in her studies. She interpreted her findings to mean that the lower numbers of cells meant that they never developed and that meant that the abnormalities had to have occurred before thirty weeks gestation when the missing cells should have been formed. More recent findings have led researchers to question that conclusion.

Researchers noticed that the patterns observed from specimen to specimen seemed to change depending on the age of the individual, implying that there may be an ongoing process, at least in some of the individuals studied. The early research on brain structure in autism led scientists to spend a great deal of time trying to pinpoint which part of the brain was abnormal, an effort that may have led to missing the proverbial forest for the trees. Each researcher seemed to have their favorite candidate for the area of abnormal brain development that would best explain the behaviors seen in autism.

Is autism caused by insufficient development of the amygdala, a specialized area in the temporal lobe that is critical for emotional responses, that was found to be smaller than usual in the early autopsy specimens? Or was the problem in the cerebellum, an area that Eric Courchesne advocated as a prime candidate based on his findings that a part of the cerebellum (called the cerebellar vermis) was consistently smaller than normal? Is the problem in a particular area of the brainstem (called the inferior olivary nucleus), as championed by Patricia Rodier based on postmortem studies and animal models using valproic acid? Or is the problem located in the frontal lobes, the part of the brain that is crucial for complex reasoning? The debate about which area was of the foremost importance continued on for quite some time and still does to some degree. However, the focus has shifted away from where the problems lay to the recognition that ASDs are more of a whole-brain condition. It has become clear that autism has more to do with how different parts of the brain connect with each other than it does with specific defects in any one part of the brain.

The reason that the early studies of postmortem brain tissue were somewhat misleading was that they were primarily based on a handful of specimens from older individuals with autism. It was initially assumed that the brain structure in older individuals with autism would be similar to the brain changes in younger individuals, but that assumption has not turned out to be true.

In an attempt to look more closely at the brain changes during the earliest stages of autism, neuroscientists started to actively look for brain specimens from younger children. Researchers looking at the brains of four year olds found that the amyadala (an area of the brain located in the temporal lobe that is crucial for processing emotions and social behavior) was larger than normal, not smaller than normal as had been suggested previously. They also found that the larger the amygdala was, the more social impairment there was. Other researchers found higher numbers of specialized brain cells in various parts of the brain, not less as had been reported previously. A postmortem study on the brain of a single three year old, the youngest specimen studied thus far, confirmed the finding that there were more, not less, brain cells in the brains of children with ASDs.

The brain changes seen in the younger children that have been studied point to a problem with too much brain growth. The epicenter of the increased brain growth was in the frontal and temporal lobes, areas that are crucial for high-order thinking and understanding and reacting to emotional situations. The results were unexpected. Clearly, there was a difference between the findings in older individuals with ASDs and younger children with ASDs. In an attempt to find out what changes take place during the early stages of ASDs, efforts turned to obtaining brain scans at the earliest possible ages.

White Matter in ASDs: Information from MRI Studies

In 2001, Eric Courchesne and his group at the University of California, San Diego performed the first brain MRI studies on young children with autism to see what was going on with their brains as ASDs first became apparent. Their study measured "brain volume" as a way to measure the size of the brain. The study showed that 90 percent of children between the ages of two and three have brain volumes that are larger than average (between 12 and 15 percent larger).

The next question asked was what parts of the brain accounted for the increase in volume? There are two main parts to the brain: an outer gray matter section and an inner white matter section. White matter is made up of the projections (or axons) that leave the nerve cell bodies and travel to make connections with other nerve cell axons. These axons are wrapped in a substance called myelin that acts like an insulator to increase the speed that messages are sent from the control center to the next nerve cell. The gray and white matter can be thought of a system that functions similarly to a computer: the gray matter acts like the circuit boards, and the white matter acts like cables.

MRI studies from a number of different researchers have demonstrated that individuals with ASDs have increases in both the gray and white matter of the brain. However, the majority of the growth seen in the MRI studies of individuals with ASDs was attributable to increases in white matter. The areas with the highest increase in white matter were the frontal lobes, the temporal lobes, and the amygdala, all areas in which abnormalities had been detected in autopsy studies.

Courchesne reviewed the medical records for the children in his MRI study of brain volumes looking to pinpoint when the accelerated brain growth begins in children with ASDs. Pediatricians typically record height, weight, and head circumference (the measurement of the size of the head just above the eyes) at routine visits. Head circumference in children can be used as a rough estimate of brain size, because the skull grows in response to brain growth. Courchesne found that a rapid increase in head circumference during the first year of life was seen in 71 percent of the children with ASD in the MRI study (Courchesne 2003).

The infants with ASDs started out with head circumferences that were typically a little below average at birth. During the first few months, the brains of children with ASDs went through an accelerated growth period, with the head size increasing more rapidly than normal to an average size slightly above the eightieth percentile as early as six months of age. An interesting additional finding was that children with PDD-NOS showed accelerated early brain growth that was greater than the TD children but less than the children with autism (peaking at an average around the fiftieth percentile). Later studies showed that the brain growth slowed significantly after reaching a peak at age four and then dropped below the normal rate of growth after age five. The result of the rapid early growth followed by a growth slowdown is that most adults with ASDs do not end up with heads that are larger than normal.

It has long been recognized that many children with ASDs had head sizes that were significantly larger than normal (macrocephaly), but the timing of the increase was not clear until Courchesne's study was published in 2003. The finding of accelerated brain growth starting during the first year of life suggests that this phenomenon is an integral part of the process that leads to ASDs in a significant number of children.

Additional studies by Dr. Natacha Akshoomoff in association with Courchesne showed that the extent of the white matter increase predicts how the children fared over time. The more white matter changes the child demonstrated on MRI, the less well they tended to do on cognitive testing. Greater increases in white matter predicted lower functioning in ASDs.

Although the information from these studies is proving valuable in the effort to sort out the biologic basis for ASDs, it is important to recognize that there is currently no statistically valid way to use head circumference as a reliable screening test or to assist with the diagnostic process on an individual basis. There are many children who do not demonstrate this accelerated brain growth pattern yet have an ASD, and many children who do show this pattern who do not have an ASD. For now, the only way to assess for an ASD is to go through the *DSM-IV* criteria for the PPDs along with all of the other parts of a comprehensive evaluation discussed in Chapters 3 and 4. Perhaps brain growth patterns will someday be used as a way to subtype the ASDs, but that has not happened yet.

Functional MRI Studies: What Is Wrong with How the Brain Processes Information?

To more fully understand what is going on within the brains of individuals with ASDs, researchers turned to a relatively new technology called functional MRI (fMRI). Instead of producing a static picture of the brain (like a regular MRI), fMRI allows researchers to see what parts of the brain are active in real time during tasks that are presented to the research subject in the fMRI scanner.

By comparing the patterns of brain activation in individuals with ASDs with patterns seen in TD individuals, researchers can determine whether there are significant differences in brain processing that might explain some of the behaviors seen in the ASDs. Functional MRI studies of face processing tasks have been particularly revealing with respect to the neural circuitry necessary for normal social interactions.

Face Processing in ASDs

Many studies have shown that individuals with autism remember faces in unusual ways. Instead of using facial expressions or a general impression of the face, individuals with ASDs focused on specific details, like the presence of a hat or glasses, to recognize a person's face. TD subjects had trouble recognizing faces that were upside down, but face recognition was not affected by orientation in individuals with ASDs, suggesting that context did not play as much of a role in the autistic individuals.

The specific parts of the brain required to process faces were not known until these fMRI studies were conducted. Initial studies of facial recognition demonstrated that all normal control subjects used an area in the frontal lobe called the fusiform gyrus when they gazed at faces. In fact, the finding was so consistent that some researchers started to refer to the area as the fusiform face area. A ground-breaking study using fMRI demonstrated that individuals with autism use an area of the brain usually reserved for objects when viewing human faces. The study seemed to explain why persons with ASD did not seem to find faces particularly informative and also why individuals with autism often treat people like objects (e.g., using an adult's hand like a tool, backing up into an adult's lap like it was a chair, and climbing over people to get to desired objects).

The situation turned out to be more complex than the original study suggested, as is often the case. After dozens of studies were done to clarify the brain circuitry for face processing by using many different conditions (e.g., recognizing familiar faces versus nonfamiliar faces or cartoons instead of pictures, and processing faces versus objects), researchers realized that the area they originally thought was specific for face processing was really an area in which typical individuals process items of considerable interest. The fusiform face processing area was not just for face processing; it is an expertise center. Because TD infants preferentially look at faces from the first few moments of life and continue to do so, they become experts on the nuances of the human face. Every single one of the TD subjects in the study used the fusiform gyrus when looking at faces.

Researchers postulated that the gaze abnormalities in children with autism limits their familiarity with faces; they do not become experts on the general subject of the human face. In 2001, an fMRI study was published that showed that the subjects with autism used other areas of the brain to process faces that were not used by the TD subjects, indicating that the normal neural network was disrupted. Each individual with autism had unique patterns of activation (all of which were abnormal), suggesting that each brain had found its own solutions to the abnormal wiring situation.

Fortunately, autistic subjects are able to develop expertise for the faces of people who are important in their lives. An fMRI study demonstrated that the faces of highly familiar adults were processed in the usual area of the brain, the fusiform gyrus. This finding confirms the impressions of countless parents and family member who report that the child's use of eye contact is much better with them. A related study showed that an intervention program that was proven to help children with ASDs recognize unfamiliar faces did not result in normalization of the face processing brain circuitry, suggesting that the typical pathway is not repaired but alternative pathways can be formed to circumvent the problem areas.

The Mirror Neuron System

Several lines of evidence have suggested that the mirror neuron system does not function optimally in individuals with ASDs. The mirror neurons are nerve cells in the brain that are activated when a person watches someone else perform movements, including those involved in facial expressions of emotions and speech production. The complex system is responsible for imitation that occurs naturally, without the need to think about the response. Automatic imitation has been shown to be the primary type of imitation that is hampered in the ASDs. Multiple areas of the brain, including the motor control s and the emotional control centers, must be connected through the mirror neuron system to allow for the effortless coordination of imitation. Disruption of the mirror neuron circuitry would provide an explanation for many of the problem areas in ASDs including difficulty with spontaneous imitation, language dyspraxia and failure to understand and develop a wide variety of culturally appropriate facial expressions, and difficulty with empathy.

Studies in HFA using fMRI revealed that the lower the level of activity in the mirror neuron system, the greater the severity of the individuals disability. Thinning of the brain in the areas corresponding to the mirror neurons suggests that the number of mirror neurons is reduced, consistent with the theory that failure of typical neural development underlies the deficits seen in ASDs.

Putting It All Together: Poor Communication between Separate Brain Areas as the Cause of ASDs

The amassed data on brain circuitry in ASDs points to problems with abnormal connectivity as the biologic basis of the brain dysfunction. The white matter is supposed to function like efficient cables, connecting brain areas separated from one another into an efficient network. If there is a problem with the cables, the brain cannot function as an integrated whole. Individuals with ASDs experience their greatest limitations in tasks that require a great deal of interconnection, commonly referred to as "higher-order thinking." Without access to rapid cross-talk, individuals with ASDs may find it easier to focus on tasks that are concentrated in localized brain areas.

Do the Biologic Findings Match Up with the Main Cognitive and Social-Emotional Theories? Weak Central Coherence, Theory of Mind, and Executive Function

Researchers have conducted a vast number of experiments to clarify how individuals with autism approach intellectual tasks and perceive the social world around them. From these experiments, several theories have evolved that have been proposed as explanations for the observed cognitive and social patterns in ASDs, Weak central coherence, deficits in theory of mind (ToM) and deficits in executive function are three of the most prominent theoretical concepts that have emerged.

Weak Central Coherence

Uta Frith observed early on that children with ASDs did not seem to be compelled to pull together complex topics into a unified whole but rather tended to preferentially focus on individual details. The drive to integrate things into meaningful wholes, and form a coherent picture out of parts, is a drive that is very strong in most TD individuals. The TD human brain is programmed to make sense of the information that is taken in: TD individuals strive to see the forest for the trees. Individuals with ASDs do not have strong abilities to integrate information into a central concept but often demonstrate strengths in perceiving specific details. The ability to synthesize information into a central concept or coherent whole is weak in individuals with ASDs. Inadequate or abnormal connections between separate brain areas due to white matter abnormalities would be expected to impair the individual's ability to synthesize complex information. Weak central coherence is well explained by the MRI findings.

ToM

ToM is the name given to indicate a person's ability to get inside another person's shoes and understand what they might be thinking or feeling. Individuals have varying degrees of deficits in ToM, sometimes referred to as "mind blindness." Limitations in empathy are often attributed to deficits in ToM. Do the MRI findings explain the deficits in ToM? Yes, they do. Underconnectivity between separate parts of the brain would be expected to disrupt the complicated neural circuitry that allows for perspective taking and empathy. The mirror neuron system may be just one example of this type of complex circuitry that is necessary for full expression of ToM.

Executive Function

"Executive function" is the term given to the brain processes that filter incoming information and preferentially direct attention toward the most important input. Executive function skills are concentrated in the frontal lobes and are known to comprise a higher-order thinking process. The attention problems seen in ADHD are caused by deficits in executive function.

Individuals with ASDs have attention difficulties that stem from a related but different brain malfunction: their attention problems arise from an inability to rapidly change their focus, referred to as problems with "set-shifting." Set-shifting requires the higher-order brain function controlled by the executive function brain system.

The inertia that results from getting stuck on the current focus of attention (such as a spinning top, a fan, or rays of light filtering through a window) results in disengagement from the surrounding social milieu. The failure to take in the complicated social world results in missed opportunities to learn, further distancing the child with an ASD from the typical developmental course.

Causes of Increased Brain Growth

The findings from the MRI and fMRI studies all point to an abnormal pattern of brain growth as the structural brain change underlying the abnormal connectivity seen in ASDs. The exact cause of the gray and white matter changes are still not known.

One theory for the excess white matter is that the normal process called "pruning" does not take place on schedule. In TD brains, the number of connections between nerve cells (called synapses) expand rapidly during the first two to three years of life. Think of these synapses as branches (called axons and dendrites) coming off a central tree (the neuron). At birth, each neuron has 2,500 synapses. By age two to three, there are 15,000 synapses for each neuron. Over the next few years, there is an orderly reduction of the number of connections as the brain starts to preferentially use the most helpful pathways and discard the rest. The selective elimination of the weakest limbs is frequently referred to as "pruning."

To use a different analogy, the pruning process allows the brain to form the equivalent of "superhighways" for necessary tasks, eliminating the slow and unnecessary "side roads." If there is something wrong with the process that controls the formation and removal of synapses, it is possible that more and more side roads will be built, resulting in a confusing maze of indirect roads with no highways to be found. The brain could easily become bogged down by the presence of so many inefficient connections, creating a noisy and distracting environment that would make higher-order thinking extremely difficult.

Mutations in the neurexin and neuroligin (CNTNAP2 and Neuroligin-3) gene families have been shown to be capable of causing ASD. Both these families of genes control the process of synapse formation. The synapse-related gene families are under intense scrutiny and may end up offering an explanation for the dysregulated brain growth seen in some individuals with ASDs.

Genetics Interacting with the Environment: The G×E Concept

The view of autism as a brain-based condition that is controlled through genetic mechanisms took hold in the sixties and has been essentially unchallenged by the scientific community until recently. The underlying premise of ASDs as strongly genetically determined is that a certain amount of the brain dysfunction is "hardwired" and cannot be prevented or repaired, but that view is now up for reconsideration.

In the majority of medical conditions with complex inheritance patterns, it is becoming clear that genetics can predispose an individual to developing a disease, but genetics are not enough; there must be an environmental factor to push the individual over the edge.

The interaction of genes with the environment is referred to as "G by E" interactions, usually written as G×E ("G" stands for genetic makeup or "genotype" and "E" stands for environment). The concept is intuitively obvious based on observed patters in other medical conditions. For example, some women who are at a high risk for breast cancer because of their genes will develop breast cancer, but others do not. Studies have shown that several environmental factors, such as diet, alcohol intake, exercise, and hormone use, all modify the risk of breast cancer; all these lifestyle issues and exposures are examples of the environment interacting with genetic makeup.

Could the risk of developing an ASD be related to G×E interactions? Most scientists and researchers are convinced that genetic vulnerabilities interacting with environmental factors play a significant role in ASDs, but the details remain to be elucidated.

Genetic Variants That May Influence How an Inflammatory Reaction Affects the Brain: An Example of a Possible G×E Interaction

A current area of research interest that is likely to prove important in ASDs is the possibility that variations in the efficiency of biochemical pathways designed to prevent harm to the body may make some individuals more prone to brain injury. Research is being directed toward glutathione, a compound used by the body to protect against a process called "oxidative stress."

Most people are familiar with the concept that antioxidants are good for us, but less people are familiar with the meaning behind the word "oxidation." Antioxidants help to disarm harmful biochemical compounds called free radicals that are created on an ongoing basis in our bodies. Free radicals attack cells and cause damage if given the chance (the attack results in oxidation). If everything is working as intended in our bodies, we do not have to take antioxidant supplements because our bodies have built-in systems to disarm the harmful free radicals.

A potentially important study released in 2007 by neurologists at the Robert Wood Johnson Medical school showed that a higher than expected number of mothers who have a child with an ASD have a genetic variant that results in less available glutathione to detoxify free radicals. With less glutathione to serve as a buffer, more damage to cells occurs by the oxidative process.

How does this finding fit into the G×E paradigm? The genetic variant is the inefficient pathway for regeneration of the active form of glutathione, which limits the mother's ability to disarm the dangerous free radicals. During pregnancy, if any situation arises that causes free radicals to build up (e.g., infection, or inflammation from autoimmune disorders), the brain of the fetus may be injured by excessive oxidation. Without some kind of stress during the pregnancy, the developing fetus will not experience a problem from the fact that its mother has this genetic variant. A 2008 study investigated the role of maternal stress in ASDs. Mothers who were pregnant during times when major hurricanes hit their communities in Louisiana were compared with controls to see whether the rate of ASDs was higher as a result of the physiologic stress reaction. What they found was surprising: the rate of ASDs was higher in the stressed population.

A related but different G×E interaction leading to an ASD might occur if the child is the one with the inefficient form of the glutathione detoxification system. If the child is faced with an environmental challenge that requires the use of the glutathione system, they may not be able to generate an adequate response. Multiple recent studies using a variety of different methods have shown that oxidation goes on at a higher rate in individuals with ASDs. Something is either driving the generation of free radicals, limiting the production of free-radical scavengers, or both. Could some individuals with ASDs have defects in the biochemical pathways used to disarm free radicals? Research in this area is still in its infancy, but the theory seems to have a rational scientific basis (in other words, it is "biologically plausible").

Theoretically, an unlimited number of variations on the G×E theme could be involved in different individuals with ASDs. A nonfunctional or inefficient version of a gene that is unable to adequately perform a necessary job sets up a situation in which the fetus or young child is at risk for an ASD. If an environmental factor tips the balance, an ASD can result. Admittedly, the stress theory is complex, but researchers have already determined that it is unlikely that a simpler answer will be found to account for all cases of ASDs.

7

What Causes Autism? Part 2: Controversial Theories and New Ways of Thinking about ASDs

When trying to solve a mystery like autism—a mystery that is guaranteed to have more than one answer—there is definitely a place for thinking "out of the box." Looking past the mainstream theories for the causes of ASDs has the potential to pay off with valuable insights. To expand the conventional approaches to ASDs, complementary and alternative medicine (CAM) approaches are increasingly being sought out.

The organization at the center of the CAM movement for ASDs is "Defeat Autism Now!" (DAN), founded by Bernard Rimland and colleagues in 1985. (see Sidebar 6). DAN draws a mixed coalition of professionals from a variety of fields, plus family members of individuals with ASDs who work together to develop alternative theories for the causes of ASDs. The DAN group believes that autism can be triggered by modifiable environmental factors and, thus, can be cured. Exposure to toxic substances and over vaccination are viewed as two of the key factors responsible for the autism epidemic. Detailed discussion of the DAN philosophy can be found on the DAN website at http://www.autism.com.

All of the DAN theories are consistent in one belief: the problems with the brain in ASDs are not caused by irreversible abnormalities in brain structure but result instead from modifiable factors that have not been adequately

The Legacy of Bernard Rimland, Ph.D. (November 15, 1928–November 21, 2006)

Bernard Rimland was a young father and husband, just a few years out of graduate school with a Ph.D. in psychology, when he began his quest to help his son, Mark. Rimland knew from the first few months of Mark's life that something was not right. The family pediatrician told Dr. Rimland that he had never seen a child with Mark's unusual behaviors. It was not until Mark reached two years of age that Rimland, with his wife's help, finally found a textbook with a brief description of autism, a condition that was not even mentioned in Rimland's doctoral psychology courses. He embarked on a search to learn all that was known about autism. It was clear to Rimland from the beginning that autism was a condition with a biologic basis.

His 1964 book *Infantile Autism: The Syndrome and Its Implication for a Neural Theory of Behavior* is widely credited with starting the process that brought down the view of autism as an emotional disturbance. In 1965, Rimland founded the National Society for Autistic Children (now known as the Autism Society of America). In 1967, he established the Autism Research Institute to serve as a clearinghouse for information on treatment for ASDs.

Rimland always believed that autism could be cured if the right interventions were used. He continually challenged the mainstream medical approach to autism, often with little or no attempt to veil his hostility. Whether or not Rimland's alternative approaches to treatment of ASDs are ultimately proven effective, his lifetime devotion to children and families with ASDs has helped push the ASD syndrome into public consciousness.

investigated by mainstream scientists. The brain, gut, and immune system are viewed as innocent bystanders that can be damaged by a wide variety of exposures, with ASDs as the result. GXE interactions are seen as the main cause of ASDs.

The mainstream scientific and medical researcher communities have been largely dismissive of CAM approaches to ASDs, standing by the genetic and engineering studies that have shaped the traditional approach to theories about causation. Research done by proponents of CAM interventions has been criticized by respected mainstream experts as junk science. A less antagonistic approach has been adopted recently by some mainstream researchers and clinicians who remain open to alternative theories proposed by the CAM groups while recommending a cautious approach to the use of treatments that have not been proven, particularly if there is any possibility that harm may result. The CAM groups are not mollified by these minor concessions. There is a core group in the CAM ASD community that believes that big business controls medical researchers to such an extent that data are deliberately misinterpreted to discredit the CAM theories about ASDs and the government is in collusion by refusing to fund the studies that they feel would prove their theories. The mainstream researchers and government agencies vociferously defend their moral character and scientific conclusions, and the standoff continues.

Celebrities including Doug Flutie, a former National Football League quarterback, and former Playboy bunny and actress Jenny McCarthy have devoted themselves to the cause of bringing autism to the attention of the public, while publicly declaring their opinions that vaccines caused their children to develop autism. Politicians joined the fray with Representative Dan Burton leading the charge for more investigation into a possible vaccine-autism link, motivated by his belief that vaccines caused his grandson's ASD. Senators Chris Dodd and Rick Santorum took up the reins by authoring Senate Bill 843, the combating Autism Act which passed in August 2006, authorizing close to $1 billion of federal funding for autism research with a specific mandate for more research into a possible autism-vaccine link. In the 2008 presidential primaries, candidates were pressed for information regarding their planned strategies for confronting the increased prevalence of ASDs. In a well-publicized statement made during a campaign trail stop in response to a question from a citizen about the cause of ASDs, John McCain made the controversial statement that "there's strong evidence that indicates that it's got to do with a preservative in vaccines."

Many parents of children with ASDs are not content to wait for conventional medicine to test the CAM hypotheses. The CAM supporters expresses disdain for the idea that carefully controlled scientific study is needed to answer the questions, maintaining that there is no time to waste. Recent studies have shown that many parents of children with ASDs are sufficiently satisfied that the CAM theories have merit to try the proposed treatments, with 32–74 percent reporting past or current use of CAM for ASDs.

The battle lines are drawn with very little acceptance of the "proof" offered by either side. One thing that is certain is that the current situation, with polarized views and antagonism on both sides, benefits no one. Dogmatic adherence to any one point of view is never the best way forward. When the answers are finally known, it is very likely that truths will be found on both sides of the rift.

Fortunately, times are starting to change, with well-respected researchers beginning to acknowledge that there are likely to be useful clues hidden within the controversial claims and calling for increased funding to examine alternative theories. The net of scientific inquiry is being spread wider because of the advocates for the alternative theories who have pushed for a change in the paradigm. In this chapter, some of the controversial theories on the causes of autism are examined in the context of what is and is not known about each theory.

VACCINES

Since vaccines were introduced on a large scale starting with the diphtheria-pertussis-tetanus (DPT) vaccine in the late thirties, the medical profession (with occasional exceptions) has stood solidly behind the use of immunizations to reduce the incidence of life-threatening disease. Doctors on the front lines welcomed the virtual disappearance of polio, measles, rubella, tetanus, and hemophilus influenza B in the age of vaccines. At the same time, there have always been individuals with concerns that immunizations might not be such a good idea. The 1932 publication of A *Shot in the Dark* raised concerns about the safety of the DPT vaccine, the first call to arms for the antivaccine contingent.

The DPT vaccine reemerged into the public consciousness in the eighties when vaccine manufacturers were sued based on claims that children had suffered irreversible brain damage after a bad reaction to the pertussis component of the vaccine (pertussis is the medical name for the bacteria that causes whooping cough). Careful review by the Institute of Medicine in 1991 failed to find definitive evidence implicating the DPT vaccine in permanent brain injury, but there was enough evidence to suggest that the DPT vaccine might causes a temporary (not permanent) irritation of the brain. The estimates of the chance that the DPT caused a temporary interference with brain function ranged for zero (no association) to a maximum of ten cases per 1 million children vaccinated, a very rare reaction.

National Vaccine Compensation Program

The DPT controversy and ensuing lawsuits led to the passage of the National Childhood Vaccine Injury Act of 1986 (Public Law 99–660) in October of 1988. The law created the National Vaccine Injury Compensation Program and court system. The vaccine injury cases are heard by special judges (officially titled "special masters") who determine if it is more probable than not that the plaintiff was injured by a vaccine. If the answer is yes, compensation is provided from a trust that is funded by a tax on vaccines. The trust was established to protect vaccine manufacturers from the high costs of litigation so that they would be willing to continue to supply vaccines. The replacement of DPT by a safer vaccine in 1996 (called DTaP, for diphtheria, tetanus, and acellular pertussis) brought an end to most of the public outcry over DTP.

It did not take long for the dockets to fill with over 5,000 cases from parents alleging that vaccines caused their child's autism. The special vaccine court (part of the U.S. Federal Claims Court) agreed to hear a total of nine test cases covering the alleged connection between vaccines and autism. The cases are divided into three sets of three, each representing one of the three main arguments made in the pending cases: (1) vaccines and thimerosal cause autism, (2) thimerosal causes autism, and (3) MMR causes autism. No decision has been rendered in any of these test cases but the court's decisions on these three arguments for vaccine causation of autism will undoubtedly have enormous consequences (see the Timeline for hearing dates).

The Hannah Poling Case: Mitochondrial Dysfunction as an Example of a Hidden Cause of Regression

Deliberations continue on the test cases, with no policy decisions issued to date. Meanwhile, a verdict rendered in November 2007 provided compensation for a child (Hannah Poling) who was developing normally until nineteen months of age, when she received five vaccines. Shortly after the vaccinations, Hannah developed a fever, followed by prolonged seizures and the onset of a regressive form of autism. Did the vaccines cause Hannah's autism? Certainly not in the way that most people writing the news stories seem to think.

Hannah had an inborn metabolic problem called a mitochondrial disorder that had not been diagnosed. Mitochondria make energy for the body. When a person has a severe mitochondrial disorder, their body does not produce enough energy for the brain, resulting in devastating neurologic problems from their very first days of life. However, some people have mitochondrial disorders that are more subtle. They are able to make enough energy to get by, but just barely. Anything that increases the body's demand for energy, such as a fever or an illness, can push the person over into a severe energy shortage that can cause brain damage. That is what happened to Hannah.

If she did not have a mitochondrial disorder, she would have recovered from her vaccine-related fever without any problems; most people can easily handle the metabolic demands of a fever. It was the fever that caused Hannah's energy demands to outstrip her energy supply. The immunizations were the direct cause of Hannah's fever, but it could easily have been the flu or some other childhood infection that pushed her energy demands past what she could make.

The CDC and other public health authorities issued statements saying that the medical details of the case were so unusual that the court's decision should not be interpreted as a blanket statement that vaccines can cause ASDs, but that is not how the press presented the situation. News headlines emphasizing that this is the first case in which the courts have ruled that a child's autism was caused by vaccines are not doing justice to the medical complexity of Hannah's situation. Hannah's case was not one of the test cases selected to set precedent for the 5,000 cases awaiting adjudication because Hannah's case is substantively different.

The case does raise an important question: how often do children with ASDs have an underlying mitochondrial disorder as a cause of their developmental issues? The percentage varies considerably depending on the study. In a study from a neurology clinic where children with ASDs were all tested for mitochondrial disorders, 7.2 percent had the condition. That is an estimated 72,000 cases of mitochondrial disorders may be hidden among children with ASDs in the United States. Could mitochondrial disorders be even more common? Some experts estimate that the figure is closer to 20 percent or perhaps even higher (estimates as high as 65 percent have been offered, but those numbers are almost certainly too high). Processing of mercury may be hindered in mitochondrial disorders, resulting in increased oxidative stress, another possible pathway to ASDs.

Should every child with an ASD be evaluated for a mitochondrial disorder? The expert consensus is "No." For one thing, the evaluation is not simple; multiple samples of blood are often required to see whether there is any evidence of a mitochondrial disorder. The vast majority of the time, a muscle biopsy is needed to definitively answer the question. Even if a mitochondrial disorder is diagnosed, there are no surefire ways to get around the energy supply and demand mismatch in these disorders. Hannah's case was tragic because she had a devastating disease, not because vaccines caused her to have autism.

The MMR Vaccine

The MMR vaccine has long been at the epicenter of the controversial theory that vaccines cause ASDs. Suspicions fell on the MMR vaccine shortly after the introduction of the vaccine into the United States (followed shortly by introduction in the United Kingdom) during the eighties. Many parents alleged that their child was developing normally until receiving the MMR vaccine. Within days to weeks of receiving the shot, they reported that their children lost their language and withdrew socially (regressed).

The medical establishment took the position that these observations were a coincidence of timing. The MMR vaccine is usually given between twelve and fifteen months of age, just when parents of children with ASDs most commonly start to worry that their child is not developing as expected and the most common time period for regression (even in children who do not receive the MMR vaccine). A common medical aphorism was used to dismiss the parental concerns: "Association is not causation." Just because two events occur near each other in time (the MMR vaccination and the realization that a child has an ASD) does not mean that one necessarily caused the other.

Rimland countered by claiming that the regressive subtype of autism was unheard of before the introduction of the MMR. However, Kanner's original series of eleven children contained a child who regressed at twelve months of age, well before the MMR vaccine. Multiple studies have since shown that there is no evidence for a regressive subtype of ASD associated with the MMR vaccine (but there is definitely a regressive subtype of autism). Still, a strong and very vocal contingent continue to believe that the MMR vaccine caused their child's ASD. An examination of how this theory was catapulted into the mainstream is infomative.

Dr. Andrew Wakefield and the "Triple Jab" Scare

In 1988, Dr. Andrew Wakefield, a GI surgeon at the Royal Free Hospital in London, thrust the MMR vaccine into the spotlight when he began to promote his theory that the MMR vaccine causes autism through inflammation of the intestines. The first salvo in his still ongoing crusade to prove the MMR-autism connection came in the form of a 1988 paper published in *Lancet*, entitled "Ilio-nodular Lymphoid Hyperplasia, Nonspecific Colitis and Pervasive Developmental Disorders in Children." In this very small observational study, Wakefield described his investigations of twelve children with different types of regressive developmental disorders (ten of the twelve had ASD diagnoses). All twelve children were ostensibly referred to Wakefield for evaluation because they had a PDD diagnosis (or a diagnosis that Wakefield thought was similar enough) and had GI symptoms consisting of abdominal pain, diarrhea, and bloating, symptoms that could be caused by an inflammatory condition of the bowel. (Wakefield later admitted that many of the children also had constipation, a condition that is not seen in patients with inflammatory bowel disease).

Wakefield used a procedure called colonoscopy to examine the bowels of these twelve children, but he did not examine any TD children for the study as controls. He reported finding a recognizable pattern of findings that he believed was caused by inflammation of the large intestine (referred to as "colitis" in medical terminology).

Wakefield had long felt that the measles vaccine included in the MMR was a cause of colitis. He had previously failed to prove a connection between measles and common types of colitis (e.g., Crohn's disease and ulcerative colitis), but Wakefield was not about to give up. He asked the parents of the twelve children in his study to remember how soon their child's regressive developmental disorder started after receiving the MMR vaccine. He reported that the majority of the children developed abnormal behavior within a very short time (most within a few days) after receiving the MMR vaccination, an association that he suggested implicated the MMR vaccine as a likely cause of ASDs.

Wakefield's claim caused a general panic that started in the United Kingdom and spread like wildfire. His findings and conclusions were instantly met with widespread criticism from pediatric specialists in bowel diseases (gastroenterologists). The first point of contention was that Wakefield made it seem like "ilio-nodular lymphoid hyperplasia" was a new GI disease that he had discovered when it is in fact a common finding in many children that is not considered a disease at all (seen particularly frequently in children with chronic constipation, a condition that was present in many of the children in his study). His claims that inflammation of the colon was present were disputed by experts who reviewed the biopsy specimens taken by Wakefield and found nothing amiss. Although Wakefield described the biopsy findings of inflammation as "subtle," other experts called them "normal."

Despite the controversy, Wakefield was not deterred in his quest. His theory was that the "autistic enterocolitis" was caused by live measles virus establishing a homebase in the gut after the MMR immunization. He reported finding live measles virus in the gut and hiding in the lymphocytes (circulating cells of the immune system), but other researchers failed to find the measles virus in the intestines of children with ASDs. Experts criticized Wakefield's studies and challenged the accuracy of his findings.

Wakefield was so sure of the MMR-autism connection that he urged parents to avoid the vaccination, replacing the three-in-one vaccination with separate vaccinations that are not widely available. Tony Blair, then the prime minister of the United Kingdom, refused to answer when asked if he was willing to give his own children the "triple jab," further fueling public panic. As a result, measles outbreaks occurred in England and Wales for the first time since the introduction of the vaccine in 1988.

In 2004, Wakefield left his position at the Royal Free Hospital in London by "mutual agreement." He moved to Austin, Texas, and established his own center, funded by organizations that believe in the MMR-autism connection. He has performed colonoscopies on more than 150 children and continues to stick by his earlier claims. The arguments between Wakefield and world-renowned specialists in gastroenterology have raged on in medical journals and in the press. The CAM community continues to support his findings, whereas the mainstream GI specialists dispute his claims and chastise him for his irresponsible criticism of the MMR vaccine.

Smear Tactics or Breaches of Professional Ethics and Flawed Research? Wakefield under Attack

After Wakefield's initial studies, evidence emerged that he had a significant conflict of interest in the promotion of the MMR vaccine as a cause of ASDs. Wakefield did not disclose to the editors of the journal that he had received a substantial sum of money from legal sources representing parents who felt that their children were injured by the MMR vaccine, nor did Wakefield mention that several of the children in his 1998 case series were specifically sent to him by lawyers trying to gather evidence for a MMR-autism link. Years later, an investigative reporter claimed that Wakefield had taken out a patent for an antimeasles vaccination before the release of his 1998 paper that stood to make him rich if the triple jab was abandoned.

When the conflict of interest information was revealed, ten of the thirteen coauthors of Wakefield's original paper withdrew their support of the paper's conclusions. *Lancet*, the esteemed British medical journal that had published Wakefield's paper, removed the paper from its electronic database. Wakefield is currently involved in a hearing in front of the U.K. General Medical Counsel to determine whether he engaged in professional misconduct. Was his research flawed? Did Wakefield misrepresent his findings? Did he commit a serious breach of ethics? Or was he hounded out of his job by the medical establishment? Whatever the final result of the trial, he will always be a hero in the CAM movement for attempting to investigate parental concerns about a possible link between MMR and ASDs.

The Gut-Brain Theory of ASDs

The DAN group has a complex theory that they proposed to explain how the gut (intestines) may interact with the brain to produce behaviors that we recognize as ASDs. The theory starts with the assumption that something disturbs the function of the intestines, perhaps the measles vaccine, or a gluten or casein allergy, an immune system dysfunction, or some type of genetically determined gut abnormality. Injury to the gut is postulated to be the first step in a cascade that ends in an ASD. We have already talked about the lack of evidence to support the role of the MMR vaccine in gut injury. Let us briefly look at the evidence for and against a role for gluten and casein in ASDs.

Gluten- and Casein-Related Bowel Disease

Immune responses directed at gluten (the main protein in milk) cause damage to the lining of the small intestine, a condition called celiac disease. Symptoms usually consist of abdominal pain and bloody diarrhea. The presence of celiac disease can be demonstrated with a highly specific laboratory test (the test looks for the antibody that cross-reacts with gluten and gut proteins). Traditional medical providers acknowledge that gluten exposure exacerbates celiac disease because there is medical proof: the offending antibody can be detected in the blood of individuals, and the lining of the small intestines appears highly abnormal when examined through an endoscope or when looking at a biopsy of the bowel under a microscope. When gluten is removed from the diet, the gut heals.

Similarly, individuals with allergies to the main protein in milk products (casein) can have antibodies against the milk protein that lead to gut injury accompanied by bloody diarrhea and abdominal pain. However, studies of children with ASDs do not confirm a higher rate of celiac disease or milk allergies. The role of gluten and casein in the DAN theory of autism causation is less straight forward than a simple gluten or milk allergy.

Leaky Gut and the Opiate Theory

Normally, the intestines permit absorption of a variety of small-sized nutritional building blocks into the bloodstream (e.g., sodium, potassium, vitamins, minerals, fat, and small pieces of protein called peptides). The key is that only small substances are allowed to pass into the bloodstream from a normally functioning gut. If the gut is injured, the barrier keeping the larger substances out is breached. The malfunctioning gut becomes "leaky." The leaky gut allows bigger peptides into the bloodstream. Peptides are little proteins, and the role of most proteins is to perform various functions in the body. It is theoretically possible that the peptides that leak through could have some degree of physiologic activity elsewhere in the body.

In the DAN theory, pieces of gluten and casein are thought to pass through the leaky gut into the bloodstream, travel to the brain, and disrupt brain function. How do these peptides throw a wrench into the normal brain processes? The theory is that the peptides from the incomplete breakdown of gluten and casein act like opiates in the brain (heroin or codeine are two example of opiates). Claims that individuals with ASDs act like they are under the influence of opiates are clearly inaccurate, but it is true that social interactions are partially governed by the body's natural opiate system. It is theoretically possible that proteins with opiate-like effects could affect the brain. Many other small peptides function in both the gut and the brain, making a gut-brain autism connection biologically plausible.

Peptides from the bloodstream are processed by the kidneys and dumped into the urine for disposal. DAN researchers claim that the opiate theory is supported by the finding that there is an abnormal pattern of peptides in the urine of some children with ASDs. Furthermore, the DAN-associated researchers claim that these peptides have been conclusively demonstrated to include the incomplete breakdown products of gluten and casein (called gliomorphin and casomorphin). No piece of scientific evidence is accepted as truth unless other scientists can replicate the findings. Researchers that are not part of the DAN consortium have not found any evidence for the presence of abnormal opiate peptides in the urine of children with ASDs.

Is There Any Epidemiologic Evidence Implicating the MMR Vaccine as a Cause of the Regressive Subtype of ASDs?

Between the release of Wakefield's case study suggesting a role for MMR in the regressive subtype of autism, in 1998 and 2008, 190 papers have been published on the topic of MMR and ASDs. The studies focus almost exclusively on epidemiologic investigations involving tens of thousands of children to see whether any changes in the rate of ASDs could be statistically linked to the use of the MMR vaccine.

Reviews of the epidemiologic evidence by multiple groups of experts in the United States (including the CDC, AAP, the Food and Drug Administration [FDA], and the Institute of Medicine) and reviews by similar groups in the United Kingdom have all failed to find a link between MMR and ASDs. Many different approaches have been used to look for any possible association, but none have shown a link.

Two convincing studies looked to see whether there was a sudden change in the statistics for ASDs when MMR was introduced or withdrawn. The introduction of the MMR vaccine in 1988 did not lead to a sudden jump in the number of children with ASDs (the rate of ASDs continued to go up at the same pace that was observed before the introduction of the MMR vaccine). On the flip side, the withdrawal of the MMR vaccine from use in Japan starting in 1993 did not result in a drop in the number of cases of ASDs in Japan. Estimates of the prevalence of ASDs in the United States started to rise before MMR was introduced and have continued to rise, although the percentage of children receiving the MMR vaccine has not changed significantly over the past fifteen years.

The comprehensive 2004 report from the Institute of Medicine acknowledged that the statistical procedures used in the epidemiologic studies may not be powerful enough to detect the occurrence of a very small number of cases of regressive autism linked to MMR, and that was enough to keep the issue open.

The 2006 discovery of a defect in the CNTNAP2 gene in a child with a regressive form of autism demonstrates that a genetic defect limited to the brain can cause a regressive form of autism. CNTNAP2 is a gene that controls the way that nerve cells in the brain connect with each other. It is likely that most of the regressive forms of autism will turn out to have genetic causes related to the formation of synapses as the brain develops. One thing is for certain—it does not make sense for a parent with a newly diagnosed child to assume that the MMR vaccine is at fault. As Dr. Courchesne points out, the abnormally rapid brain growth that starts well before the MMR vaccine is given at twelve months of age cannot be explained by a vaccine that has not yet been given.

Mercury as a Possible Cause of ASDs: The Thimerosal Story

Thimerosal is the common name for a preservative used to kill potentially harmful microbes in a wide variety of products that need to be sterile for safe use. Thimerosal has been around since 1928, when it was referred to as mercurolate, a substance commonly used as an antiseptic for wounds.

Most users of products with thimerosal did not give the preservative a second thought until concerns exploded in the wake of a 1999 safety assessment of thimerosal in childhood vaccines conducted by the government agency responsible for medication safety (the FDA). Before the safety review, most parents and healthcare professionals were not aware that the main ingredient in thimerosal is mercury, a substance that even schoolchildren know to be toxic. The review concluded that there was no evidence that thimerosal exposure had caused any harm to children but conceded that there was enough reason for concern that thimerosal should be phased out of use in vaccine preparations as a precautionary measure.

It is common knowledge that mercury, a member of the class of elements called heavy metals, is a dangerous substance for humans. Medical familiarity with mercury toxicity goes back to the 1900s, when workers in the hat industry were stricken with a mysterious neurologic deterioration that was eventually traced to exposure to mercury in felt.

Mercury contamination of Minamata Bay in Japan by an unscrupulous corporation caused thousands to develop devastating nervous system diseases during the fifties. Affected adults showed a wide variety of symptoms: numbness, slurred speech, changes in vision, involuntary movements, and problems with their coordination. Pregnant mothers who consumed fish from the contaminated bay gave birth to children with birth defects, cerebral palsy, and severe brain damage.

Without question, high levels of mercury, like high levels of other heavy metals such as lead, plutonium, and cadmium, are toxic to the human brain. Organizations committed to the belief that mercury poisoning is a major cause of ASDs have sprung into existence. Groups such as SafeMinds and Generation Rescue claim that the symptoms of mercury toxicity closely parallel the symptoms seen in children with ASDs. Neurologists and other doctors who have worked with individuals with mercury poisoning are very clear that the core symptoms of ASDs bear no relation to acute (sudden) or chronic mercury poisoning.

Still, it is reasonable to wonder how it came to pass that a preservative made from a toxic substance continued to be used in a product that is given to babies and young children once it became clear that mercury is bad for the brain. There are several parts to the full answer, but, despite all the public health arguments to the contrary, it is likely that there simply was not enough attention paid to the issue as the number of childhood immunizations increased.

The use of thimerosal was justified based on the longheld belief that ethyl mercury (the kind of mercury in thimerosal) is less toxic than methyl mercury (the kind that comes from the environment and ends up in the food chain). The form of mercury that poisoned the residents around Minamata Bay was methyl mercury (also referred to as organic mercury). Methyl mercury is generally believed to be more readily absorbed into the human body and less easily excreted, leading to greater toxicity than ethyl mercury.

The second reason for allowing ethyl mercury to be used as an antimicrobial is that most toxic substances have thresholds for toxicity. If the exposure to a substance is at a low enough level, then harmful effects are not expected. Almost all of us have measurable blood levels of lead and mercury. As long as the levels are low enough, humans do not seem to have trouble from the heavy metal exposure. Thimerosal is an extremely effective preservative that prevents deaths from vaccine contamination, and experts felt that the low level of exposure would not be dangerous to the children receiving the vaccines. Were the decision makers right?

As the number of required childhood vaccinations containing thimerosal increased over the years (from a total of three separate shots containing thimerosal in the first six months of life in the eighties to a maximum of nine separate shots with thimerosal by 2001), little attention was paid to the possible adverse effects from the higher total mercury dose given to each child. The FDA reviewed the situation in great detail in 1999. The first hurdle to overcome was the absence of reliable safety guidelines. The EPA had established safety guidelines for methyl mercury but not for ethyl mercury. To add to the confusion, the EPA guidelines gave figures for safe daily doses of methyl mercury, but the exposure to ethyl mercury in the vaccines occurred intermittently. For small babies, the maximum amount of mercury received in a set of immunizations could exceed the recommended average daily dose per kilogram, but it was not clear whether that was or was not a significant problem. It is important to note that the FDA based their conclusions on the maximum possible thimerosal exposure from the required childhood vaccinations; many children did not receive the maximum amount because of combination vaccines that include two or three separate vaccines in one shot and the variability in thimerosal content in the hepatitis B, DTaP and Hib vaccine preparations from different manufacturers. For example, of the four DTaP vaccines on the market during the nineties, two never contained thimerosal, and one contained only trace amounts. Similarly, only one of the four brands of Hib vaccines contained thimerosal. Vaccines that never contained thimerosal as a preservative include MMR, chicken pox, polio, IPV, rotavirus, and the pneumococcal vaccine. The FDA concluded that the amount of ethyl mercury contained in childhood vaccinations was probably a safe amount. However, they decided to recommend that thimerosal be removed from all childhood vaccines as expediently as possible as a precautionary measure.

A flurry of studies followed that measured mercury levels in babies and documented rapid excretion of ethyl mercury within the first few days, but the results were not enough to hold back the rising tide of concern. The antimercury groups countered with theories that the mercury level in the blood may decrease rapidly, but that did not mean that the mercury was gone. They theorized that the mercury was sequestered where it could continue to do harm but cannot be measured (there is no scientific basis for their theory). Epidemiologic studies looked for evidence of harm to the developing brain based on the amount of exposure to ethyl mercury in vaccines. Studies using a variety of different approaches in many different countries failed to show a link between exposure to ethyl mercury and ASDs or other neurodevelopmental disorders.

Probably the strongest evidence against thimerosal as a major cause of ASDs comes from a 2008 study that showed that the removal of thimerosal from childhood vaccines did not result in a slowdown in new cases of ASDs. The study used data from the California DDS showing that the prevalence of ASDs has risen at a steady rate between 1995 and 2008. Thimerosal has been virtually absent from childhood vaccines since 2001 (although a few vaccines still have trace amounts of thimerosal, the maximum amount of ethyl mercury that a child could receive by six months of age from routine immunization decreased from 187.5 µg before 2001 to less than 3 µg after 2001). If thimerosal exposure was the cause of a significant number of cases of ASDs, the prevalence rate for autism should have declined sharply between 2004 and 2007. The absence of a drop in the rate of ASDs after the huge reduction in methyl mercury burden is strong evidence that thimerosal is not a major cause of ASDs.

Although thimerosal has been cleared based on epidemiologic evidence, there is emerging evidence that concerns about ethyl mercury are warranted. Studies by Dr. Isaac Pesah at the University of California, Davis M.I.N.D.

Institute have shown that even very small concentrations of thimerosal can be highly toxic to brain cells. In fact, ethyl mercury may be more toxic than methyl mercury. The cautionary decision to remove thimerosal was well advised, but a clear link between thimerosal and ASDs or other neurodevelopmental disabilities has not been demonstrated.

ENVIRONMENTAL EXPOSURE TO MERCURY AS A POSSIBLE CAUSE OF ASDS

Over the past ten years, there has been increasing recognition of the toxic effects of environmental mercury for all individuals, not just for those with ASDs. As mercury from coal-burning electric plants and other industrial processes increasingly contaminates the environment, elemental mercury works its way into the food chain, turned into methyl mercury, and taken up by humans through consumption of contaminated fish. As a result of the environmental and food chain contamination, levels of methyl mercury are rising in all individuals.

As the dangers of neurodevelopmental problems for developing babies and infants exposed even to low levels of methyl mercury are recognized, FDA recommendations have progressively limited the recommended amount of fish intake for pregnant women. Our environment is becoming increasingly contaminated, and the developing child is at the most risk for injury, a wakeup call for us all.

Genetic Predisposition to Mercury Toxicity: A G×E Theory

Anti-mercury groups such as DAN, Generation Rescue, and SafeMinds continue to believe that autism is caused by mercury toxicity from thimerosal. To explain why some but not all children are damaged by mercury, the groups proposed that only a fraction of children have a genetic inability to adequately process mercury. The theory is that the children who developed ASDs after receiving immunizations containing thimerosal cannot process mercury, resulting in a build up to toxic levels in the child's system. Interestingly, studies by Dr. Jill James have shown that the glutathione system that prevents damage from the harmful substances in the body called free radicals is also involved in detoxification of mercury and other heavy metals. Genetic researchers have shown that there are variant forms of the genes involved in the glutathione system that make this process more or less effective. Is it possible that some individuals have an inefficient gene variant controlling their detoxification system for heavy metals and are thus at more risk of harm from small doses of environmental mercury? The theory is biologically plausible.

Is there any evidence that the level of mercury is higher in children with ASDs? CAM advocates routinely report high mercury levels in children with ASDs, but the results are obtained through a handful of "specialized" laboratories that are not monitored for accuracy or quality, making the results questionable. Preliminary results released in 2008 from the University of California, Davis M.I.N.D. Institute C.H.A.R.G.E. (The Childhood Autism Risks from Genetics and the Environment) Study, the largest ongoing study looking at environmental factors in ASDs, did not demonstrate any differences in the blood levels of mercury measured in children with or without ASDs. The caveat is that these blood levels were drawn years after the children last had a vaccine with thimerosal. Still, the study argues strongly against the theory that mercury gets trapped in the body and needs to be treated with chelation (see Chapter 8 for information about chelation).

Consequences of the Antivaccine Movement

The anti-mercury movement threw in their support with the anti-MMR groups and those who decried all vaccines with or without mercury. The coalescence of so many voices urging avoidance of childhood vaccines was enough to tip the balance of public opinion, resulting in a downturn in immunization rates. Doctors and public health officials have been worried from the beginning that the widespread avoidance of childhood immunizations would result in epidemics of previously controlled diseases, and that fear is starting to become a reality. Recent studies have shown that one of four children are not receiving the recommended vaccinations in the United States. A recent CDC study showed that the percentage of children receiving their recommend immunizations dropped from 81 percent to 72 percent in 2005. The consequences of the drop have followed quickly. A CDC report from April 2008 documented sixty-eight measles cases in California and Arizona. At the same time, measles and mumps infections increased seventeen fold in the United Kingdom between 1998 and 2007 as a result of parents choosing not to immunize their children. Although modern medical care in developed countries minimizes deaths from measles, it is still a potentially fatal disease that has made its way back to threaten children after it was declared eliminated in most developed countries in the year 2000.

How many avoidable deaths attributable to failure to immunize are too many? For doctors and public health workers, even a few preventable deaths are too many. Concerns about rare episodes of polio infection from oral polio immunization were enough to push the entire U.S. vaccination program to shift to a safer injectible vaccine. What is the right thing to do? Now that mercury is out of all of the routine childhood immunizations (with the exception of yearly flu vaccine), there is no longer a reason to avoid the recommended shots if mercury is the main concern. Does the MMR cause ASDs? The preponderance of evidence would say no. Still, there will be those that feel that immunizations cause ASDs and preventing ASDs is the highest priority no matter the costs in terms of disease, and there will be others that feel that the decrease in immunization rate does not prevent ASDs but subjects innocent children to unacceptable risks. Each group is convinced that truth is on their side.

The Toxic Load Theory of ASDs

Although mercury toxicity has received the lion's share of publicity as a suspected cause of ASDs, groups like DAN have a much broader theory that includes the possibility that a wide variety of environmental toxins and acquired conditions that exceed the body's ability to respond appropriately can trigger ASDs. Almost all the proposed remedies for ASDs are aimed at "detoxifying" affected individuals. Both children and adults are said to benefit from detoxification. Testimonials are commonplace, but multiple reviews of proposed biomedical interventions, including a 2007 review by Lynne Huffman and colleagues at Stanford University for the upcoming California guidelines on treatment of ASDs, failed to find convincing evidence for any of the alternative treatments. Lack of definitive evidence does not always equate to ineffectiveness. In many cases, more studies need to be done to definitively answer the questions about efficacy.

Environmental Toxicants

The toxic load theory in CAM approaches to ASDs has historically been focused on toxins from yeast, bacteria, mercury and metabolites of gluten, and casein. However, there are more insidious toxins lurking in the environment that are acknowledged by both CAM users and conventional medical and public health providers: environmental toxins. We are all exposed to potentially harmful environmental toxins. Why would some children develop autism but others did not? The theory is that children with ASDs have genetic vulnerability to environmental exposures that render them more susceptible to harm from the toxic substance. Without exposure to the particular environmental trigger, the child would not develop an ASD.

The list of environmental agents felt to be possible causes of ASDs include all of the known substances that can cause harm to the developing nervous system, including heavy metals, arsenic, most pesticides and herbicides, PCBs, phthalates (plasticizer), and polybrominated diphenyl ethers (brominated flame retardants). In addition, there are countless other chemical compounds in the environment that have not been studied for neurotoxicity but are likely to be dangerous to the developing brain.

The pervasiveness of environmental toxicants that can reasonably be thought of as harmful is so great that even a newborn baby is not safe from contamination. A 2005 study of newborn blood samples (taken from the umbilical cord) revealed 287 measurable chemicals. Of those, 217 are toxic to the brain and nervous system, and 207 have been shown to cause birth defects. The list of chemicals in the umbilical cord blood includes mercury, flame retardants, and pesticides (including dichloro-diphenyl-trichloroethane [DDT], which was banned decades ago). A 2003 study of breast milk revealed similar findings.

Children born since the forties (when the end of World War II led to conversion of many of the weapon-related manufacturing companies to chemical manufacturing) have been exposed to an exponentially increasing burden in potentially toxic environmental chemicals, many of which persist for long periods of time. The likely role of environmental toxins in the current increase in neurodevelopmental problems, including ASDs, ADHD, LDs, and childhood mental health disorders, is one area that mainstream medicine and CAM providers agree on.

Antibiotic Overuse: Bacterial and Yeast-Related Toxins

Antibiotics are given to kill specific bacteria that are causing infections. For example, penicillin is given to kill the bacteria that causes strep throat, but antibiotics also kill other bacteria in the body, some of which are helpful bacteria. Killing the normal gut bacteria allows overgrowth of other bacteria and yeast. In the CAM community, yeast overgrowth has been proposed as a cause of a wide variety of problems ranging from chronic fatigue syndrome to fibromyalgia. A complicated theory proposed by DAN implicates toxins from yeast and other bacteria as causes of brain dysfunction. There is no solid scientific evidence to support this theory despite a smattering of uncontrolled case reports of improvement with antifungal medications and antibiotics directed to specific gut bacteria that can flourish after antibiotic exposure.

Infections as Triggers of Brain Dysfunction

Immune dysfunction is considered a significant issue for children with ASDs by the CAM practitioners. Infections of any kind, including the mild infections caused by vaccines made from weakened but living viruses in vaccines called "attenuated strains" (e.g., MMR and chicken pox), are viewed as stresses on the child's already inadequate immune system that lead to negative effects on brain function. The DAN group claims that receiving multiple vaccine strain viruses "overwhelms" the child's immune system. Vaccine experts counter by pointing out that humans are constantly bombarded with viruses, bacteria, and yeast that require our immune systems to respond almost constantly, not just with vaccinations. They also point out that the total amount of foreign material in childhood vaccinations has been drastically reduced over time, despite increases in the number of vaccines given as a result of improvements in vaccine technology, leading to less, not more, immune activation from vaccines.

IMMUNE SYSTEM ABNORMALITIES AS POSSIBLE CAUSES OF ASDS

Over the past twenty-five years, a handful of scientists have maintained that the immune system is important as a cause of ASDs. It was not until the explosion of autism awareness and the commitment to more funding for ASD research that a broader spectrum of immunology researchers began to pay closer attention to the role of the immune system in ASDs.

Parents of children with ASDs have long felt that there was something wrong with their child's immune system, citing a high incidence of allergies, recurrent ear infections, colds, and multiple courses of antibiotics as proof. It has not been proven that children with ASDs get sick more often than other children, but it is starting to become clear that some individuals with ASDs have immune systems that are not regulated the way they should be.

Organized research into the role of the immune system in ASDs took longer to catch on than other areas of investigation because there was so much disagreement in the early studies that it did not appear to be a fruitful avenue to pursue. Some researchers found antibody responses to vaccines that were much higher than expected, whereas others found very poor responses. Researchers reported abnormalities in a wide variety of cells of the immune system only to have their results refuted by other immunologists who found different abnormalities. The conflicting information made it seem, at first, as if there was no solid evidence of a link between immune dysfunction and ASDs.

The search for genes that are linked to ASDs turned up several genes that are involved in regulating immune system activity. The discovery that complex interactions take place between the immune system and the nervous system that influence brain development, function, and maintenance further served to raise interest in the immune system's possible role in ASDs. As more data were gathered, patterns started to become more clear. There is now a consensus that the immune system does not function correctly in some children with ASDs. It is still too early to know precisely what percentage of children with ASDs have dysfunctional immune systems or whether any particular subtype (early onset or regressive) is more or less likely to show immune system abnormalities, but data are now being gathered to answer those questions.

Early Studies Suggest There Is a Link between the Immune System and ASDs

The first hint that the immune system might play a role in the development of ASDs came in 1971 when researchers noticed that children with autism had a higher number of family members with diseases caused by a malfunctioning immune system (referred to as autoimmune diseases or disorders). The immune system is designed to attack outside invaders such as bacteria and viruses (nonself) but spare all parts of the body that have a legitimate right to be there (self). When the immune system mistakenly launches an attack on the body in which it resides, the assault is referred to as an autoimmune reaction (*auto* for self). Autoimmune reactions can cause significant damage to whichever part of the body is under attack. Many autoimmune diseases affect the nervous system (e.g., multiple sclerosis and systemic lupus erythematosis). A 2005 study further implicated the immune system in ASDs by showing that mothers with asthma and allergies during pregnancy have twice the risk of having a child with an ASD (both conditions involve an activated immune system).

Maternal Immune Reactions as a Possible Cause of ASDs

In 2003, a researcher named Paulo Dalton collected a blood sample from the mother of a child with an ASD (who also had a child with severe language delays and a TD child). All of the blood cells were removed from the sample, leaving behind a pale yellow fluid called serum that contains antibodies and circulating chemical messengers that control the function of the immune system (called cytokines and chemokines). The mother's serum was injected into pregnant mice, and the baby mice were allowed to develop.

When the newborn mice arrived, they demonstrated unusual social behaviors (similar in some ways to autism), suggesting that something circulating in the mother's bloodstream interfered with fetal brain development. When the brains of the baby mice were examined, some of the maternal antibodies were found attached to a specialized group of fetal brain cells in the cerebellum called Purkinje cells (cells that have been shown previously to develop abnormally in the brains of individuals with ASDs). The experiment confirmed that maternal antibrain antibodies and possibly other circulating factors in the mother's serum were able to cause neurodevelopmental problems in the developing mice.

In 2007, Andrew Zimmerman and colleagues showed that antibodies taken from the mothers of twelve children with ASDs bound to rat fetal brain cells, whereas the antibodies from mothers of TD children did not. The authors suggested that circulating maternal antibodies directed at brain cells that are present only in the very early stages of brain formation might cause ASDs in some children.

These studies make an intriguing case for maternal anti-brain antibodies having the potential to influence brain development, but there are problems with the theory that maternal antibrain antibodies cause ASDs. If all that was required was the presence of the antibrain antibodies, then each and every child born to a mother with these antibodies would have an ASD, but that was not the case with the families in the study. Maternal antibrain antibodies might be part of the picture, but they are far from the whole picture.

Autoimmunity and ASDs: Do Individuals with ASDs Make Antibodies against Their Own Brain?

Researchers have reported finding higher levels of autoantibodies in some individuals with ASDs than are present in normal control subjects. It would be easy to assume that these auto-antibodies caused the child's ASD, but the situation is not that simple. The problem is that many of the control subjects also make the same antibrain autoantibodies but do not have an ASD, making it clear that something else besides the autoantibody must make the difference between an ASD and typical development.

Researchers at the University of California, Davis M.I.N.D. Institute may be on to a lead. Using serum samples from thirty individuals with ASDs, preliminary results revealed that 20 percent of the subjects with ASDs showed antibodies to a particular cell in the cerebellum, but none of the controls or siblings showed a reaction (Wills et al. 2007). The researchers are not claiming that the antibodies are the cause of damage to the developing brain, but that is one of the possibilities. Another possibility is that something is abnormal about the cells in the cerebellum that stimulated the formation of the autoantibodies. The autoimmunity story is still unfolding.

Inflammation and the Immune System

Evidence from multiple sources point toward an ongoing inflammatory process in the brain of individuals with ASDs. Furthermore, the inflammation seems to be centered in the same areas in which the increased white matter is found. It is not yet known whether the inflammation is the cause of the white matter changes seen on the MRI studies conducted by Courchesne's group or whether the inflammatory process occurs as a result of the brain changes. What is known is that the immune system and the brain each influence each other: the immune system is important for brain development and normal brain development is important for a normally functioning immune system.

The immune system is the key player that controls of the inflammatory response. Evidence of an ongoing inflammatory response in the brains of individuals with ASD has been demonstrated through measurement of factors that promote inflammation (cytokines and chemokines) in the spinal fluid and direct observation of immune system cells in the brain.

Specialized cells in the brain, called glial cells, are always on the lookout for any intruders in the central nervous system. When glial cells find something that triggers an immune response, they look different from when they are resting. Glial cells that are in an activated state (switched on to promote an immune response) have been found in spinal fluid samples taken from individuals with ASD (spinal fluid bathes the brain so it is an easy way to measure what is going on in the central nervous system). Measurements of the levels of many cytokines, soluble factors that influence the activation of the immune system, are higher in children with ASDs, consistent with increased immune system activity in the brain. Recent studies by Vargas and colleagues found evidence of ongoing immune activation in postmortem brain specimens from persons with ASDs.

An interesting link between brain development and the inflammatory process was shown in a 2003 experiment by Limin Shi and colleagues. Shi was following up on an initial experiment that showed that maternal infection with the influenza virus during pregnancy resulted in a higher risk for both autism and schizophrenia. Dr. Shi wanted to know whether it was the viral infection itself or just the inflammatory process that caused the problems with brain development. Instead of infecting the pregnant mice with live influenza virus, the mice were injected with pieces of genetic material known to activate the immune system. The immune system responded by releasing cytokines that cause inflammation. The offspring developed the same behavioral abnormalities as they did when the mouse actually had the flu, proving that it is the inflammatory process itself, not the viral infection, that causes the brain abnormalities.

Summing Up: Immune System, Inflammation, and Brain Development

So where does this all leave us with respect to the question of whether or not immune system interactions can cause ASDs? We can say with confidence that there is an ongoing interplay between the immune system, inflammation, and the development of the brain that is very complex. There are many known ways to disturb the delicate balance (maternal antibrain antibodies, infection, a vigorous inflammatory response, and stress), and there are likely to be many more ways that we have not found yet. It is possible that perturbations in the immune system occurring at different times, combined with specific genetic vulnerability, may lead to a variety of brain-based changes, including ASDs, other neurodevelopmental problems, or psychiatric conditions. The details are still far from clear, but expect to hear more about the immune system in ASDs in the coming years.

OPENING UP NEW FRONTIERS FOR RESEARCH: AUTISM AS A BRAIN DISORDER OR AUTISM AS A DISORDER THAT AFFECTS THE BRAIN?

Mainstream researchers have primarily taken the approach that autism is a disorder that arises from the brain. Meanwhile, a broad coalition of parents and professionals have refused to accept that there is an unchangeable genetic flaw in the brains of individuals with ASDs that can never be completely repaired. Instead, they favor theories that allow for the possibility that the process harming the child's brain can be interrupted or even reversed.

The autistic spectrum may be broad enough to accommodate both conceptions. Martha Herbert, a prominent pediatric neurologist at Harvard University, is a strong advocate for expanding mainstream scientific research to look for possible metabolic, biochemical, and immunological causes of ASDs (Herbert 2005). It is not possible to know how many children who currently receive a diagnosis of an ASD have a potentially treatable cause unless we look more systematically. It is far past time to expand the mainstream medical horizons and start to consider seriously the possibility that the genes that control brain development may not be abnormal in all children with ASDs: perhaps the brain is downstream from the real problem in some of the kids that are diagnosed with an ASD.

8

Conventional Early Childhood and Educational Interventions for ASDs

For a full forty years after Kanner and Asperger published the first descriptions of autism, no effective interventions for ASDs were developed. The initial view that autism was caused by "refrigerator mothers" led to disastrous attempts to salvage the child by subjecting both the mother and child to psychoanalytic therapy or, worse yet, taking the child away from the family. Children with ASDs were routinely turned over to state-run hospitals at the suggestion of well-meaning doctors who honestly believed that institutionalizing children with ASDs was the right thing to do.

Children with ASDs were sometimes sent to special schools, but there was hardly any information available to guide teachers in their attempts to educate these difficult to reach children. Whether or not a child made progress depended almost entirely on the ability of teachers and parents to develop their own insights into effective teaching methods. For a firsthand account from the director of the Ives School for Special Children between 1966 and 1972, read Virginia Walker Sperry's book *Fragile Success* (Sperry 2001). The prevailing opinion of doctors and psychologists was that there was nothing that could be done to change the course for children with autism. As a result, organized efforts to find effective treatments were few and far between.

This hopeless view of ASDs was the norm until a psychologist named O. Ivar Lovaas at UCLA developed the first effective early intensive behavioral intervention (EIBI) program. In 1987, Lovaas reported the groundbreaking results from the Young Autism Project showing that a behaviorist approach to autism treatment (often referred to by the acronym DTT for discrete trial training) was a highly effective intervention method. The success of DTT opened the door for others to tackle the job of developing techniques to help children with ASDs overcome the barriers that block their educational progress.

Since the late eighties, the number of options available to parents of young children with ASDs has expanded exponentially. For the uninitiated, the myriad program names and acronyms feel overwhelming: DTT; pivotal response training (PRT); developmental individual-difference relationship-based (DIR); social, communications, emotional regulation, and transactional supports (SCERTS); Treatment and Educations of Autistic and Related Communication-Handicapped Children (TEACCH); relationship development intervention (RDI); the Denver model; responsive teaching; and a host of others. Despite the differences in names, the common goal of all conventional interventions is to assist each child to develop to her fullest potential.

The overwhelming majority of research on intervention has focused on the development of EIBIs. Programs directed toward teens and adults are few and far between. The few existing programs for teens and adults with ASDs (e.g., Lifeskills and Education for Students with Autism and Other Pervasive Behavioral Challenges, or TEACCH) will undoubtedly be joined by research-based options in the coming years.

Whether or not complete and absolute recovery from ASDs is attainable is still a matter of contention, and will likely depend on the cause of, the individual's ASD. Every intervention program aims to improve the child's ability to function in the world to the maximum extent possible, regardless of cause. In this chapter, we will delve into the mechanisms that allow effective intervention programs to produce profound changes in brain function. We will then turn our attention to the important components of effective intervention program for ASDs, including the recent focus on "manualized" programs (i.e., the availability of a "how-to" guide so that the research-based intervention can be implemented outside of the research setting). Finally, we will take a look at some of the most well-known intervention programs and the available evidence to support them.

NEUROPLASTICITY

There seems, at first, to be a contradiction between the conventional view that most ASDs are caused by defects in brain connectivity that are predetermined by genetic glitches and the finding that conventional intervention works. How can an intervention improve the outcome for children with ASDs if the problem causing the ASDs is a malfunction in brain development? The answer lies in a concept referred to as neuroplasticity.

The brain is constantly asked to rewire during the course of each individual's life. Each time we learn new skills or become more proficient in old ones, the brain pathways used in those skills are strengthened. The time of greatest growth and change in the brain is during the first few years of development. Many of these brain changes are outwardly visible as babies grow into toddlers. The newborn who is unable to hold her head up or reliably follow moving objects with her eyes gains these skills by two months of age as the brain matures. The infant is able to sit, then crawl, then walk because of changes going on in the brain that allow motor development to proceed in an orderly manner. By the time the child is twelve months of age, she is able to learn language because the brain has laid down the appropriate infrastructure to do so based on the toddler's experience with listening to the language of others and experimenting with sounds of her own. Each acquired skill is made possible by a combination of observation, experimentation, and brain readiness; if any of the components are missing, progress does not occur.

On a cellular level, development proceeds through the ongoing processes of synaptogenesis and pruning. Synaptogenesis means creating synapses, the process of making new connections from neuron to neuron. Pruning is the process of removing unnecessary connections. You can picture a neuron like a tree trunk. The connections with other nerve cells are like the branches. As skills are honed, the branches that are useful for the skill are strengthened while the extraneous connections are pruned away.

Experiments comparing the brain structure of young animals raised in a environment filled with opportunities for discovery and mastery of skills with animals raised in a barren environment have shown that the connections between nerve cells are better developed in animals with a broader range of experiences. Experience changes the brain wiring by altering the number and location of synapses to fine-tune skills. Neuroplasticity is the name for the overall process of forming and removing synapses to alter the pathways used for neurons to communicate with each other. The connections between brain neurons are constantly changing in response to our experiences to make the lines of communication as efficient as possible.

Neuroplasticity is the underlying explanation for why EI works for the majority of children with developmental delays or learning disabilities. With the advent of a technique called fMRI, the effects of intervention on brain circuitry can actually be seen on a brain scan. For example, children with dyslexia who receive effective intervention have demonstrable brain changes that accompany improvement in their measured reading skills. Before intervention, children with dyslexia do not use the same part of the brain to process written material as proficient readers. After intervention, the connections in the brain shift to allow dyslexic individuals to use the same areas as proficient readers. Taking advantage of neuroplasticity in young children with ASDs is the basis for the improvements seen with conventional interventions.

For many years, common wisdom dictated that neuroplasticity went away after the early childhood years. We now know that is not true; neuroplasticity continues at least into the young adult years and most likely (albeit to a lesser extent) throughout the life span. Whether or not parents decide to pursue CAM interventions for ASDs, it is absolutely essential that conventional interventions be started as early as possible to take advantage of neuroplasticity.

ESSENTIAL COMPONENTS OF ASD INTERVENTION PROGRAMS FOR YOUNG CHILDREN WITH ASDS

In 2001, a panel of experts was charged with the task of reviewing the accumulated information about conventional treatments for children with autism from birth to age eight and formulating recommendations to assist with treatment choices. The 307-page report entitled *Educating Children with Autism* is strongly recommended as a first stop for anyone wanting to carefully review supporting evidence for established intervention programs. The entire report is available online for free from the National Research Council (http://www.nap.edu). The conclusions and recommendations section (Chapter 16) succinctly summarizes the state of the art in intervention for ASDs as of 2001 (although the specific treatment options have changed somewhat since then, the basic principles have not).

The important components of an acceptable program for young children with ASDs outlined by the expert committee consist of the following: (1) entry into an intervention program as soon as a diagnosis of an ASD is seriously considered; (2) a minimum of twenty-five hours per week of systematically planned developmentally appropriate intervention per week, provided twelve months per year; (3) parent training in the intervention process; and (4) ongoing evaluation of the child's progress with appropriate adjustments made to the program when indicated.

ESSENTIAL FEATURES OF INTERVENTION PROGRAMS FOR ADOLESCENTS AND ADULTS

To date, very little attention has been directed toward developing appropriate intervention programs for older teens and adults with ASDs. A recent systematic review of all intervention studies published in the English language turned up 600 studies on EIBI compared with a paltry thirty studies of adult interventions. There are no expert panel consensus guidelines on research-based treatment for older teens and adults with ASDs because there has been very little research. The absence of carefully developed guidance for adults has not escaped parents, who often find themselves without adequate options once their son or daughter finishes in the public school system at age 22.

In 2007, the California Legislative Blue Ribbon commission on autism listed expansion of services for adolescents and adults with ASDs as one of the top priorities for the state. The same dialogue is going on all across the country. As the number of individuals with ASDs entering adulthood swells, the urgency of the issue is becoming clear.

There is universal agreement that the goals for adults with ASDs include maximizing communication abilities, attaining skills that allow for the highest degree of independence possible (e.g., cooking, washing clothes, and managing money), identifying areas of strength and matching those strengths to possible employment options, and providing opportunities to develop a social network. ABA principles continue to be effective in adulthood for teaching and managing disruptive behavior. Social skills groups have been found to be effective for adults. Most adults with ASDs spend their days in sheltered workplace jobs and day programs, where the quality of the teaching and training they receive varies widely. For more functional individuals attempting to get a higher education, it is encouraging to note that many colleges and universities are starting to provide regular monitoring and guidance to improve their chances of graduating.

THE SPECTRUM OF INTERVENTION TECHNIQUES

Trying to sort out the details of each and every available intervention program is nearly impossible, even for professionals involved in teaching children with ASDs. To simplify the task, the available intervention techniques can be divided into more manageable groups. One way to think about programs is to divide them by age groups between programs designed for preschool-aged children (often referred to as early childhood intervention programs), school-aged educational programs, and interventions directed to adults. Given the current emphasis on diagnosing ASDs as early as possible, most of the focus in this book (and in research studies) is on the EIBI programs.

Another way to cut across the spectrum of EIBI programs is to split them up by other distinguishing features such as who controls the flow of the program (adult or child directed) and where the program is administered (controlled or natural setting). Examples of a controlled setting include clinics that are set up in a consistent manner or programs conducted with the child seated in a chair at a table. "Naturalistic" refers to programs that are conducted in the child's usual environment (e.g., at home, at the park, at the store).

Early interventional approaches can also be subdivided by the grounding principles used in the intervention program. The three most common approaches to intervention programs for ASDs are based on behavioral, developmental, and relationship models. The behaviorist approach focuses on teaching the child to complete specific tasks in a structured way to build the necessary skills. The developmental approach provides a developmentally appropriate progression to help the child develop the missing skills. The relationship-focused EIBI models use social interactions as a vehicle for developing the skills lacking in children with ASDs.

Although these distinctions can provide some structure for a survey of available programs, the reality is that there is a large degree of crossover from one theoretical bent to another within the comprehensive EIBI programs and amongst the other focused interventions (e.g., speech and language, social skills, and treatment of SPDs). In this chapter, we will look at a few representative programs out of the vast number of available options and assess what is and is not known about the effectiveness of these interventions.

JOINT ATTENTION: THE ESSENTIAL COMPONENT FOR ALL INTERVENTION PROGRAMS

There is one key feature that must be present for an intervention program to succeed: joint attention. JA is essential for learning. The earliest learning in infancy starts with parents paying attention to what the infant is interested in and directing their attention to the same item so that they can share the experience. An infant that seems fascinated with the moon prompts the parent to look at the moon along with the child, point to the moon, and enthusiastically say, "Moon!" Shared experiences provide the building blocks for language acquisition, social awareness, and the vast majority or early childhood learning. In any EIBI program, the first step is to establish joint attention. Whether the chosen intervention program uses adult-directed activities or allows the child to direct the course of the intervention program, no progress will be made unless joint attention is established. The same is true for behavior-based programs, developmentally oriented programs, and relationship-based programs; each program uses different tactics but all are aiming to establish joint attention, the prerequisite for learning.

COMPREHENSIVE EARLY CHILDHOOD INTERVENTION PROGRAMS

Selecting the best intervention program for one's child is an enormously difficult decision for parents. The amount of research on the topic is daunting and the writing is often in a technical style, making it hard to know what to make of the available studies. A thorough review that succeeds in putting the results into perspective was published in 2008 by Sally Rogers, Ph.D., and Laurie Vismara at the University of California, Davis M.I.N.D. Institute. The interested reader is referred there for a digestible discussion of the topic (Rogers and Vismara, 2008).

A highly desirable feature of an EIBI program that has not been emphasized until recently is the availability of a manual detailing exactly how to provide the program outside of the research setting (referred to as "manualizing" the program). Research studies showing that a particular program helps individuals with ASDs are encouraging and informative but are not particularly helpful unless they can be used in a nonresearch, real-life, community setting. Programs that come with a how-to manual have a distinct advantage over programs that do not.

The Lovaas Method

The Lovaas program is the prototypical example of an EIBI program based on applied behavioral analysis principles in a controlled setting that is adult-directed. O. Ivar Lovaas, a psychologist at UCLA, used the principles of operant conditioning (described by B. F. Skinner in the thirties) to shape the behaviors of preschool children with ASDs. Operant conditioning is based on the use of positive and negative reinforcement (rewards and punishment) to shape desired behaviors. Lovaas initially included mild forms of punishments in his program (a loud "No" or a slap on the thigh when an incorrect response is given). Negative reinforcers are no longer used because it is now recognized that using positive reinforcement without punishment is equally effective in modifying behavior. Programs that use operant conditioning principles to modify human behavior are now generally referred to as applied behavior analysis (ABA), and the professional who directs the program is referred to as a behavior analyst. ABA has a long track record of success for teaching a variety of skills in widely different setting; it is not a technique specific to ASDs.

During the late sixties and seventies, Lovaas started using ABA techniques with institutionalized nonverbal children with autism and was encouraged by the results. He designed a program for young children (ages two to four) that could be provided in the home setting that has come to be known by a number of different names, including the Lovaas method, the UCLA Program by Dr. Lovaas, and the Lovaas Model of Applied Behavioral Analysis. Many people use the term "DTT" as a shorthand for the Lovaas method, but that practice is not correct. DTT is the technique that Lovaas used to design his curriculum, not the program itself. Lovaas's program is manualized (i.e., the exact progression of the Lovaas program is described in a manual). Two children receiving DTT intervention from independent behavioral analysts may be receiving very different programs (just having the abbreviation DTT in the title does not mean that the curriculum being used is effective). The Lovaas curriculum is available through the sanctioned Lovaas Institute treatment centers (located throughout the United States or on a consultation basis).

DTT is a teaching method that is accomplished through a series of trials (referred to as "massed trials" by behaviorists). Each trial has a clear beginning and end. In this context, "discrete" means separate and distinct. A discrete trial has an unvarying structure. The person in charge of the DTT program (often referred to as an "interventionist" or "program manager") asks the child to complete a task. For example, the interventionist might place a block on the table, then give the child a block and say, "Put with same." The desired response is for the child to put the block with the other block. The child's response to the request is documented. The interventionist's response to the child's action is entirely dependent on whether the requested task is completed correctly or not. If the child's response is incorrect, they are told to try again. If the child does not respond at all, the interventionist models the correct response for the child (by placing their hand on the child's hand and "motoring" the child through the correct response, commonly referred to as hand-over-hand prompting). For the first few discrete trials of a new task, any attempt by the child to respond correctly, even if imperfect, is rewarded with whatever the child responds to most favorably: praise, treats, high-fives, tickles, or some other pleasurable reward. The program manager requests the same task over and over, using prompting if needed, until the child consistently performs the task correctly without any prompting (referred to as "fading" the prompt). Eventually, the child learns to perform the task when asked without needing a reward (referred to as fading the reward). In ABA terminology, these key steps are referred to as prompting, shaping (the successive refinement of the desired behavior), and fading. The program is 100 percent adult directed. The program manager keeps track of the child's responses and uses those data to determine when it is time to move on to teach a new skill. The child participates in the program but does not influence the content of the curriculum in any way.

Lovaas developed a standardized curriculum for his DTT program that specified every detail of how the program was to be administered (described in detail in the manual). When a provider of intervention to children with ASDs uses the term DDT or "table time," they are probably referring to a structured

ABA-based intervention, but they are not necessarily referring to a program that follows the Lovaas curriculum.

In the Lovaas method, the interventionist follows a predetermined sequence of activities designed to develop skills that the child must master before moving on. The curriculum is not individualized to the child. Lovaas laid out the entire curriculum in his 1981 book entitled *Teaching Children with Developmental Disabilites: The ME Book* (the manual was revised in 2002). The first task is to prepare the child to learn by teaching the child to come to the table and sit down at the start of the session. Once that skill is mastered, the program then proceeds to include simple cognitive and receptive language tasks such as matching objects or pointing to the correct picture of an object named by the adult interventionist. Words are taught to develop an expressive language lexicon, followed by phrases and more advanced skills involving imitation and structured play.

In O. Ivar Lovaas's classic 1987 study, he compared the outcome for children (ages two to four) with autism who received ABA interventions of varying intensity. Nineteen of the children received the intensive ABA in-home program (forty hours per week for two years), whereas the other nineteen children received the same intervention but for only ten hours each week. A separate group received the standard community-based treatment outside of the DTT clinic that did not involve any ABA. The results were impressive: at age seven, nine of the nineteen children (47 percent) in the forty-hour-per-week group had improved dramatically, showing significant gains in IQ testing (thirty points on average for those completing two years of the program). These nine children were able to attend a mainstream first-grade class with minimal supports. Lovaas considered them to have "recovered" from autism. Only one child out of the children in the comparison groups was considered recovered (2 percent). An additional 40 percent of the children in the forty-hour-per-week group improved significantly but still required special education (considered a "good outcome" but not recovered), whereas 10 percent did not make substantial gains (considered a "poor outcome").

A follow-up study of the same children at age thirteen showed that eight of the nine improved children had maintained their gains and continued to function in mainstream classes. Clinicians examining the children reported that they were unable to distinguish the recovered children from the other children in the classroom. In comparison, only one child from the less intensive treatment groups had a comparable outcome.

The Lovaas study results generated controversy for two main reasons: because the results were so much better than expected that many experts expressed doubt that the children could do that well, and Lovaas' use of the term "recovered." Lovaas felt that there were three separate groups in the ASD population: a group capable of recovery, a group capable of marked improvement that fell short of recovery, and a group that does not respond to treatment. The word recovery applied to a disorder that was thought to be attributable to brain abnormalities present at birth created a firestorm of dissension. Experts declined to believe the results until other researchers could show that the results were not a fluke. The way that all proven treatments become accepted as effective is through replication of the results by independent researchers.

The long-awaited first well-designed replication study was published by Smith and colleagues in 2002. Since then, multiple other studies have been published that examine the Lovaas method with slight variations (e.g., changes in number of hours, site that the program is provided, other interventions used at the same time, and/or whether the 2002 manual for the Lovaas method was used or not). The gains made by the children with ASDs varied in quantity from study to study, but there were important common trends that can no longer be disputed. Taken together, the studies confirmed that the Lovaas method of ABA treatment can lead to increases in cognitive test scores in a subgroup of children with ASDs. Even so, studies showed that as many as 50 percent of the children did not make gains, with the lowest gains in the children with autism and better results for PDD-NOS.

In the 2002 study there were no individuals who could be considered recovered. However, a 2005 study did show a significant subgroup (50 percent) who tested in the normal IQ range and were functioning successfully in regular education classrooms with fluent language skills and regular social interaction with peers (this group would likely be called recovered by Lovaas).

Over the years, Lovaas has modified details in his original DTT curriculum (the revised manual from 2002 entitled *Teaching Individuals with Developmental Delays: Basic Intervention Techniques* is available through PRO-ED [http://www.proedinc.com]). Many other programs for autism using the DTT methodology have emerged that go by a variety of names, including ABA-based, ABA/DTT, early intensive behavioral intervention (EIBI), and early intensive behavioral treatment (EIBT).

DETERMINING INTENSITY OF TREATMENT

Once it was known that ABA-based programs were effective, efforts turned to determining how much is enough. A 1998 study by Bryna Siegel and colleagues looked at how many hours per week are needed for substantial improvement. The study compared a group of preschoolers with ASDs receiving twenty-five hours per week of ABA-based intervention to a group receiving thirty-five hours of the same treatment. Both groups obtained equal benefits.

Many other studies have been done that show substantial improvements with ABA treatments with even less hours (as few as twelve per week) for shorter periods of time (as little as one year). Duration (months) of treatment was shown to be more important than number of hours per week in one study. The 2001 recommendation from the National Research Council expert committee on education for children with autism is for "a minimum of 25 hours," but the exact form of treatment is not specified. The twenty-five-hour-per-week number is more of an educated guess than it is a research-proven truism.

Cost Issues in EIBT

"Intensity" is a term used to refer to the number of hours of treatment provided for a condition. Should cost factor into the decisions about intensity of treatment for ASDs? In the best of all possible worlds, the answer would be no. Reality dictates that there needs to be a careful balance in which the appropriate intervention is provided in a cost-effective way. The difference in costs between ABA programs provided twenty-five versus forty hours per week is substantial. Although costs for an ABA program vary greatly depending on the area, average costs run $30-50 per hour (even more in big cities with higher cost of living). Providing a twenty-five-hour-per-week program instead of a forty-hour program results in a savings of $30,000 per year (or more).

A 1996 cost-benefit analysis assessment concluded that provision of an appropriate EIBT program for children with ASDs would be expected to result in improvements in the child's level of functioning and that the treatment would pay for itself several times over during the course of the child's life. Savings per child were estimated at $200,000 by age twenty-two and an astounding $1 million by the age of fifty-five. In the preschool population, limiting hours of intervention to the bare minimum (or below, as is often the case) is clearly not well advised, even if the strategy is cost effective in the short term.

Of course, cost is not the only limiting factor in service provision for preschoolers with ASDs. There are many other factors limiting the provision of services. A significant problem with EIBI is the shortage of appropriately trained interventionists. Because of the increasing demand for EI programs, poorly trained interventionist are able to hang up their shingle and provide services that do not conform to one of the research-proven programs (referred to as problems with "fidelity" of the intervention, meaning that the program delivered is not a true replica). Parental preference for the style of intervention must also be heavily weighted, as do the individual characteristics that may make a child more or less likely to succeed with a particular intervention.

Unfortunately, there is no proven formula that can accurately predict which children do best with which treatments.

Eclectic Treatment Programs

It is common practice to add up all of the hours spent in any form of active intervention (e.g., early intensive behavioral programs, other school programs, play groups, and speech therapy) and use the total to meet the recommended twenty-five hours of intervention. The term "eclectic" is used to describe these types of intervention services because a variety of different styles of intervention are often combined, resulting in a mix of controlled and naturalistic settings, led by adults or the child. Are these kinds of programs a reasonable way to meet the twenty-five hours of intervention that were initially recommended based on the early ABA-based treatment studies?

A 2005 study compared preschool children receiving twenty-five to forty hours of one-to-one intensive behavioral therapy (similar to the ABA-based programs) with children receiving a combined total of thirty hours of intervention through school special education services (termed eclectic interventions). The speech and cognitive gains made by the children in the ABA-based treatment group were larger than the gains made by the children in the eclectic group. A 2007 study extended the findings that intensive ABA-based treatment was superior to an eclectic program to include children starting treatment between ages four and seven.

The researchers both concluded that ABA-based interventions are superior to other intervention programs. The two studies taken together suggest that combining multiple different treatment approaches may not be such a good idea. It is possible that efforts to maintain a common approach among the providers of an eclectic program (e.g., mainstream teachers, special education teachers, speech therapists, and classroom aides) could lead to the same degree of gains as the ABA-based intervention. At the very least, the study results merit an effort to make sure that all of the interventionists in the school program are using similar strategies.

In many regions there are not enough qualified providers of intensive ABA-based programs to provide services to all of the children diagnosed with ASDs. In addition, funding may not be available (a forty-hour-per-week EIBI program costs a minimum of $60,000–90,000 per year). Research efforts have demonstrated that programs using ABA methodology provided by parents with a limited number of hours for training and supervision hours can be as effective as programs provided by trained interventionists. A high research priority should be placed on developing strategies to train parents in EIBT methods.

PRT: ABA in a Naturalistic Setting

Dr. Robert Koegel, a Ph.D. graduate student in psychology who trained in DTT under Lovaas, felt there had to be a better way to help children with ASDs learn. He wondered whether the tightly controlled, artificial setting used for DTT led to robotic learning that might not be accessible to the children in other settings (i.e., might not generalize to other environments). Starting in 1979, he set to work on an intervention program that came to be called PRT, a kinder, gentler ABA-based intervention.

PRT broke away from the Lovaas-style DTT in four main ways. PRT abandons the requisite table and chairs in favor of providing intervention in the child's real-world settings (termed naturalistic settings). Instead of using a fixed curriculum like the one developed by Lovaas, PRT takes advantage of the child's interests to teach useful skills. Rather than using rewards that have nothing to do with the task being requested, PRT uses natural consequences as rewards (e.g., the child that requests a soda using words gets the soda for the reward). The fourth departure from the Lovaas approach is the recognition that parent training in the intervention techniques is crucial. Instead of using trained program managers to work directly with the child, the fundamentals of ABA are taught directly to the parents who can then apply the principles to all areas of the child's life.

The use of the word "pivotal" in the name of the intervention is intended to convey that gains in important (pivotal) areas can create opportunities for learning in other areas (a concept that the Koegel's refer to as "collateral learning"). For example, learning to ask or answer questions provides the child with a highly useful skill that can be used to acquire more language, get needs met, or approach another child socially. The idea is that all of these skills are tightly interconnected so that advances in one area can create a chain reaction of advances in other areas.

PRT is based on the ABA concept of rewarding desired behaviors. The main difference is that the interventionist picks situations that involve activities known to be of great interest to the child rather than relying on a set curriculum that is not individualized to the child. For example, if a child likes watching a toy train go around and around the track, the PRT trainer might suggest that the parent put her hand in the way of the train and say to the child, "Go?" in a questioning voice. The child who really wants the train will eventually make some attempt to communicate and that attempt is rewarded by letting the train go. Over time, the child learns to say, "Go" clearly. PRT has been shown to generalize better that DTT. Improved generalization means that a child who learns the meaning of the word "go" while playing with the train is more likely to use "go" appropriately in other circumstances.

There is quite a bit of research documenting the effectiveness of the various techniques used to develop PRT, but only one study has been conducted to prove the effectiveness of the PRT program over the long haul. The long-term follow-up study of ten children published in 1996 demonstrated very good outcomes (see *Educating Children with Autism* for details). There are no research studies directly comparing DDT with PRT.

RELATIONSHIP-BASED INTERVENTION PROGRAMS

The idea behind relationship-based intervention programs is that the social relationship between an attentive adult and a child is a necessary foundation for developing emotional awareness, social reciprocity, imitation, and other skills needed to function in daily life. Most relationship-based programs are developmentally oriented, meaning that the programs try to follow on the typical sequence of social and emotional development in an effort to help the child.

The Origins of Relationship-Based Intervention Programs

The first programs that focused on creating a social world for children with ASDs were those developed by insightful parents and teachers through trial and error. Before there were intervention programs from which to choose, parents like Clara Claiborne Park (author of *The Siege*) and Eustacia Cutler (Temple Grandin's mother, author of *Thorn in My Pocket*) figured out their own ways to break into their child's autistic world.

In the seventies, the parents of a child diagnosed with severe autism at eighteen months of age wrote a book entitled *Son-Rise: The Miracle Continues* about the transformation of their mute autistic child with a measured IQ of 30 into a typical child through their self-made intervention program. The story captured public attention when it was made into an NBC television movie.

The book recounted the family's focused efforts to engage with their son, Raun Kauffman. Raun's mother started out by spending hour after hour with Raun, her attention focused on whatever interested him. As she persisted in her efforts to engage him (what we now would call a child-led method of achieving JA using the child's interests in a naturalistic setting), she slowly made social inroads. The couple developed and marketed the Son-Rise program, promoting the idea that parents need to find ways to develop a loving rapport with their child. The program was originally operated by Raun's parents out of the Options Institute campus, located on 100 acres in Western Massachusetts. The program is now operated by the Autism Treatment Center (a division of the nonprofit Options Institute), with the self-proclaimed recovered Raun Kauffman at the helm. There is no research base to support this program, but it does focus on recognized areas of importance—JA and parent education.

Floortime

In the eighties, Stanley Greenspan, a child psychiatrist and brother of the recently retired chairman of the Federal Reserve, Alan Greenspan, developed the most widely known child-led treatment program for ASDs. The official name for Greenspan's comprehensive program is DIR/Floortime, but it is often referred to simply as "floortime." DIR is a developmentally based intervention program (unlike the behaviorally based Lovaas method and PRT). The concept behind DIR is to meet the child at whatever developmental level they are at and then go back to pick up the developmental milestones the child might have missed. Greenspan uses the analogy of a developmental ladder that can be climbed through a combination of interactions with appropriate specialists (e.g., SLPs and occupational therapists) and social interactions between the child and parent.

Floortime intervention requires the parent to literally get down on the floor to engage in play with their child for twenty-to thirty-minute sessions worked into the day as often as possible. In much the same way as is true for TD children, the social relationship with the parent is the core from which all other skills develop. Skills learned in other parts of the DIR program are practiced and solidified in the floortime sessions.

RDI

RDI was developed by a psychologist named Steven Gutstein in conjunction with Rachelle Sheely. The program goal is to improve the quality of life in children with ASDs by working on the core deficits of ASDs: failure to develop friendships, trouble feeling empathy, difficulty expressing love, and limitations in sharing experiences. RDI is an adult-directed intervention that trains parents to be the child's main interventionists. Although the individual components of the program are research based, there have not been any independent studies done to prove the effectiveness of the RDI program. A 2007 study conducted by Gutstein reported impressive results, with sixteen of sixteen children treated with RDI losing their ASD diagnostic label after completion of the program. The study was limited by the fact that there was no control group for comparison. The phenomenal results seem a bit too impressive to be true, a warning sign that the initial results may be overly optimistic. In general, an intervention program that has not been replicated by an independent researcher should not be considered to be a proven treatment. The program is highly marketed to parents through workshops and publications, another reason for caution about accepting claims of efficacy at face value.

PROGRAMS DRAWING ON MULTIPLE PERSPECTIVES: BREAKING THE BOUNDARIES

Over the past ten years, efforts have been made to take the important lessons learned from the best-studied intervention programs for ASDs and develop new approaches to help children with ASDs. Perhaps the biggest paradigm shift over the past decade has been the increasing recognition that successful intervention programs, in the home or in the schools, must include placing a high value on parent education and participation.

Autistic Learning Disabilites: Individualizing Approaches to Treatment

Bryna Siegel is an influential developmental psychologist who directs the PDD clinic at the University of California San Francisco, a part of the Langley Porter Psychiatric Institute. She has been at the forefront of autism treatment issues for more than twenty years. Her route to autism research started with a doctorate in education, credentials that give her an extremely useful perspective on autism interventions.

Siegel is a prolific and eloquent writer. In her 2003 book *Helping Children with Autism Learn*, she presents an alternative way to approach the learning process for individuals with ASDs. Rather than packaging a program with a catchy acronym, she empowers parents and teachers to better understand and concentrate on interventions for the specific areas in which individuals with an ASD are most in need of assistance. By taking a close look at each individual, assessing their areas of strengths and weaknesses related to their particular manifestations of ASDs (termed "autistic learning disabilities"), and using areas of strength to help overcome areas of weakness, parents and teachers can develop an approach to learning that is fitted for the individual.

In recognition of the crucial role played by parents in the treatment of ASDs, Siegel participated in the development of a one-week program called "Jump-Start—Learning to Learn." The program was developed in 2004 as a national model program to assist families of individuals with ASDs by helping them to understand their child's particular autistic learning disabilities. Empowering parents with the knowledge they need turns every hour of parent-child contact into potential intervention time. The recommended twenty-five to forty hours of intervention are amplified exponentially by parents who more fully understand how to help their child learn, twenty-four hours a day, seven days a week.

SCERTS

SCERTS is a program developed by experts in speech and language issues in ASDs (Barry Prizant, Ph.D., director of childhood communication services at Brown University; Amy Wetherby, Ph.D., a professor in the communication department at Florida State University; and Emily Rubin, M.S.) in conjunction with a pediatric OT with extensive experience in special education planning (Amy Laurent, Ed.M., OTR/L). The SCERTS program is an integrated approach that emphasizes the importance of social communication, primarily through child-initiated communication in natural environments. The "ER" of SCERTS stands for emotional regulation, a key area that children with ASDs need to learn to manage for maximum progress to be made. Transactional supports refer to all the ways that the child can be supported in their efforts to learn to communicate and regulate their emotions. Implementation of the program requires a high level of family participation in recognition of the crucial role family members plays in a child's development. Assessments are provided for parents to monitor progress as they progress through the transactional supports program goals. The SCERTS program is manualized.

The SCERTS model is intended to be a team approach, to take advantage of the skills of professionals familiar with ASDs while using the SCERTS curriculum as a common structure. SCERTS trainings are made available through ongoing workshops with supporting teaching manuals available for purchase. Although the SCERTS model makes use of research-based information to construct a program that covers all of the core deficits seen in ASDs, there are as of yet no studies proving the effectiveness of the comprehensive program. Studies are currently underway to compare the SCERTS model with other interventional programs. Additional information is available at http://www.SCERTS.com.

EDUCATIONAL INTERVENTIONS

Structured Teaching: TEACCH

The TEACCH program was one of the first structured educational programs for children with ASDs. Starting in the sixties, Eric Schopler and colleagues at the University of North Carolina at Chapel Hill worked to develop an optimal teaching structure for individuals with ASDs. The program is built around the observation that children with ASDs have different needs in the classroom that must be accommodated if they are to thrive. The TEACCH program attempts to honor the "culture of autism," modifying the classroom and other environments to better suit the needs of individuals with ASDs. TEACCH is an adult-led program that aims to help the individuals function more independently. The techniques are designed to be used in the classroom (a controlled setting) and at home (a naturalistic setting).

The TEACCH program is designed to capitalize on the tendency for individuals with ASDs to be visual learners, thrive on order and predictability, prefer quiet, organized environments, and have a preference for independence. The classroom environment is highly structured, with learning activities designed to be completed by the child without verbal instructions. The "work" for each day is laid out in an organized fashion with a left-to-right structure: work to be completed is picked up by the child on the left of the desk, completed at the desk, and placed in a finished basket on the right. The TEACCH learning structure does not directly teach language or social skills, but the organized, predictable classroom creates an environment that sets the child at ease and allows for other intervention strategies to be incorporated. A number of studies incorporating the TEACCH approach with other interventions (e.g., speech therapy) have demonstrated good results.

Special Education versus Mainstream Classrooms for Children with ASDs

With the passage of the Americans with Disabilities Act of 1990, schools were mandated to provide appropriate education for all in the "least restrictive setting." Determining the most appropriate school setting that still meets the least restrictive setting requirement is a difficult process, particularly if there are differing opinions.

During the preschool years, it is usually possible to include children with ASDs in mainstream education. An integrated preschool is an option that works well for socialization experience in the school system. Children with and without developmental issues share the preschool. A special education support staff is provided to help children with DDs integrate into the preschool classroom. Decisions regarding the desirability of mainstreaming become more complex as the children with ASDs progress in school. With each passing year, the behavioral requirements for the TD peers become more and more demanding, accentuating the behavioral differences between the TD students and the children with ASDs.

The issue of whether or not to mainstream children with ASDs can be an emotional one for everyone involved, and there is no single answer that applies to all children with ASDs. The decision must be made on a case-by-case basis, based on which setting is likely to provide the best opportunity to learn. Options include full-time placement in special education, part-time inclusion, or full-time inclusion. Children needing high levels of support to function in the classroom are probably best served in special education classrooms where their individual needs can be better accommodated. One-on-one classroom aides can be used in a mainstream setting, but if the child is isolated with her aide, then she is not really fully included and is probably not benefitting from the mainstream placement. The option to mainstream is always open; rushing the process before the child is ready is not likely to be beneficial.

FOCUSED INTERVENTIONS

A multitude of intervention techniques have been developed to help children with ASDs to develop skills in specific areas. These focused interventions differ from the comprehensive treatment models because they target a particular area. However, even focused interventions do more than just affecting a single aspect of the child's ability to function. Improvements in any given area provide opportunities to grow in other core deficit areas; language skills, social skills, and improved self-regulation (i.e., the ability to maintain an even keel) are intricately intertwined.

Speech Therapy

Developing the ability to communicate is the single most important goal for individuals with ASDs. All speech therapy techniques are not created equal, and access to an experienced speech therapist is a crucial component to any ASD intervention program. Covering the range of specific speech therapy approaches is beyond the range of this text, but a few key points bear mentioning.

Sign Language

The use of sign language has been shown to facilitate the development of language. There is no evidence to support the idea that encouraging sign language will somehow delay language development.

Visual Aids and Other Forms of Augmented and Alternative Communication

If a child does not use enough sign language or oral language to communicate effectively, a variety of visual supports can be used. The Picture Exchange

Communication System (PECS) is a copyrighted program that uses simplified drawings (called icons) to represent items or actions that the child may desire. The child is asked to give the adult the appropriate icon to make a request. The requested item is given to the child as a reward for communicating. The icons are placed in a binder that the child keeps with him. Over time, the child learns to make spontaneous requests of increasing complexity. Instead of using the PECS icons, many professionals feel that it makes more sense to present the child with actual pictures of desired objects or activities given the difficulties that children with ASDs have in understanding abstract concepts. Pictures of upcoming activities can be arranged chronologically to let the child know what is coming next. Visual picture schedules are like the day planners that so many neurotypical individuals rely on. There is comfort for everyone in having some idea about what is coming next. Picture schedules can reinforce or substitute for the verbal input that children with ASDs have difficulty processing.

An alternative strategy to help the child with communication is to use an assistive communication device. "Assistive communication" refers to the use of technology to help the child communicate. An amazing array of assistive communication devices are available. A common device uses recorded spoken voice that is accessible at the push of a button. The child can use the menu of recorded phrases to request desired items or activities. Although some children with ASDs benefit from assistive technology, the vast majority of children with ASDs do not use this mode of communication.

Speech Apraxia

Children with severe developmental apraxia of speech, or DAS (the term most commonly used by speech therapists to describe dyspraxia of speech), may benefit from techniques that have been refined to address the motor-planning problems seen in apraxia. For more information, see the National Institutes of Health website, http://www.nidcd.nih.gov/health/voice/apraxia.htm.

The Hanen Programs

The Hanen Centre is a nonprofit organization based in Toronto, Canada, that has been influential in developing programs to treat children with speech and language delays for more than thirty years. From the inception, the Hanen Centre recognized the enormous benefits that could be reaped by training family members to incorporate language learning opportunities into their social relationship with their child. The focus of the Hanen early language intervention programs is to teach parents to become their child's most skilled language facilitators. In 1999, the Hanen Centre developed a program specifically for young children with ASDs called *More Than Words*. The program is presented to a group of parents and family members of children with ASDs over a three-month time period. The Hanen-certified SLP running the training uses a combination of one-on-one sessions with the parents and child, small-group sessions focused on teaching effective techniques to the parents, homework assignments for the parents to try with their child, and videotaped sessions to give parents feedback. The Hanen Program encourages parents to follow their child's lead and make use of situations that occur in the course of everyday life to develop the child's language skills (child-led, naturalistic setting).

A research study comparing the same number of hours spent in either the More Than Words program or traditional, office-based speech therapy convincingly showed that the Hanen program resulted in superior language gains. In 2006, the Hanen Centre released a follow-up program called *TalkAbility*. The program uses the same basic principles and methodology to teach parents of verbal children with ASDs (ages three to seven) how to improve their child's social skills.

SPD

Treatment for the sensory issues in ASDs are commonly sought out with over 80 percent of individuals with ASDs receiving some form of sensory intervention and 92% of families expressing satisfaction with the results. The medical community has long been skeptical about treatments proposed for sensory integration dysfunction (SID), more recently referred to as SPD. SID is a concept that was introduced by Jean Ayres, an OT. Her nomenclature and interventions have been the main template for all sensory integration therapy that has followed. Part of the problem with acceptance lies in the diagnostic terminology and explanations for proposed treatments used in sensory integration therapy. For example, a child with autism who swings obsessively would be described as having a "craving for vestibular input" that is treated by interventions aimed specifically at the vestibular system (the vestibular canals in the inner ears provide information on movement and equilibrium). The vagueness in the terminology, lack of objective measurement of the dysfunction, and lack of clear standardization of treatment have made it difficult for sensory treatments to be take their place along with other accepted treatments for ASDs.

Sally Rogers and Sally Ozonoff performed a comprehensive review of all of the theoretical papers and studies on the underlying physiologic abnormalities in sensory dysfunction published since 1960. They did not find strong evidence for any of the prevailing hypotheses used to try to explain SPD but did find proof that sensory symptoms are "more frequent and prominent" in children with ASDs (Rogers and Ozonoff 2005). Studies of the effectiveness of sensory integration therapy have been of insufficient size to draw any statistically valid conclusions, but the situation is starting to change. A recent pilot study headed by Beth Pfeiffer at Temple University compared two groups of six to twelve year olds with ASDs who were treated with traditional fine motor OT or sensory integration therapy for eighteen treatment sessions over six weeks. A series of scales measuring behavior were used to monitor the effects of the treatments. Both groups showed significant improvements, but the children in the SIT group showed more progress in specific behavioral areas including a decrease in restricted and repetitive behaviors. A larger study is planned.

Stepping back from SPD terminology, and the question of underlying cause, few professionals working in the field of autism would have difficulty acknowledging that children with ASDs demonstrate a confusing mixture of failure to respond to some sensory input, a strong preference for others, and significant distress from still others. Whatever the physiologic explanation is, there does seem to be a split between sensory input that produces a state of contentment and that which creates an anxious, agitated state. It makes intuitive sense that providing a child with activities that are enjoyable or calming and working to reduce the negative reaction to distressing sensory input would help a child to better regulate their emotional state. Children who are not frightened or nervous or upset are better able to participate in activities designed to address the core deficits in ASD.

Desensitization to situations that cause anxiety or distress is a tried and true form of behavioral intervention. Similarly, engaging in pleasurable activities is a recognized way of modulating our emotional states. Breaking through the under responsiveness to sensory experiences demonstrated by children with ASDs will provide more opportunities for joint attention. If SPD treatment is looked upon as a combination of desensitization, techniques to improve mood regulation, and a way to achieve joint attention, the benefits to the child with an ASD seems clear.

The issue that still remains is to how to determine how much and what kind of intervention is appropriate for each child. Research studies of specific interventions for well-defined target behaviors need to be conducted with careful measures of changes in the target behaviors. Equipment commonly prescribed for children with ASDs such as weighted vests, and swings need to be studied, just as the separate pieces of a comprehensive behavioral program are studied before the program is assembled.

Social Skills

Many programs have been developed for the express purpose of improving social skills. Although the details of how the programs are set up differ, the goals of each program are the same: help the child respond appropriately to social overtures from peers and learn ways to reach out to others to start and maintain meaningful social relationships. Let us take a look at the most common types of social skill interventions to see what is available and what is known about the effectiveness of the intervention.

School-Based Social Skills Programs

School is a place where children go to learn, but the learning is not limited to academics; the exposure to peers provided in the school setting has a profound effect on the development of social skills. The situation should be the same for children with ASDs except that they need extra help learning to navigate the social world. As the number of children with ASDs has increased, schools have raced to develop effective social skills programs. After one look at the books available on the topic or a perusal of the huge number of speakers at conferences presenting their own spin on how to set up a social skills program, it becomes clear that a vast number of alternatives are available. How are schools to make informed decisions?

A study released in 2007 provided important information for schools to use when selecting appropriate social skills programs. The researchers pooled together fifty-five studies on various social skills programs used in the educational setting in a type of study called a meta-analysis. The idea behind a meta-analysis is to take studies done on small groups of individuals and estimate what the results would be if there was one big group of study participants. Studies of the school-based social skills programs were all based on small numbers of subjects. In statistical analysis, studies with few subjects yield results that could be off by a significant amount. When all fifty-five studies were combined, the number of subjects increased to 147 children, still not a huge sample considering the importance of the question. The researchers found that the school-based programs resulted in little change in the targeted behaviors. Furthermore, the small improvements seen in the program setting were often not apparent in the classrooms. However, that does not mean that there is no point in including social skill training in the school curriculum; social skills are hugely important for the quality of life of individuals with ASDs. The researchers made several useful observations from the study. Perhaps most importantly, they concluded that social skill programs provided in the child's usual classroom resulted in the most improvement. They noted several problems with the studies that may have contributed to the dismal results and made recommendations to correct the deficiencies. Their suggestions were to increase the amount of time devoted to social skill programming, make sure that the programs are actually being implemented correctly, and individualize the program to address each child's skill deficits.

Peer Play Groups

Play is one of the primary tools used by children to gain mastery in the social world. Children have the opportunity to learn and practice social skills during imaginary play and interactions with other children during play. Children with ASDs often miss out on the chance to develop their social skills because they do not tend to engage in imaginary play nor do they seek peer interactions. Peer play groups for young children have become a cornerstone of EI strategies for ASDs, largely as a result of the work of Adriana Schuler and Pamela Wolfberg. The integrated play group concept that they pioneered involves using TD children who are considered to be "expert players" to teach the children with ASDs (the "novice players") how to play. Some researchers have criticized the peer play strategy by suggesting that the children with ASDs are simply learning to pretend to play rather than truly expanding their imaginary abilities. Although their criticism may be based in truth, it is likely that pretending to play is a useful tool for increasing positive peer interactions, which ultimately will benefit the child.

Social Stories

Carol Gray developed a technique called Social Stories to help children with ASDs know what to do in various social situations. There are several requirements for an acceptable social story, including that the writer has to attempt to adopt the child's perspective, the language used must be within the child's grasp, and desired behavioral responses should be expressed as positive statements (e.g., "I will use a quiet voice" as opposed to "I will not shout"). The technique is purported to be effective for individuals with ASDs in the mild MR range up to the highest-functioning individuals.

Social stories can be written for any situation that is difficult for the child to comprehend, from knowing how to behave while standing in line to clarifying how to thank someone for a birthday present. The idea is for the child to have an appropriate script ready for social situations that have proven difficult to manage using their instincts. Alternatively, social stories can be used to try to eliminate undesirable behaviors. A study on the effectiveness of social stories in the elimination of undesired behaviors in three students was published in 2008. The authors demonstrated a decrease in disruptive behaviors (chair tipping, talking in a loud voice, and cutting in line at lunch) following the use of Social Stories.

A comprehensive review of the research studies on social stories published in 2006 revealed that there were only eleven published reports on social stories that included data (the others were case reports that just described the improvements). All of the studies on children with ASDs were very small.

The review revealed that Social Stories can be effective, but the results are highly variable. The available studies do not provide enough information to know whether there are particular characteristics (e.g., specific PDD diagnosis, IQ, and verbal skills) that make the stories more or less likely to be effective. It is notable that there were very few individuals with low cognitive scores included in any of the studies, leaving the question unanswered as to whether Social Stories are, as claimed, effective for the lower-functioning individuals with ASDs. Although it seems reasonable to assume that children with higher cognitive and verbal skills (e.g., children with HFA/AS) may respond better to Social Stories, the data are not available to make those kinds of distinctions.

Emotional Skills

To have successful social interactions, individuals must be able to recognize emotions in themselves and others. Without this awareness, individuals with ASDs cannot respond appropriately to others or successfully convey their own feelings. Recognition of emotions in themselves and others is a particular area of difficulty for many individuals with ASDs.

Comic Book Conversations

Carol Gray developed a technique called Comic Strip Conversations that allows an individual with an ASD to draw out their feelings and thoughts using various colors to express different emotions. Some children with ASDs are much more able to express themselves through drawing compared with verbalization of their thoughts and feelings. There is little to no research available to support this technique, but it may be a useful tool for children who feel more comfortable expressing themselves in nonverbal ways.

Recognition of Emotions from Facial Expressions

Various strategies for teaching children with ASDs to recognize common facial expressions have been developed. A variety of computer programs for teaching awareness of the emotional meaning of facial expression have been shown to facilitate the learning process for children with ASDs. Simon Baron-Cohen and colleagues developed a DVD-ROM entitled *Mind Reading* that was shown to improve performance in recognition of emotions from facial expressions over a fifteen-week usage period (Golan and Baron-Cohen 2006). Another computer program called *FaceSay* has also been shown to improve recognition of emotions over a six-week period (with more improvement seen in AS compared with autism). Attempts to show that improved skills are associated with changes in brain function have not yet been successful. An fMRI study done by the Yale University group looked at children who had completed an effective computer-training program on recognizing facial expressions. The hope was that the gains in abilities would show up as a normalization of their fMRI scans when looking at faces. Although their abilities improved in tests of facial recognition, the fMRI scans did not demonstrate a shift in brain activation patterns used to process faces. Additional studies attempting to link improved skills with changes in brain circuitry are likely to be done in the future.

Social Groups

Just as TD children progress from play dates to social groups, individuals with ASDs benefit from the same progression. Facilitators explain the ins and outs of social rules and then provide opportunities for the skills to be practiced in a nonthreatening environment. The group activities are customized depending on the age and skill levels of the participants. For example, adult social groups might address appropriate conversation topics in formal and casual situations, learning the boundaries between friendship and romantic relationships, developing skills for independent living (e.g., how to manage a checking account, applying for a job, interviewing skills, and how to keep the job once hired). We all need social groups to provide support, and individuals with ASDs are no different.

Video Modeling

Video modeling is a technique that has been used successfully to teach a variety of skills. The approach is based on the idea that visual representation of desired behaviors can help individuals with ASDs develop a visual image of the behaviors that are being taught. Video modeling can be used as both a template for desirable behaviors or a way for a person to view their own behavior and assess how close they are to the modeled behavior. Multiple studies have documented the utility of video modeling for individuals with ASDs.

SPECIAL CONSIDERATIONS: HFA AND AS

The appropriate interventions for a child with a high-functioning form of autism will differ from those used for a child with classic autism, but the differences are mainly accounted for by the level of language and intellectual skills used in the programs: the same core deficits are targeted. The primary focus of intervention programs for individuals with HFA/AS is the development of social language skills (pragmatics) and other important social skills that the person will need to succeed. A wide variety of programs are used to help individuals with ASDs develop social skills, but solid research has not been done on specific programs aimed at higher-functioning individuals.

A 2008 article entitled "Social Challenges and Supports from the Perspective of Individuals with Asperger Syndrome and Other Autism Spectrum Disorders" provides valuable insight into the social needs of individuals with HFA/AS. Eighteen adults with ASDs (fifteen with AS, two with HFA, and one with PDD-NOS) were asked to share their experiences with social difficulties and comment on interventions that were helpful. Six major themes emerged with regard to social difficulties: feelings of intense isolation, difficulty initiating social interactions, challenges in communication, longing for intimacy and social connectedness, desire to contribute to the betterment of the world, and efforts to develop greater self- and social awareness. Several major and minor themes emerged with regard to recommended social supports. Helpful external supports included shared interest activities, structured social activities, and small-group and partner interactions. In the area of communication, alternative modes of communication were a significant benefit, whereas instruction in interpreting and using social cues was felt to be of less importance but helpful nonetheless. Finding creative outlets was a very important self-initiated support.

Jet Fuel Only is the name of a teen rock band started by Daniel Goodson to help his oldest son with HFA/AS (Sawyer), and his middle son with speech articulation issues (Evan), build their self-esteem and gain social acceptance. The band has been profiled in *People* magazine and has appeared on the *Rachael Ray Show* (check out their website at www.jetfuelonlyband.com).

There are several excellent books and documentaries available that paint a picture of what life is like for an individual with HFA/AS that others with ASDs can relate to easily. A highly recommended book for adolescents with HFA/AS is *Freaks, Geeks and Asperger's Syndrome* by a British teen named Luke Jackson. The author pokes fun at the neurotypical world in a way that amuses and informs other adolescents with ASDs. Another glimpse into the life of a teen with HFA/AS can be found in the documentary *Normal People Scare Me*, produced by a fifteen year old named Taylor Cross. Collaborating with a noted filmmaker, he interviews a number of individuals with HFA/AS who share their experiences (available from http://www.normalfilms.com).

For older individuals with ASDs, there are many good books available by adults with ASDs. Temple Grandin has written several books that may be helpful, including *Emergence—Labeled Autistic* and *Thinking in Pictures*. A 2006 documentary called *Today's Man*, produced by the sister of an adult with HFA, gives an intimate look into Nicky Gotlieb's attempt to fit into the neurotypical world. Internet chat sites for individuals with HFA/AS can be particularly helpful in developing a sense of community (although a parent or other responsible adult should monitor the site to make sure the individual with an ASD is not duped into any unwise or dangerous transactions). Blogging is another popular social outlet.

MEDICATION USE IN THE TREATMENT OF ASDS

No medication can cure a child, adolescent, or adult with an ASD. Medications should never substitute for concerted efforts to try to find other ways to help individuals with ASDs cope with the world around them, but that does not mean that medications cannot help persons with ASDs to function better. Many of the behavioral characteristics that are common in ASDs can greatly interfere with educational programs, home life, work possibilities, and myriad other life issues. Aggression, agitation, hyperactivity, inattention, irritability, repetitive behaviors, and self-injury are common issues that can limit the opportunities for learning and negatively impact the quality of life for individuals with ASDs. Psychotropic medications are the types of medications used in the field of psychiatry. These medications work on the brain to change how the brain works. It is impossible to overstate the message that medications are never a first-line response to difficult behaviors. Behavioral techniques should always be used to determine the underlying cause of any problematic behavior and attempts should be made to help the individual cope without resorting to medications. The possibility that a disruptive or unusual behavior might be attributable to illness or pain must always be carefully evaluated. If it proves impossible to adjust the environment or make other changes to decrease the individual's anxiety, agitation, or other symptoms that interfere with everyday life, then a medication trial should at least be considered.

Prevalence of Psychotropic Medication Use in ASDs

The percentage of individuals with ASDs treated with psychotropic medications is substantial and increasing rapidly. A 1995 survey showed that 30 percent of children with ASDs were given at least one psychotropic drug. Six years later, the figure had risen to 46 percent. Whereas only 8 percent were using more than one drug in 1995, the figure rose to 21 percent in 2001. The most current statistics are astounding and disturbing, even for conventional medical practitioners who believe that these medications can help smooth out the emotional regulation problems that make life so difficult for individuals with ASDs.

A 2008 study published in the journal *Pediatrics* used the Medicaid insurance database to show that 56 percent of individuals with ASDs were on at least one psychotropic medication, with 20 percent of those taking three or more medications. Perhaps the most surprising finding is the prevalence of medication use in the very young, with 18 percent of children as young as newborn to two years of age and 32 percent of children three to five years of age taking medications that affect brain neurotransmitters. Other studies looking at different populations also come up with extremely high estimates, with psychotropic medication use estimated at 45 percent in children and adolescents and a whopping 75 percent in adults with ASDs. Increasing age, lower levels of adaptive skills, and more challenging behaviors are all factors associated with higher rates of medication use.

Coexisting Mental Health Problems or Symptoms of ASDs?

At least half of all individuals with ASDs are diagnosed with "comorbid" mental health conditions (i.e., the mental health issues are thought of as coexisting with autism). In a 2008 study of adults with ASDs, psychiatric diagnoses were common: anxiety in 50 percent, obsessive-compulsive disorder in 50 percent, depression in 21 percent, with a smattering of other diagnoses including Tourette syndrome and bipolar disorder in an additional 5–10 percent. Many experts disagree with the idea that individuals with ASDs have superimposed mental health conditions, finding it more logical to conclude that commonly observed symptoms (e.g., anxiety, agitation, aggression, obsessive-compulsive disorder, and inattention) are part and parcel of the ASD. The comorbid approach attributes the problematic symptoms to psychiatric conditions, whereas the other approach sees the person's mood and behavioral issues as stemming from the neurobiologic conditions that causes ASDs. Which of the two views is correct cannot be easily teased out, and the difference in views turns out to be primarily theoretical, with little relevance when it comes down to selecting medications for use in ASDs. The accepted approach is to target medications toward the observed symptoms. An anxious-appearing individual with an ASD may benefit from antianxiety medications, whereas a hyperactive and inattentive person with an ASD might benefit from the class of medications used to treat a person with ADHD. The problematic behaviors are referred to as the "target" behaviors. Whether or not the medication "works" is determined by watching for a decrease in the target behaviors while monitoring carefully for side effects. The balance of improvement in the targeted symptoms with an acceptable side-effect profile (preferably no side effects, but that is hard to achieve) determines whether or not the medication is continued.

A slightly different approach is to categorize symptom complexes that tend to group together and try to treat the entire group of behaviors. A system that subdivides the behavioral symptoms in ASDs into five categories has been used at the University of Kansas. This approach is not commonly used, but perhaps it should be. The categories used by the psychiatrists there are as follows: seizure-related behavioral symptoms (primarily side effects of seizure medications); a hyperactive-inattentive impulsive-distractible symptom cluster; tics, Tourette syndrome, and movement disorders; a compulsive-sameness oriented-explosive symptom cluster; a mood disorder symptom cluster (e.g., Treatments are selected according to the group that best fits the individuals's symptoms).

Types of Psychotropic Medications Commonly Used to Treat ASDs

Virtually every psychotropic medication that psychiatrists have at their disposal have been used in ASDs at some point in time. At first it may strike the layperson as odd that medications used for psychotic disorders, depression, anxiety, ADHD, and seizures are all commonly prescribed for individuals with ASDs. It took many years to dispel the notion that children with autism were not similar to those with childhood schizophrenia, so why are antipsychotic medications still used? Why are seizure medications used in children who do not have seizures? The answer is that it is common for a drug to be approved for a specific condition only later to be found useful in an entirely different circumstance. There are countless examples of expanded uses for medications, such as the use of anticonvulsant medications to treat bipolar disorder and migraines, two conditions that have nothing to do with seizures.

Psychotropic medications can help with a variety of brain-related conditions. Any medication that affects the chemical messengers in the brain (referred to as neurotransmitters) will have a broad range of effects because there are only a limited number of brain chemicals that must control an amazingly diverse set of brain-related phenomenon. The big three neurotransmitters are serotonin, norepinephrine, and dopamine. Antidepressants and antianxiety medications mainly affect serotonin but have variable effects on norepinephrine. Antipsychotics (also referred to as neuroleptics) primarily affect dopamine but have effects on the other neurotransmitters as well. Anticonvulsant medications, used as mood stabilizers, are the least well-characterized medications with respect to how they affect neurotransmitters. The result is that, even for the best-trained psychiatrists, it is a trial-and-error process to come up with a medication combination that works the best for any individual, whether the medications are used to treat mental health disorders or ASDs.

The main targets of pharmacologic intervention are anxiety, obsessive-compulsive behaviors, depression, impaired ability to focus, hyperactivity, sleep problems, self-injurious behavior, agitation, and aggressive behaviors. The same types of medications used to treat these symptoms in persons without ASDs are used for persons with ASDs. The most common medications used in children with ASDs are the antipsychotic medications (used in 13.7 percent of children with ASDs). Other medications used frequently included antidepressants (12.2 percent), anticonvulsant medications used as mood stabilizers (5.7 percent), and antianxiety medications (1.6 percent).

Antipsychotic Medications: First-Generation and Atypical Antipsychotics

During the forties and fifties, institutionalized patients with autism were often treated with antipsychotic medications such as haloperidol (e.g., brand name Haldol). Although it is tempting to think of the early institutions as places where patients were sedated into submission by uncaring doctors (and there is some truth to that view), there are many studies supporting the use of antipsychotic medications in ASDs. For many years, Haldol was the medication with the most evidence supporting its use in autism. More current studies have confirmed the previous results. For example, a 2001 study showed that haloperidol decreases irritability and hyperactivity in individuals with ASDs. The main problem with the typical or first-generation antipsychotic medications is the high rate of side effects. There are many side effects from typical antipsychotics: tremors and unsteadiness; bothersome feeling of restlessness that results in the need to move legs or other body parts (called akathesia); a dangerous medical condition called neuroleptic malignant syndrome that can result in high body temperatures and even death; to the most feared, a permanent side effect called tardive dyskinesia. Affected patients with tardive dyskinesia are subjected to an involuntary procession of facial grimaces and mouth and tongue movements that can be stigmatizing and life-altering. A major shift in usage of medications with antipsychotic properties occurred in the nineties when atypical antipsychotics were introduced, the single most prescribed class of medications for ASDs. Atypical antipsychotics are widely considered to have a safer side-effect profile with respect to motor movements, but there are other serious health issues that should not be underestimated. Weight gain on the atypical antipsychotics can be dramatic, with weight gains of forty to sixty pounds occurring commonly, even in children. Atypical antipsychotics also cause high blood sugar levels (independent of weight gain). The amount of weight gain varies depending on which antipsychotic is used, with risperidone associated with the most weight gain and ziprasidone associated with the least (so-called "weight neutral").

The only drug in any class that has been studied well enough to receive FDA approval specifically for use in children with ASDs is the atypical antipsychotic risperidone (Risperdal). A 1998 study of risperidone showed improvement in behavioral symptoms in 57 percent of the study population. A well-publicized large clinical trial published in the *New England Journal of Medicine* in 2001 found that 56 percent of children with ASDs taking risperdone had a significant decrease in symptoms of irritability (e.g., tantrums, aggression, and self-injurious behavior). Other medications in the same class are also used commonly in behavior management (without FDA approval) for individuals with ASDs, including olanazpine (Zyprexa), ziprasidone (Geodon), and aripiprazole (Abilify).

Serotonin in ASDs

Studies have repeatedly shown that individuals with ASDs have high circulating levels of a neurotransmitter called serotonin. Because high serotonin is a consistent finding in ASDs, researchers tried treating with a psychotropic medication that is known to decrease serotonin. Although the approach seemed logical, the results were disappointing.

In contrast, medications that increase the concentration of serotonin at the nerve ending (called selective serotonin reuptake inhibitors [SSRIs]) are effective. A 1996 study of fluvoxamine (Luvox), a drug used to treat obsessive-compulsive disorder, showed that 56 percent of individuals with ASDs had less repetitive thoughts and behaviors and less aggressive behaviors during treatment. Improvement in language usage was also seen. Other medications in the SSRI class that have been shown to be effective in treating explosive outbursts, aggression, self-injurious behavior, and obsessive behaviors by as much as 50 percent are fluoxetine and sertraline (brand names Prozac and Zoloft). Older medications in a class called the tricyclic antidepressants also affect serotonin and have been found effective in controlling movement disorders (e.g., tics and Tourette syndrome).

Medications for Inattention, Impulsivity, and Hyperactivity: The ADHD Medications

The most commonly used medications for ADHD are the stimulant medications (e.g., methylphenidate or Ritalin, dextroamphetamine or Dexedrin, and a variety of newer stimulant preparations, including several long-acting preparations). Approximately one-third of children with ASDs show a decrease in hyperactivity and impulsivity with an increase in attention when given a stimulant. Individuals with ASDs without ID are more likely to respond to stimulant medications. A major side effect of stimulant medications is decreased appetite, which can be a limiting factor in children with ASDs, who often are not big eaters. Newer nonstimulant medications (e.g., atomoxitene or Strattera) are also showing promising results for treatment of maladaptive behaviors in ASDs.

Other medications used for ADHD, including clonidine and guafacine, have been shown to be effective in reducing maladaptive behaviors in ASDs. Both medications are in a class called alpha-2 blockers. They function by blocking adrenaline-like effects in the brain and body. These medications can be sedating and are often used to help with sleep and with tic disorders.

Mood Stabilizers: The Anticonvulsant Medications

The use of mood stabilizers in the treatment of ASDs is exceedingly common. Lithium was the first mood stabilizer that was used to control mood swings in manic depression (now called bipolar disorder). Because of the significant side effects of lithium, the anticonvulsant medications have primarily replaced the use of lithium. Multiple small studies have supported the use of valproate in individuals with ASD to decrease frustration and explosive behaviors. Improvements in social behaviors and language have also been reported. Currently, the most frequently used mood-stabilizing drugs are valproic acid (Depakote), lamotrigine (Lamictal), and oxcarbazepine (Trileptal). Typically, a mood stabilizer is used in conjunction with other medications (most often an SSRI or atypical antipsychotic). Although these medications are all anticonvulsants, the mechanism of action is not related to seizure control.

Opiate Blockers

To test the theory that excess opiates are involved in ASDs, a medication that blocks the effect of opiates in the brain (called naltrexone) has been studied in many small trials over short time frames with variable results. A 2006 review of all of the evidence concluded that a trial of naltrexone in children with ASDs with self-injurious behavior is warranted. Improvement in hyperactivity, agitation, irritability, temper tantrums, social withdrawal, and stereotyped behaviors along with improved eye contact and attention may also be seen. The most common side effect was transient sedation. Most clinicians have not been impressed with naltrexone, and it is rarely used in actual practice.

Anticholinergic Medications

Donepezil is a medication used to help patients with Alzheimer's disease think more clearly by increasing the brain concentration of a neurotransmitter called acetylcholine. Based on studies that showed a decrease in the acetylcholine-producing neurons in ASDs, a pediatric neurologist named Dr. Michael Chez decided to investigate the possibility that medications to increase acetylcholine concentrations in the brain might improve symptoms in ASDs. In 1999, he conducted a pilot study of donepezil in ASDs that showed improvements in language with treatment. In 2000, Chez conducted a placebo-controlled trial of fifty-one children who received a total of six to twelve weeks of treatment that also showed benefits. A small follow-up study done by other researchers in 2002 did not confirm the gains in language that Chez claimed (but there were some other areas of behavioral improvement noted). In 2003, Chez published the results of a double-blind, placebo-controlled study showing statistically significant improvement in expressive and receptive language and decreases in the severity of overall symptoms in a group of forty-three children with ASDs (ranging in ages from two to ten). In 2005, Dr. Chez again reported speech gains from short-term treatment with yet another anticholinesterase medications (called rivastigmine). It is clear that Dr. Chez feels there is merit in the use of anticholinesterase medications, but it is not as clear why no other researchers are picking up the banner and running with it. In the absence of other researchers confirming these intriguing findings, the anticholinesterase medications are not being used as standard treatments for ASDs.

Melatonin

Melatonin is a natural hormone produced by the pineal gland in the brain that is involved in the natural circadian rhythm that regulates sleep. Several studies have shown improvements in sleep-wake cycles in persons with DDs of all types when treated with melatonin. A 2008 study of 107 children ages two to eighteen given melatonin for sleep revealed that 25 percent no longer had sleep problems, and 60 percent reported improved sleep. There was no increase in seizures (a theoretical side effect). The doses used by children in the study ranged from 0.75 mg up to 6 mg at night.

Final Thoughts on Psychotropic Medication in ASDs

Temple Grandin, a successful professional with HFA, attributes her ability to function in the neurotypical world to taking an antianxiety medication (Temple takes a tricyclic antidepressant). Depression is also common in ASDs, particularly for the higher-functioning individuals who eventually realize that they do not fit in. Helping a person to overcome anxiety and depression allows her to pursue a fulfilling life, whether she has an ASD diagnosis or not. The use of psychotropic medications needs to be assessed on an individual basis. Combinations of medications are often needed to achieve optimal results, but there is not an exact formula. There is no substitute for close monitoring by a professional who actively seeks information to determine whether the benefits of the prescribed medications are outweighing the risks.

9

CAM Approaches to Treatment: "Biomedical" Interventions

Alternative treatments for health conditions have always existed in parallel with mainstream medical approaches, and autism is no exception. The proponents of CAM treatments for ASDs refer to these alternative interventions as "biomedical" treatments. As discussed in Chapter 7, proponents of biomedical treatments for ASDs believe that the brain in ASDs is essentially an innocent bystander, damaged as a result of a breakdown in function somewhere else in the body. Biomedical treatments are based on the belief that ASDs can be cured (or at the very least greatly improved) by the judicious use of various vitamins and supplements, dietary modifications, and eliminations of toxins, bolstering the dysfunctional immune system, and treatment of harmful infections to decrease the stress on the body.

The popularity of the alternative treatments for ASDs is enormous. Recent studies have shown that the majority of children with ASDs are given some form of CAM treatment with estimates for usage of up to 87 percent, with about half of the CAM users trying more than one "treatment." Most studies show that the use of specially formulated vitamins and supplements are the most popular form of CAM, followed by the GFCF diet. Two percent of families are using mercury chelation.

A recent major review of the medical literature on all CAM treatments for ASDs was headed up by Lynne Huffman, M.D., at Stanford University for the upcoming publication *Autistic Spectrum Disorders: Guideline for Effective Interventions* (sponsored by the California DDS, and tentatively scheduled for release in late 2008). The review did not find adequate evidence to consider any of the CAM treatments to be proven. More study is needed before any conclusions can be drawn.

VITAMINS AND OTHER NUTRITIONAL SUPPLEMENTS

The first vitamin to be recommended by Rimland (well before DAN was ever started) was vitamin B6 (also called pyridoxine), often given with magnesium to increase absorption. Although Rimland claims that at least sixteen studies have verified the positive effects of pyridoxine and magnesium, experts in the analysis of clinical studies do not agree. The studies on B6 have yielded conflicting results. A 1997 study that was designed in an acceptable manner—randomizing children with ASDs to a treatment group or a control group in a double-blinded manner (meaning that neither the researcher nor the parents knew whether the child was receiving B6 or a placebo)—did not show a benefit from B6 supplementation.

The list of recommended vitamins and supplements has grown over the years to include dimtheylglycine, vitamin A, vitamin B12, vitamin C, glutathione, various amino acids, a prescribed mix of essential fatty acids from various sources, zinc, tetrahydrofurfuryl disulfide, probiotics, and a host of others. The research data are not convincing, with studies done on small numbers of children yielding mixed results. Behind most of the recommendations, there is some theoretical support. There is evidence that many of these vitamins and supplements can affect the brain. For example, well-designed studies out of Harvard University have shown that essential fatty acids found in fish oil can help stabilize the course of mild bipolar disorder. Additional study is needed using carefully constructed clinical trials before any definitive conclusions can be reached. The M.I.N.D. Institute is currently recruiting children with ASDs for a clinical trial of vitamin B12 because of the theoretic possibility that vitamin B12 supplementation might decrease oxidative stress (see Chapter 6 for details on oxidative stress in ASDs). Other mainstream research institutions are following suit with better designed studies to get answers about CAM treatments.

Many conventional practitioners are wary of the fact that all of these supplements are available from specialty companies that sprang up to fill this special niche for ASDs and all are expensive. The costs for an ongoing supply of several of these supplements can run more than $200 per month, severely taxing the budget of many parents who use CAM treatments for their children with ASDs.

SECRETIN: THE BROKEN PROMISE

Worldwide attention was focused on secretin after a published report (based on experience with just three children) suggested that administration of a single dose of secretin resulted in significant improvements in autistic children. After several years of intensive research efforts failed to confirm its effectiveness, secretin has almost faded out of memory. A close look at how the secretin story unfolded is necessary to appreciate how a single individual believing strongly in a link between a treatment and a sudden recovery from autism led to the largest research expenditure ever directed to any proposed ASD treatment. Perhaps the best reason to resurrect the secretin story is to place the sequence of events into perspective as yet another example of the dramatic rise and ultimate fall of a promised cure that failed to deliver. The secretin story is a cautionary tale for parents who are tempted to rush out and try a new cure for autism before the data are in, no matter what the cost.

Victoria Beck, the mother of a child with autism named Parker Beck, was the first to proclaim that a single injection of the gut hormone secretin brought her child out of autism, allowing him to speak his first words. Parker was being evaluated for diarrhea by a pediatric gastroenterologist. As part of the medical workup, secretin was given to measure the function of his pancreas (an organ that releases important enzymes to aid digestion). After just a single dose of secretin, his mother noted an increase in his language and an improvement in his social responsiveness that lasted for several months. In response to her observations, a gastroenterologist named Dr. Horvath published a description of three children with ASDs who showed improvement in language and social skills after receiving a single dose of secretin (one of the three children was Parker Beck). Before any research studies were done, thousands of children received injections of secretin, causing a worldwide shortage of supplies that allowed some unscrupulous providers to charge exorbitant prices for the injection. Personal accounts of miracle cures flooded the ARI and the airwaves. In the introduction to her 1999 book *Confronting Autism: The Aurora on the Dark Side of Venus*, Bernard Rimland wrote, "I have encountered no treatment modality, in my 40 years of experience, which is nearly as promising as secretin."

The first trials looking at secretin used a single dose, just like Parker Beck received. In contrast to the reported situation with Parker Beck, no improvement was documented with a single intravenous injection. Advocates for secretin suggested that repeated treatments might be necessary to see the full beneficial effects (although Parker Beck only had one injection). In response, trials using multiple doses over longer time periods were conducted. Studies failed to confirm a significant difference between the secretin treatment group and the group that received a placebo injection. The children in both the treatment and the nontreatment groups improved by the same amount; the secretin group had no effect. Advocates for secretin raised the issue that synthetic human secretin might be better than the secretin obtained from pigs or humans. Although one study suggested that there might be a subgroup of children with GI symptoms who responded to synthetic secretin, most other studies did not find a difference between the secretin and placebo groups. Review of twenty-two studies led to the conclusion that there was no proof of a clear benefit from secretin.

Repligen, the company that had bought the rights to synthetic secretin when it seemed that there was money to be made, tried but failed to come up with results that could convince the FDA that secretin should be approved for use in ASDs. Nevertheless, some DAN providers continue to use specially formulated secretin preparations that they claim are effective (e.g., for use on the skin or to be taken under the tongue). These preparations are not monitored by the FDA, and it is not known whether they are even absorbed well enough to potentially have an effect.

The conventional medicine interpretation of the lesson from the secretin story is that association is not causation: just because a child demonstrates improvement after using one or another of the CAM treatments does not mean that the treatment caused the improvement. Parents and healthcare providers would be well-advised to view reports of miracle cures with skepticism. The CAM interpretation is that secretin helps some children with gut-related causes of ASDs, making it worth a try, even if the studies did not show a benefit.

GFCF DIETS

Proponents of the GFCF diet recommend removing the gluten and casein to prevent pieces of partially digested gluten or casein from entering the bloodstream and, from there, going to the brain. Most studies of GFCF diets in ASDs are not designed well enough to draw any conclusions. However, a 2002 study with an acceptable design seemed to support the presence of the peptides and improvement off the GFCF diet. In the recent review of CAM treatments sponsored by the California DDS (conducted by Lynne Huffman, M.D., and colleagues at Stanford University), an insufficient, number of high quality studies of the GFCF diet were available to support the treatment. As with many of the CAM treatments (with the exception of secretin, which has been thoroughly discredited), more research is needed in this area to draw a definitive conclusion.

A controversial aspect regarding the GFCF diet is whether or not it is worth getting a specialized laboratory test to see whether gluten and casein peptides are present in the urine. Reports of an abnormal pattern of peptides in the urine of children with ASDs have primarily been made by a single researcher named Karl Reichelt. Reichelt claims that the abnormal protein pattern clears on the GFCF diet and (tests for the peptides are available through the Great Plains Laboratory).

Studies done by the RepliGen Corporation (the company that bought the rights for synthetic secretin production) did not find any evidence of opioid peptides in the urine of autistic children: no gluten peptides, and no casein peptides. The tests done by RepliGen used far more sophisticated equipment than was used by the Great Plains Laboratory, making it very likely that the RepliGen results are the correct results. At the present time, it does not appear that there is any reason to obtain a urine peptide test from one of the specialty laboratories that offer this unproven test. Even if there is no evidence an abnormal peptide pattern is not found, CAM adherents still recommend a trial of the GFCF diet for six to twelve months, claiming that it can take that long to see improvement. Failure to see improvement is often attributed to small amounts of hidden gluten in food instead of ineffectiveness. The proponents of GFCF diets claim that even a tiny amount of gluten can prevent the diet from working, foisting the blame for any failure of the diet onto the parents for lack of vigilance. Those with a more cynical bent feel that the laboratories that offer unproven tests (e.g., measurement of urinary peptides) are preying on the desperation of parents who will do anything to help their children.

MERCURY CHELATION

As soon as the CAM autism community became aware of the presence of mercury in thimerosal, efforts began in earnest to find ways to remove the mercury that they believed was trapped in the bodies of children with ASDs. Mercury chelation is the hottest topic in alternative treatment for ASDs at the present time, despite medical concerns that chelation might not be safe for the child. Up to this point in time, one child has died during chelation (as a result of intravenous administration of the wrong chelation agent). The conventional medicine opinion is that one child is one child too many. Experimenting with new techniques on children is a dangerous paradigm. For a fascinating perspective on the rise of mercury chelation treatment, read the article entitled "My Involvement with Autism Quackery" on the Autism Watch website, a site dedicated to presenting the scientific data on ASDs (http://www.autism-watch.org/about/bio2.shtml).

The same laboratories that measure the abnormal peptides alleged to be from gluten and casein reported high levels of mercury in the hair, urine, and blood samples from children with ASDs. The accuracy of the measurements from these laboratories is questioned by conventional medicine experts for two main reasons. The first issue is that none of the specialty laboratories are certified by the regulatory agencies that ensure accuracy in the licensed laboratories that are typically used for routine medical tests. The second reason to doubt these laboratory results is that studies done in routine laboratories do not confirm the presence of wildly elevated mercury levels. Studies of TD individuals have shown that approximately one-third have mild to moderately elevated mercury levels related to environmental contamination. The CAM providers counter that a special protocol needs to be followed to extract the stored mercury before an accurate measurement of the individual's mercury level can be obtained, but experts from prestigious institutions say there is no scientific evidence for their claims.

Multiple different protocols have been developed to remove the mercury that CAM supporters think is poisoning children with ASDs. The technique used is called chelation. To chelate a heavy metal (e.g., lead or mercury), a medicine is given that binds the substance and facilitates clearance from the body. The DAN protocols have used various combinations of intravenous medications and application of specially formulated topical preparations containing chelation medications. None of these alternative protocols for chelation have been adequately assessed for effectiveness or safety. The methods used to "remove" mercury have been derived purely on the basis of trial and error by the DAN physicians.

There are many reasons to think that chelation for suspected mercury toxicity is unlikely to be effective. The first reason is that there is no evidence that excess mercury is stored anywhere in the body. Although excess lead is stored in bone for long periods of time, there are no clear storage sites in the body for mercury. Preliminary results from the Childhood Autism Risk from Genetics and the Environment Study do not show any difference in the mercury levels measured in children with ASD and TD children.

Although not very much is known about treatment for high mercury levels, there is quite a bit of knowledge about chelation for lead poisoning. A major lesson to be taken away from the lead poisoning story is that removal of lead by chelation does not reverse the developmental problems caused by the high lead levels before treatment. By extension, it is not likely that brain damage that might have occurred from mercury poisoning would be expected to resolve with chelation.

Attempts to obtain approval for a clinical trial of mercury chelation sponsored by the National Institute of Mental Health are stalled because of ethical concerns about treating children with a potentially dangerous medication (the chelating agent DMSA).

HYPERBARIC OXYGEN THERAPY

Hyperbaric chambers were initially developed to help scuba divers with the bends but the uses have greatly expanded since that time. The chambers pressurize oxygen, which allows the oxygen permeate into the body tissues. Hyperbaric oxygen therapy (HBOT) has been found to be helpful in the healing of difficult-to-heal wounds, such as the ulcers that form in the feet of diabetics as a result of their poor circulation. The theory behind HBOT for ASDs is based on studies that show that parts of the brain in individuals with ASDs receive less blood flow compared with TD individuals. The hope is that the pressurized oxygen will get to the under-oxygenated areas of the brain and restore normal function. The only evidence supporting HBOT for ASDs are testimonials. Despite the very high cost of treatment, many parents are turning to HBOT as pricey HBOT centers proliferate.

TREATMENT OF INFECTIONS AND IMMUNE SYSTEM BOOSTERS

Treatment with antifungals for suspected yeast overgrowth and antibiotics designed to kill bacteria that can overgrow in the gut (e.g., vancomycin) are recommended for children who have been on multiple courses of antibiotics. Antiviral medications are also used.

Treatment with antibodies (immunoglobulins) has been studied at the University of California, Irvine by Dr. Gupta. Treatment was offered only to individuals with ASDs who had test results showing a deficiency of antibodies (a finding that is not specific to ASDs). Preliminary reports were promising, but a controlled clinical trial did not confirm the effectiveness of the treatment. Once again, the CAM proponents interpreted the findings as proof that a subset of individuals with ASDs benefited. Other unproven immune system boosters (e.g., colostrum, transfer factor) are routinely recommended but have not been carefully studied.

CONCLUSIONS ON BIOMEDICAL TREATMENTS FOR ASDS

The list of CAM treatments used for ASDs continues to grow. It is incumbent on the medical system to design appropriate trials with adequate numbers of subjects to answer the question of efficacy for CAM approaches to ASD treatment. Without adequate numbers of subjects in the studies, the diversity in the causes of ASDs allows the persistent belief that any one of the CAM options might help a specific subgroup of individuals, leading well-meaning parents to take a shotgun approach to avoid missing a treatment that might help their child. If the treatments are found to be effective, mainstream practitioners need to made aware. Parents will have to make their own cost-benefit analysis and decide for themselves which CAM treatments they want to try, if any. The main hope of the conventional practitioners is that parents will not forgo proven mainstream interventions because they are distracted by unproven theoretical biomedical interventions.

10

Outcome

The very first question most parents ask the clinician at the time of diagnosis is "Where on the spectrum is my child?" They desperately want to know whether their child's ASD is mild, moderate, or severe. What they really want to know is what is going to happen to their child. Will he be able to go to kindergarten? Will she be able to have a job, live by herself, get married, and have children? What will happen to them when we get older? What will they do after we pass away? Their questions are completely understandable; any parent would want to know the same things. The reality is that, most of the time, it is not possible to provide an answer, especially not an answer that has the degree of certainty that most parents would like.

The outcome for individuals with ASDs is highly variable. Let us first take a look at the older follow-up studies to see what we can glean about outcome and then look to see what we can say about the outcome for children who have been identified at younger ages and had the advantage of contemporary intervention programs. Finally, we will look at what information we currently use to try to make predictions about the future.

THE FIRST FOLLOW-UP STUDY: KANNER'S ORIGINAL ELEVEN CHILDREN TWENTY-EIGHT YEARS LATER

Kanner's initial report that brought infantile autism into the medical and psychiatric lexicon was based on eleven children, ranging in age from two to eight years old when he first saw them. What became of the children he described so eloquently? The head social worker from Kanner's original clinic at Johns Hopkins Medical School was dispatched to find out. Let us check in on Donald T., Fredrick W., and Richard M. (the three vignettes presented in the introduction to this book).

Donald T.

Donald's parent's placed him on a tenant farm when he was nine years old. The social worker visited Donald at the farm a few months before his twelfth birthday. Fortunately for Donald, the couple he was placed with had the natural ability to think of ways to help Donald. The couple used motivating situations to develop Donald's abilities in an astoundingly similar manner to current intervention methods. For example, they used Donald's obsession with counting to teach him how to plow rows in the field. They used his preoccupation with measurements by having him dig a well and report on its depth. He made good academic progress at a small country school where his peculiarities were accepted. When the social worker checked in with the family, Donald was a thirty-six-year-old bachelor, living at home with his parents. He had received a B.A. degree at age twenty-five and taken a job as a bank teller, where he remained with no desire for promotion. He was an avid golf player and was involved in many community service groups. Donald's parents said, "While Don is not completely normal, he has taken his place in society very well, so much better than we ever hoped for."

Frederick W.

At the age of five, Frederick W. was enrolled at the Devereux School, one of the earliest schools devoted to treatment of children with developmental issues. He stayed at the school until he was twenty-six years old. A report from his school read as follows: "He is, at 26 years, a passive, likeable boy whose chief interest is music." At age thirty-four, Frederick was living with his parents and working at an office job. A letter from his boss described him as an outstanding employee because of his dependability, reliability, thoroughness, and thoughtfulness toward his coworkers.

Richard M.

Richard was placed in a foster home at five years of age. He went through two other foster homes before he was placed at a state school for exceptional children. At thirty-three years of age, Richard was still in an institutional setting. He was able to respond to his name, follow simple commands, and use some NVC with the staff. Richard continued to be withdrawn and uninterested in participating in structured activities.

Summary of the Kanner Follow-Up Results

Review of the outcome reports for the other eight children in Kanner's initial report were less encouraging. Two of the eleven (Donald T. and Frederick W.) had productive lives in the neurotypical world, although neither had achieved full independence. Herbert B. cannot be called a true success story, but he did escape the fate of lifelong institutionalization. Although he remained mute, he learned to help with routine chores after being placed on a farm. Later, after the farmer died, he was able to perform the duties of an orderly in a nursing home operated by the farmer's wife. Six others were institutionalized and remained there, where "they all lost their luster early after their admission." Two of the children were lost to follow-up, but what is known of their course did not suggest that they were likely to have a good outcome. Overall, the outcomes for Kanner's initial eleven children were fairly grim: two success stories, one fair outcome, and six poor outcomes with lives spent in isolation within institutions. Kanner summed up the results of the follow-up study with the simple statement that "most did not fare well into adulthood."

On the bright side, Kanner was careful to point out that the sample probably painted a picture that was more hopeless than warranted. His subjects were studied at the very beginning of the autism story, "before the days when a variety of therapeutic methods were inaugurated." This caveat is a limiting factor in all follow-up studies. By the time long-term follow-up is available, the intervention strategies for newly diagnosed children will undoubtedly have been modified, presumably in the direction of greater effectiveness. Results from long-term follow-up studies should be considered the very least we can reasonably expect.

RESULTS FROM OTHER FOLLOW-UP STUDIES ON AUTISM

A study by Lotter in 1978 came up with results very similar to Kanner's: 50–75 percent of adults with autism were living in institutions, whereas 5–15 percent had a normal or near-normal social life. A summary of findings on the long-term course of ASDs published in 1998 was equally disheartening

(Nordin and Gilberg 1998). The next round of studies, based on children diagnosed thirty years after Kanner's original report, yielded significantly more encouraging results.

A study published in 2008 by Eaves and Ho gathered data on the long-term outlook for young adults born between 1974 and 1984 who were all diagnosed with autism or a related disorder during the preschool years. Most of the children received a diagnoses of autism (57 percent), whereas the others had lesser variants that would now be considered PDD-NOS or AS. The authors first looked at test results obtained at an average age of 6 years, 8 months and retesting around age eleven. On the first round of testing, 50 percent of the subjects had verbal IQs greater than 50, 17.4 percent had verbal IQs greater than 70, and the rest were scattered fairly evenly between mild, moderate, and severe to profound MR. Because children with ASDs tend to perform less well on verbal IQ tests, the performance IQ was also reported. The number of subjects with IQs greater than 50 increased to 61 percent (a small but significant increase).

When the subjects were retested at an average age of eleven, their measured IQs were about the same and their ASD diagnosis was fairly stable (61 percent received an autism diagnosis). All of the children went to regular elementary schools where they received special education support and finished high school.

At an average age of twenty-four, the vast majority of the study participants were living at home (56 percent) or in supported living arrangements (37 percent). Only 7 percent lived independently. Thirty percent had gone on to college, but none had graduated by the time the outcome study was done. Fifty-six percent had a history of employment, mostly in volunteer positions, sheltered workshops, or part-time employment averaging five hours per week. The authors combined information about the individuals' work history, quality of friendships, and level of independence to come up with ratings that they used to generate an overall score for the outcome, ranging from very good to very poor. Individuals with "very good" outcomes had achieved a high level of independence with at least one deep interpersonal relationship and a job. A "good" rating for outcome was assigned if the person had some type of work and some friends but required some degree of support in daily living. "Fair" outcomes were given to individuals with some degree of independence not requiring special residential placement and acquaintances but no close friends. "Poor" outcomes were assigned to individuals in special residential settings with high levels of support and no friends or work. "Very poor" outcomes were given to those individuals who needed a high level of care and had no friends and no autonomy. The results were consistent with most other recent studies using similar classification schemes: 4 percent had very good outcomes, 17 percent had good outcomes, 32 percent had fair outcomes, and 46 percent had poor outcomes (no individuals had very poor outcomes).

What conclusions can be drawn from these outcome studies? It is clear that the rate of institutionalization has come down dramatically since Kanner's day, but the meaning of that improvement is not completely clear because it is no longer common practice to segregate individuals with DDs in institutions. Nonetheless, movement out of the institutions is a change to celebrate because children with ASDs who are not institutionalized, like Donald T. and Frederick W., almost certainly have a better chance to find their way back into the social world. Effective intervention, whether from natural teachers like the farmers who taught Donald T. and Frederick W. or from more modern intervention programs, gives the children the opportunity to continue their learning and improve their social skills. Compared with Kanner's initial sample, outcomes have improved over time with lower rates of very poor outcomes and higher rates of fair to good outcomes (a movement away from the worst outcomes toward more promising futures).

OUTCOME STUDIES FOR HFA AND AS

It is commonly assumed that the outcome for individuals with HFA and AS is much better than the outcome for other ASDs. Although the outcomes are indeed better when IQ is in the normal range and speech skills are better developed, the majority of studies show that higher-functioning individuals with ASDs continue to have severe impairments throughout their life that affect their independence and quality of life. A 2003 study of forty-two adults with ASDs, all of whom had IQs in the normal range or higher, found good outcomes for only 12 percent. Only one person of forty-two was employed, few had close relationships, and most required extensive supports to function. Although more individuals with AS attend college, that does not translate into a higher chance of gainful employment or marriage. A 2006 study by Saulnier and Klin compared thirty-two individuals with HFA to thirty-five individuals with AS. Despite higher verbal IQ and language abilities, individuals with AS did not fare any better with respect to real-life adaptations, a realization that is extremely frustrating and depressing for many with HFA/AS who find themselves falling through the cracks of the piecemeal government DD resources.

The poor outcome seen in the older studies of HFA/AS are likely to be partially attributable to late diagnosis and delayed intervention. EI for cognitive and speech issues is not enough for children with HFA/AS. Intervention must address the social deficits that make up the core of ASDs. A 2005 study by McGovern and Sigman at UCLA showed that the extent to which adolescents engaged with their peers predicted the level of their daily life skills. A combination of earlier diagnosis for children with HFA/AS and better intervention programs with more focus on social skills is likely to improve the outcome in years to come.

PREDICTORS OF OUTCOME

Every parent wants to know what the future holds for their child, but the urge to know is particularly strong for parents of children who have just received an ASD diagnosis. Although ASDs can be diagnosed fairly reliably as early as eighteen to twenty-four months of age, the outcome for each child is so variable that no evaluator can reliably predict how things will turn out for these young children. There are, however, some clues that can be used to take an educated guess about outcome.

The single factor that has the strongest predictive value for ultimate outcome is the child's cognitive potential. Unfortunately for parents and family members hoping for a definitive answer, the child's IQ often cannot be accurately gauged at a young age (unless there is reason to strongly suspect that the child has significant MR). IQ can easily be underestimated in a child with an ASD who is very often not interested in participating in cognitive testing. Children with language delays often receive lower IQ scores than are warranted because their language issues lower their scores. When disinterest in the testing and language delays are both present in a child, it is virtually impossible to estimate the child's true cognitive potential. To eliminate the confounding effect of language delays on IQ results, nonverbal IQ has been found to be the best predictor of ultimate outcome for children with ASDs, but even nonverbal IQ scores can underestimate IQ in young children with ASDs. Cognitive and language delays at age two are good predictors of final outcome. It is often necessary to wait until the child is five or even older to get accurate IQ test results. In children with hyperlexia (fascinations with letters that allows the child to learn to read earlier than expected), it is reasonable to assume that the child will likely test above the ID range once accurate testing is done (children who are able to count and read early are rarely mentally retarded).

A second predictor of outcome is language abilities. It is intuitively obvious that individuals with better communication skills are more likely to have a better ASD outcome, but it is not a simple matter to determine which of the young children with language delays will go on to develop adequate language skills. Researchers have shown that several behaviors predict language gains in ASDs, including response to bids for JA, rate of NVC attempts, frequency of requests, imitation abilities, and play skills. There is a direct correlation between the number of hours spent in speech therapy between the ages of two and four and language gains. The bottom line is that better developed language is crucial for an optimal outcome from an ASD. Although certain innate behavioral features affect the chance of language gains, most young children with ASDs can make great strides in language development if given the appropriate speech and language intervention. There is one discouraging caveat: failure to speak before age five has consistently been found to predict a much lower chance of developing functional verbal communication. That does not mean that it is impossible for a child older than five who has not yet developed speech to learn to speak; there are many examples of children who have broken through the language barrier at a later age, but it does mean that the chances are much lower.

Studies have shown that ASD diagnoses can be made fairly reliably in the second year of life, but that does not mean that the severity of behavioral issues and cognitive and language delays at age two are good predictors of final outcome. A 2007 study looked at thirteen children diagnosed with an ASD before thirty months of age who lost their ASD diagnosis when they were reevaluated at age four. The authors noted that children with PDD-NOS were more likely to move off the spectrum than those with an autism diagnosis (39 versus 11 percent). Surprisingly, it was not possible to predict which children would lose their ASD diagnosis. No differences were found in the symptom severity, socialization, or communication skill between the group that continued to have an ASD diagnosis and the group that did not. The significance of this study is profound. Although parents want to know the clinicians impression of the severity of their child's ASD at the time of the diagnosis, the clinicians cannot accurately predict the outcome.

A 2005 study by Tony Charman and colleagues followed twenty-six children who were diagnosed with autism at age two, who were then reassessed at ages three and seven. At each age, data were collected on symptom severity and cognitive and language skills. They found that the pattern of autistic symptom severity varied across time, with an increase in variability as the children grew older. Assessment at age two did not predict outcome at age seven, whereas assessment at age three was a reasonable predictor of all of the measured areas.

What is known about changes in ASDs during the adolescent years? A 2005 study by McGovern and Sigman out of UCLA assessed the changes in social interactions, repetitive and stereotyped behaviors, adaptive behaviors, and emotional responsiveness to the distress of others in adolescence compared with middle childhood. Individuals with HFA showed more improvements than low-functioning adolescents. The significance of the study is that change in ASDs is an ongoing process. Successful work on social skills during adolescence is likely to pay off in adult life. Outcome is a moving target that must be assessed and reassessed to gain an accurate picture of the individual's true potential. When parents ask at the diagnostic evaluation how severe their child's ASD is, perhaps the best answer is to say that the best predictor of outcome is continuing change in a forward direction. Outcome cannot be accurately predicted until the amount of progress with intervention has been assessed.

CHARACTERISTICS THAT PREDICT RESPONSE OR FAILURE TO RESPOND TO INTERVENTION

Some children with ASDs make dramatic progress with intervention, whereas others make much less impressive gains or do not respond at all. It would be helpful if there was some way to predict which children might respond better to any given treatment program, but there is far too little information to be that specific with treatment planning at this point in time.

The information that we do have has been gathered piecemeal from studies of various intervention programs. For example, a study of children who responded well to PRT demonstrated that spontaneous attempts to engage in social communication before PRT predicted response to treatment. In other words, children who demonstrated more interest in social interactions were most able to benefit from training that made the social world more available to them.

Factors associated with poor outcomes from a variety of different intervention programs include lack of JA by age four, lack of functional speech by age five, MR, comorbid medical or psychiatric disorders, extreme autistic aloofness, macrocephaly (with a pattern of accelerated brain growth starting during the first year of life), and regression. That is not a lot for parents to go on. Even the most experienced clinicians have been surprised by positive outcomes in children they thought would do poorly and poor outcomes in children they predicted would do well. For children under three, our ability to predict outcome is limited. As the child reaches the age of seven or eight, it starts to become more clear who the responders and nonresponders are likely to be.

RECOVERY FROM AUTISM: DOES IT HAPPEN?

Until very recently, autism researchers have maintained that recovery from autism is not possible. Reports of children diagnosed with autism who later showed no detectable signs of autism were met with skepticism about the accuracy of the original diagnosis. Lovaas was the first to introduce the concept of recovery. Since then, most talk about recovery has come from the CAM orientation, with vitamins, minerals, special diets, and the like assumed to be the reason for the recovery.

Nowadays, mainstream researchers are increasingly acknowledging that it is possible for a child with an ASD diagnosis to move off the spectrum. A 2007 study out of the University of Connecticut showed that 37 percent of children with a PDD-NOS diagnosis and 11 percent with an autism diagnosis at age two move off the spectrum over time. CAM proponents celebrate recovery and generally take the credit. A more even-handed approach to the recovery issue would be to acknowledge that the developmental course for many children is not as predictable as we once thought. For reasons that are still unknown, a sizeable percentage of children who look autistic in their first two to three years of life grow out of autism (or "recover," "have an optimal outcome," are "a success story," whatever you want to call it) whether they use CAM treatments or not. There appears to be more plasticity in brain development than was previously appreciated. Predicting which children with early signs of ASDs will make such significant progress that an ASD diagnosis is no longer appropriate is not currently possible, but it is not logical to attribute these cases to the use of CAM treatments when those methods are not used universally in the cases of recovery.

Remember the story of Raun Kauffman, the recipient of the first Son-Rise intervention program discussed in Chapter 8 (under relation-based intervention programs)? What does Raun's story tell us about possible outcomes for children with ASDs? Nonbelievers in the possibility of recovering from autism question whether Raun was actually autistic. However, the description of his odd repetitive interests (e.g., spinning plates) and extreme social withdrawal seems consistent with our current conceptions of autism. The caveat is that Raun was diagnosed at eighteen months, quite early for his time (early diagnosis was not common until the late nineties). Back in the days when it was felt that children with autism could not recover, the average age for an autism diagnosis was between age four and five (or later). Based on what we now know about the inability to predict outcome based on level of severity at age two, it is not hard to believe that Raun moved off the spectrum. Even when a child is not diagnosed until the third year of life (twenty-four to thirty-six months of age), there is a 32 percent chance that the child will go on to lose the ASD diagnosis by age five (Raun was said to emerge from autism around age five). You can hear Raun tell his story on the Son-Rise program website at http://www.autismtreatmentcenter.org (although there is no video of his early childhood years, so you cannot make your own diagnosis). Remember Raun's story when you listen to CAM proponents attributing recovery to treatments such as GFCF diets and mercury chelation.

EFFECTS OF ASDS ON FAMILY MEMBERS

Living with a child who has an ASD is a stressful experience, no matter how supportive and accepting the family members are of the individual's differences. Studies comparing stress levels in parents of children with ASD and non-ASD DDs show that the ASD children generate higher stress levels. There is nothing predictable about family life when a member of the family has an ASD. Fortunately, humans are a resilient species. Factors associated with an ability to adapt to the stress of parenting a child with an ASD include family connectedness and closeness, finding a positive meaning in the family member's ASD, and achieving spiritual and personal growth through the challenge of including an individual with an ASD in a family. Studies on siblings of children with ASDs have consistently demonstrated that siblings do not feel slighted by the attention directed to the child with an ASD. Instead, siblings are more likely to develop empathy and compassion for individuals with challenging life circumstances. Books by siblings of children with ASDs and support groups are becoming increasingly common.

CHANGING ATTITUDES: ASDS IN THE SCHOOLS AND WORKPLACE

The increased awareness of ASDs has brought about a benefit that is not often appreciated by the general public: increased understanding and acceptance of individuals with ASDs for who they are. In the past, the odd or eccentric child in the school system was routinely shunned and often feel victim to bullying. Social exclusion of students and workers who do not fit in still persists, but there is a growing shift toward greater acceptance of individuals with ASDs. Mainstream students are growing up alongside children with ASDs and other developmental issues who are no longer hidden away in special education classrooms for the duration of their school years.

More and more, individuals with ASDs are finding empathetic peers and mentors to act as their guides through the complex social mazes of the schoolyard and the workplace. Tolerance for differences and compassion toward others start early in a child's development. With continued patient efforts to increase understanding about ASDs, children who are being diagnosed today will have a much greater chance of a satisfying life as they move forward in the company of peers who can accept their differences and celebrate the unique gifts they bring to the human experience.

Abbreviations

AAP	American Academy of Pediatrics
ABA	applied behavior analysis
aCGH	microarray-based comparative genomic hybridization
ADDM	Autism and Developmental Disabilities Monitoring Network
ADHD	attention deficit hyperactivity disorder
ADI-R	Autism Diagnostic Interview—Revised
ADOS	Autism Diagnostic Observation Schedule
ARI	Autism Research Institute
AS	Asperger syndrome or Asperger's syndrome
ASD	autistic spectrum disorder
ATSDR	Agency for Toxic Substances and Disease Registry
BAP	broader autistic phenotype
CAM	complementary and alternative medicine
CARS	Childhood Autism Rating Scale
CDC	Center for Disease Control and Prevention
CDD	childhood disintegrative disorder
CHAT	Checklist for Autism in Toddlers
CMV	cytomegalovirus
CNV	copy number variant
COPDD	childhood onset pervasive developmental disorder

CP	cerebral palsy
CSBS	Communication and Symbolic Behavior Scale
CSBS-DP	Communication and Symbolic Behavior Scale—Developmental Profile
DD	developmental disabilities
DDS	Department of Developmental Services
DDT	dichloro-diphenyl-trichloroethane
DIR	developmental individual-difference relationship-based
DPT	diphtheria-pertussis-tetanus
DSM	*Diagnostic and Statistical Manual of Mental Health Disorders*
DTT	discrete trial training
EEG	electroencephalogram
EI	early intervention
EIBI	early intensive behavioral intervention
EIBT	early intensive behavioral treatment
EPA	Environmental Protection Agency
FC	facilitated communication
FDA	Food and Drug Administration
fMRI	functional magnetic resonance imaging
G×E	genotype and environmental interaction
GDD	global developmental delays
GFCF	gluten-free, casein-free
GI	gastrointestinal
HBOT	hyperbaric oxygen therapy
HFA	high-functioning autism
ICD	*International Classification of Disease*
ID	intellectual disability
IQ	intelligence quotient
JA	joint attention
LKS	Landau-Kleffner syndrome
M-CHAT	Modified Checklist for Autism in Toddlers
MMR	measles, mumps, and rubella
MR	mental retardation
MRI	magnetic resonance imaging
NFRR	nonfunctional routines and rituals
NVC	nonverbal communication
OT	occupational therapist
PCB	polychlorinated biphenyl
PCP	primary care provider
PECS	Picture Exchange Communication System
PEDS	Parents Evaluation of Developmental Status
PDD-NOS	pervasive developmental disorder not otherwise specified
PKU	phenylketonuria

PPV	positive predictive value
PPVT	Peabody Picture Vocabulary Test
PRT	pivotal response training
RDI	relationship development intervention
RMM	repetitive motor mannerisms
RPM	Raven's Progressive Matrices Test
SCQ	Social Communication Questionnaire
SCERTS	social communications emotional regulation and transactional supports
SIT	sensory integration therapy
SLI	specific language impairment
SLP	speech-language pathologist
SPD	sensory processing disorder
SSRI	selective serotonin reuptake inhibitor
TD	typically developing (children who do not have developmental delays or ASDs)
TEACCH	Treatment and Educations of Autistic and Related Communication-Handicapped Children
ToM	theory of mind
UCLA	University of California, Los Angeles
WISC	Wechsler Intelligence Scale for Children

Timeline

1943	Dr. Leo Kanner publishes the first clinical case series of eleven children with "autistic disturbance of affective contact," later renamed "early infantile autism."
1944	Dr. Hans Asperger publishes a paper describing four children similar to Kanner's series, choosing the name "autistic psycopathy" to describe the condition.
1956	Kanner proposes the first set of rules to diagnose early infantile autism.
1964	Bernard Rimland, PhD., publishes his text, *Infantile Autism: The Syndrome and Its Implication for a Neural Theory of Behavior*, ending the view of autism as a psychiatric problem and ushering in the era of treating autism as a neurodevelopmental disorder.
1965	Rimland establishes the Autism Society of America, still one of the largest autism support organizations in the United States.
1967	Rimland establishes the Autism Research Institute, the epicenter of the movement to find alternative treatments for autism.

1978	Michael Rutter in the United Kingdom proposes modified diagnostic criteria for autism.
1981	Lorna Wing translates Asperger's 1944 paper from German and brings it to the attention of the world's experts in autism.
1984	Autism is included in the *The Diagnostic and Statistical Manual of Mental Disorders* (*DSM*) for the first time with the publication of the *DSM-III*.
1986	Temple Grandin publishes her memoir *Emergence: Labeled Autistic*, bringing high-functioning autism into public awareness.
1987	Ivar Lovaas and colleagues at University of California, Los Angeles publish the first study showing that young children with autism can improve dramatically with intensive early intervention. His intervention program becomes the standard for effective early childhoon intervention.
1988	The image of Raymond Babbit, an autistic savant, portrayed by Dustin Hoffman in the movie *Rain Man*, becomes the stereotype for the public conception of autism.
1991	Recommendations to immunize for hepatitis B starting at birth and immunize for Hemophilus influenza B (Hib) at 2, 4, and 6 months of age increase the number of vaccines given to infants and toddlers.
1992	Asperger's disorder is included in the *DSM* for the first time with the publication of the *DSM-IV*.
1998	Dr. Andrew Wakefield, a gastroenterologist in the United Kingdom, suggests a connection between the MMR vaccine, gastrointestinal disorders, and regressive PDDs.
1998	The CDC Brick Township Study demonstrates that 1:167 children ages 3–10 have an ASD.
1998	The University of California, Davis M.I.N.D. (Medical Investigation of Neurodevelopmental Disorders) Institute is established by a cooperative effort between parents of children with autism and the University of California, Davis.
1999	The California Department of Developmental Services releases a report showing a 273 percent increase in the number of

children with autism entering the developmental services system over the ten-year period between 1987 and 1998.

1999   The American Academy of Pediatrics and the U.S. Public Health Service issue a recommendation for the removal of thimerosal, a mercury-based preservative, from childhood vaccines.

2000   Publication of the *DSM-IV-Text Revision*.

2001   Removal of thimerosal from routine childhood vaccines used in the United States is completed (except for trace amounts in hepatitis B and Hib vaccines, and the continued presence of thimerosal in influenza A immunizations, which are optional for children).

2004   The Institute of Medicine issues a report with their conclusion that the bulk of evidence does not support the theory that thimerosal causes autism. Advocates of the theory remain unconvinced.

June 2005   Robert F. Kennedy Jr. publishes "Deadly Immunity" in *Rolling Stone*, thrusting potential harm of mercury from thimerosal in childhood vaccines into the public eye.

2006   The Combatting Autism Act of 2006 passes, increasing autism research funding to an estimated $101 million in 2007 and directing further research to include examination of a possible autism–vaccine connection.

2006   Journalist David Kirby publishes *Evidence of Harm*, a book that tells the tale of an alleged government and pharmaceutical company conspiracy to suppress data suggesting that thimerosal causes autism. Mistrust of vaccinations rises precipitously.

2007   Celebrity Jenny McCarthy adds her voice to the parents and other celebrities popularizing the idea that children with autism can "recover" using a combination of early intensive behavioral intervention and biomedical treatments.

2007   The Omnibus Autism case hearings start in a special federal claims court with three cases scheduled for each of the three main theories put forth for how vaccinations may be linked to ASD. Each of the first three cases alleges that a combination of vaccines and mercury from thimerosal caused the child's autism.

2007   Comprehensive guidelines for screening, diagnosis, and management of ASDs are released by the AAP. The guidelines call for universal screening for all developmental delays and specific testing for ASDs at the eighteen- and twenty-four-month checkups.

2007   The second set of three test cases commences in the Omnibus Autism case hearings. All three cases allege that thimerosal is the cause of autism.

2008   The first case alleging a connection between ASD and vaccines (the *Cedillo* case) is decided in the plaintiffs favor without a trial by judges in the U.S. Court of Federal Claims as the first of three test cases. Almost 5,000 other cases await a hearing.

2008   California DDS autism statistics are used to show that the numbers of children in the regional center system diagnosed with autism continue to rise despite the phase-out of thimerosal from childhood vaccines that was completed in 2001, calling into question the thimerosal theory of autism.

2009   The third set of three cases alleging a vaccine link to autism is scheduled to start in the Autism Omnibus case hearings. Each case alleges that MMR caused the child's autism.

2011–2012 Anticipated date for release of the *DSM-V*.

Glossary

Adaptive behavior The level of skills a person demonstrates in various areas needed for everyday living compared to other individuals of the same age. Adaptive behavior skills are often divided into three categories: conceptual, social, and practical skills. Examples of conceptual skills include the ability to write, read, and understand money concepts. Examples of social skills include the ability to understand and obey laws and the ability to avoid victimization. Examples of practical skills include the ability to groom, use the toilet, dress, cook, eat and avoid injury. Significant limitations in adaptive behavior adversely impact the ability to participate in daily life. Limitations in adaptive behavior are assessed by using a standardized test (e.g., the Vineland adaptive behavior scales, SIB-R, or ABAS).

Affect A term used in clinical psychology and psychiatry to describe a person's demeanor. Examples include a depressed affect, an anxious affect, or a "flat" affect (a blank face that does not convey emotional experiences). Flat affect is a common finding in ASDs.

Aloof Used to describe autistic individuals who often seem to be oblivious to the presence of other individuals in their midst, preferring to follow their own interests without any social interaction.

Autisms An alternative name for autistic spectrum disorder used to indicate that individuals with ASDs may be grouped together by behaviors but are likely to have widely varying causes of their symptoms.

Biomarkers Measurable indicators of a condition used to confirm a diagnosis and/or assess the severity. Biomarkers are detectable and measurable by a variety of methods, including laboratory assays and medical imaging.

Broader autistic phenotype (BAP) The presence of traits in family members of persons with ASDs that are similar to, though usually less severe than, traits found in individuals with ASDs. BAP has been found in 15-45% of family members of people with autism. BAP-related symptoms include slow language development, pragmatic deficits, learning disabilities, shyness, obsessive-compulsive traits, and anxiety and other mood disorders.

Categorical diagnostic systems A categorical approach to diagnosis using the *DSM* results in splitting autism, PDD-NOS, and Asperger's disorder into discrete, separate categories.

Chromosomes Strands of DNA in the form of a double helix that contain genes. Each gene codes for a protein that has a specific function in the body.

Cognitive Having to do with the ability to think and reason. The phrase "cognitive level" is essentially equivalent to "intellectual abilities." IQ (intelligence quotient) is one type of measure of cognitive potential.

Comorbid A condition that can coexist with a separate medical condition. Some comorbid conditions occur together with a high frequency (e.g., autism and sleep disturbances, ADHD and tic disorders, and depression and anxiety).

Criterion Singular form of criteria.

Diagnostic criteria The essential components of a condition laid out in a systematized way that can be used for diagnosis. Each criterion attempts to summarize one of the important features that can be seen in individuals with a particular condition.

Dimensional diagnostic systems A dimensional approach to diagnostic categories recognizes that the conditions that comprise the ASDs are all interrelated and are best included under a single diagnostic label with a modifier to indicate the severity (e.g., mild, moderate, or severe).

Dysmorphic Dysmorphic is a medical term used to indicate that the formation of the fetus did not proceed in the expected way, resulting in an unusual appearance.

Echolalia A speech abnormality frequently noted in individuals with ASDs. Immediate echolalia refers to the exact repetition of words immediately or soon after the words are heard, often with similar intonation. Delayed echolalia involves the repetition of phrases or longer sections of dialogue (often from movies or video games) long after the words are first uttered.

Electroencephalogram (EEG) A tracing of the electrical activity of the brain made by attaching electrodes to the scalp, primarily used to assess for seizure disorders.

Emotional regulation The ability to maintain control of one's emotions. Emotional regulation is a developmental skill that increases with time as individuals learn various coping mechanisms.

Epigenetics Mechanisms used to control the expression of genes that do not involve changes in the DNA.

Ethyl mercury The type of mercury contained in the preservative thimerosal. Ethyl mercury has long been viewed as less toxic than the types of mercury that contaminate the air, water, and food chain (methyl mercury), but that view has recently been challenged.

False-negative A test that indicates that a condition is not present when the condition is present. The test result is "negative" but the result is in error.

False-positive A test that indicates that a condition is present when the condition is not present. The test result is "positive" but the result is in error.

Flourescent in situ hybridization (FISH) A test that uses fluorescent markers that bind to specific areas of DNA to determine if that section of DNA is present, absent, or duplicated. Tests are available for only a handful of a growing number of genetic disorders that have been localized to a particular chromosome at a specific address on that chromosome (e.g., PraderWilli/Angelman's syndrome at 15q11–13, DiGeorge/Velocardiofacial Syndrome at 22q11.2, and Sotos syndrome at 5q35).

Functional MRI (fMRI) A specialized MRI scan that allows researchers to monitor which areas of the brain are active during specified tasks. fMRI is not used as a diagnostic tool in ASDs.

Gaze monitoring Typically developing children look to see how others are reacting to them and pay attention to where the other person is looking. Children with ASDs do not engage in gaze monitoring to the same extent.

Genes Genes are separate areas on a chromosome that code for a protein that has a special function in the body. If the gene is changed in some way, the function of that protein can be affected, resulting in a change that can be disastrous or inconsequential, depending on which gene is involved and how much the gene is altered.

Gestalt Often used in psychology/psychiatry to mean a recognizable general pattern that may be difficult to characterize completely by listing the various parts.

Global developmental delay A developmental term used as shorthand to indicate that a developing child is significantly behind in all areas of development. The child fails to meet expected developmental milestones such as sitting, crawling, and walking (motor skills); first words (language skills); and the performance of tasks that are indicative of level of intelligence. Most individuals with GDD are eventually determined to have significant intellectual disabilities (i.e., mental retardation is very common in children with GDDs).

Head circumference The measured distance around the forehead (just above the eyes). This measurement is an indirect measure of brain size in young children because it is the growth of the brain that causes the skull to increase in size.

Idiosyncratic language Language that makes sense only to persons familiar with the details that led to the intended meaning. For example, a child who first discovered the joys of going down a slide at daycare may refer to all future slides as daycare.

Intelligence quotient (IQ) According to the American Association of Mental Retardation (AAMR), intelligence refers to a general mental capability. It involves the ability to reason, plan, solve problems, think abstractly, comprehend complex ideas, learn quickly, and learn from experience. Although not perfect, intelligence is represented by Intelligent Quotient (IQ) scores obtained from standardized tests given by a trained professional. IQ is reported as a numerical value, with 100 representing average intelligence.

Joint attention (JA) The process of seeking to share attention with others. Impairment in JA is a core deficit in ASDs. The techniques used to establish JA become more sophisticated as the child develops. The process starts in infancy when parents follow the child's gaze and interact around whatever has caught the child's attention. Infants typically follow a progression of increasingly sophisticated attempts to develop JA: shifting their gaze from an object of interest, to another person, and back to the object (referred to a "three-point gaze"); paying attention to whatever another person points to or looks at; and using simple gestures to direct the attention of others and share enjoyment by looking to another person when smiling. Eventually, the child learns to use language to establish JA.

Karyotype A laboratory test used to check for large problems with chromosomes. The twenty-three pairs of chromosomes are laid out in order of size (from the biggest to the smallest) along with the two chromosomes that determine gender (X and Y). The chromosomes are examined under a high-powered microscope to check for structural abnormalities such as extra chromosomes (e.g., an extra chromosome 21 is the cause of Down syndrome), lost chromosomes (e.g., a single X without another X or a Y is the cause of Turner's syndrome), and places where small pieces of the chromosome have been copied too many times (called a "duplication"), left out (called a "deletion"), or stuck where they do not belong (called a "translocation"). It is important to realize that a normal karyotype does not mean that there are no genetic abnormalities.

Language The ability to put words together correctly in a way that allows for clear communication (includes expressive language, receptive language, and pragmatics).

Longitudinal study A research study that starts at a specified time or age and follow the subjects over an extended period of time until the study concludes or the individuals in the study reach a specified age.

Mental retardation (MR) A psychologic term used to identify individuals with significantly subaverage general intellectual functioning (IQ) accompanied by significant limitations is adaptive functioning. IQ scores of 70 or below fall in the MR range. The level of MR increases in severity as the IQ drops. Individuals with MR have low skill levels in all areas. If a person has normal abilities in one area (e.g., the ability to problem solve) but scores in the MR range in another area (e.g., verbal skills), a diagnosis of MR is not appropriate.

Methyl mercury The type of mercury that contaminates the food chain (as opposed to ethyl mercury—the type of mercury contained in the vaccine preservative thimerosal).

Neologisms The fabrication of nonsensical words that are used consistently to replace the standard word for an object. Neologisms should not be confused with the normal process of language development that starts with the use of a close approximation of a new word and progresses over time to the correct pronunciation. In contrast, a child with an ASD using a neologism repeatedly produces a nonsense word that is markedly different than the standard word (e.g., *ja-ja* for "milk"). Despite repeated modeling, the child with an ASD continues to use his version of the word.

Neurodevelopmental disorder A problem with brain development that can occur during gestation or early in the course of childhood development.

Neurotypical (NT) A term coined by persons with high-functioning ASDs used to refer to everyone who does not have an ASD or other significant developmental problems (same meaning as "typically developing," or TD).

Nosology The systematic classification of diseases.

Otitis media Middle ear infection.

Otoacoustic emissions (OAE) A hearing test that assesses the ability of the cochlea to perceive sounds without the need for cooperation from the person being tested.

Pathognomonic A medical term that means the essential or defining characteristic of a particular disease or condition. "Patho" refers to pathology—the study of disease.

Perseverative play Repeating an action or behavior over and over with little variation; getting stuck on a specific activity.

Phenotype The outward manifestations of a person's genetic makeup interacting with the environment.

Personality disorders A category of mental health disorders that start in adolescence or early adulthood resulting in significant disruption of the individual's life. Some of the personality disorders could be confused with ASDs if the early history is not carefully reviewed. For example, schizoid personality disorder is defined in the *DSM-IV* as "a pattern of detachment from social relationships and a restricted range of emotional expression." Obsessive-compulsive personality disorder is "a pattern of preoccupation with orderliness, perfectionism, and control." Although some individuals with personality disorders are referred unnecessarily for ASD evaluations, it is likely that many more have been given a personality disorder diagnosis in the past when an ASD diagnosis would have been more appropriate.

Positive predictive value (PPV) The chance of having a condition (e.g., ASD) when a screening test is positive.

Pragmatics The social rules that govern spoken language (e.g., how to start or stop a conversation, indicate interest in what another person is saying, make a request, and ask or answer a question).

Primary care provider (PCP) A primary care provider is a healthcare professional who sees a patient on a regular basis. The continuity of care allows the PCP to make sure that all of the important aspects of developmental and preventative care are addressed. The PCP for most children is a pediatrician, family practitioner, or midlevel nurse practitioner or physician's assistant working in collaboration with a physician. Emergency rooms and walk-in clinics can provide treatment for isolated problems, but these health care providers do not provide primary care services. One of the risk factors for late diagnosis of ASDs is not having a regular PCP.

Prognosis The medical term for the anticipated outcome from a disease or condition.

Prosody The rhythm and melody of spoken language. Prosody can be broken down into various components, including rate, pitch, stress, inflection, and intonation—all of which tend to be abnormal to varying degrees in ASDs.

Prospective study A study where the structure and patient population are selected in advance to try to answer a specific research question. Prospective studies provide more reliable information than retrospective studies (i.e., studies where researchers try to draw conclusions by looking back in time at a group of individuals that were not preselected).

Protodeclerative pointing Pointing for the purpose of shared interest.

Receptive language The ability to understand what others say.

Regression The loss of previously acquired developmental skills.

Reliability The consistency of a test when used by different professionals trained to use the tool.

Schizophrenia A severely disabling condition marked by the gradual or sudden loss of the ability to organize thoughts in a cohesive manner along with the onset of hallucinations and delusions, usually occurring in the late teen years or in the early twenties. Schizophrenia is a lifelong condition that can be partially improved with antipsychotic medication treatment but never cured. Contrary to popular usage, schizophrenia is not a "split personality."

Screening test A test designed to identify individuals with a high chance of having a particular condition of interest (e.g., an ASD, colon cancer, or heart disease).

Sensitivity How good a test is at including individuals who have the condition of interest. Sensitivity is the number of *true positives* in a sample. A high sensitivity means that most of the true positives are picked up by the test.

Specificity How good a test is at excluding individuals who do not have the condition. Another term for specificity is *true negatives*. The higher the specificity of a test, the more certain the tester can be that the individual truly does not have the condition of interest.

Speech The verbal means of communication composed of articulation (e.g., the ability to accurately produce speech sounds) and fluency (e.g., stuttering or hesitations).

Standardized test A test that is given to large numbers of individuals in order to establish valid statistical cutoffs.

Stereotypic Used in ASDs to refer to odd speech and language or other behaviors that are performed repeatedly in a similar manner. Stereotypic speech can be as simple as repeated utterances with very little variation. Perseverative play with minimal variation from a set pattern is also referred to as stereotypic play. Stereotypic motor mannerisms consist of readily identifiable repetitive patterns of jumping, hand-flapping, or spinning in a manner that is clearly odd with little variation between occurrences.

Thimerosal An ethyl mercury–based preservative contained in some routine immunizations used in the United States prior to 2001. Thimerosal was never present in any of the "live" vaccines, including MMR, varicella (chicken pox), and polio vaccines. Thimerosal was used as a preservative in flu vaccines and Rhogam shots for pregnant women who are Rh negative, but both preparations are now available without thimerosal.

Validity A measure of how accurately a test results in the correct classification for the condition assessed.

Bibliography

American Psychiatric Association. *Diagnostic and Statistical Manual of Mental Disorders*, 4th Edition, text revision (DSM-IV-TR). Washington, DC: American Psychiatric Publishing, 2000.

American Psychiatric Association. *Diagnostic and Statistical Manual of Mental Disorders*, 4th Edition (DSM-IV). Washington, DC: American Psychiatric Publishing, 1994.

American Psychiatric Association. *Diagnostic and Statistical Manual of Mental Disorders*, 3rd Edition, revised (DSM-III-R). Washington, DC: American Psychiatric Publishing, 1987.

American Psychiatric Association. *Diagnostic and Statistical Manual of Mental Disorders*, 3rd Edition (DSM-III). Washington, DC: American Psychiatric Publishing, 1980.

American Psychiatric Association. *Diagnostic and Statistical Manual of Mental Disorders*, 2nd Edition (DSM-II). Washington, DC: American Psychiatric Publishing, 1968.

Autism and Developmental Disabilities Monitoring Network Surveillance Year 2000 Principal Investigators; Centers for Disease Control and Prevention. "Prevalence of Autism Spectrum Disorders: Autism and Developmental Disabilities Monitoring Network, Six Sites, United States" *Morbidity and Mortality Weekly Review Surveillance Summary* (2007) 56:1–11.

Autism and Developmental Disabilities Monitoring Network Surveillance Year 2002 Principal Investigators; Centers for Disease Control and Prevention. "Prevalence of Autism Spectrum Disorders: Autism and Developmental Disabilities Monitoring

Network, 14 Sites, United States, 2002." *Morbidity and Mortality Weekly Review Surveillance Summary* (2007) 56:12–28.

Baron-Cohen, Simon. *Male and Female Brains and the Truth about Autism: The Essential Difference*. New York: Basic Books, 2003.

Benaron, Lisa. "Inclusion to the Point of Dilution." *Journal of Autism and Developmental Disorders* (2003) 33: 355–59.

California Department of Developmental Services. "Autistic Spectrum Disorders: Best Practice Guidelines for Screening, Diagnosis, and Assessment." Sacramento, CA, 2002. Available at http:/www.ddhealthinfo.org/documents/ASD_Best_Practice.pdf.

Courchesne, Eric, Ruth Carper, and Natacha Akshoomoff. "Brain Overgrowth in the First Year of Life in Autism." *Journal of the American Medical Association* (2003) 290: 337–44.

Filipek, Pauline, Pasquale Accardo, Grace Baranek, Edwin Cook, Gerladine Dawson, Barry Gordon, Judith Gravil, Chris Johnson, Ronald Kallen, Susan Levy, Nancy Minshew, Barry Prizant, Isabelle Rapin, Sally Rogers, Wendy Stone, Stuart Teplin, Roberto Tuchman, and Fred Volkmar. "The Screening and Diagnosis of Autistic Spectrum Disorders." *Journal of Autism and Developmental Disabilities* (1999) 29: 439–84.

Fombonne, Eric. "Epidemiological Survey of Autism and Other Pervasive Developmental Disorders: An Update." *Journal of Autism and Developmental Disabilities* (2003) 33: 365–82.

Frith, Uta. *Autism and Asperger Syndrome*. New York: Cambridge University Press, 1981.

Gilberb, Nordin. "The Long-Term Course of Autistic Disorders: Update on Follow-Up Studies." *Acta Psychiatry Scandanavia* (1998) 97: 99–108.

Golan, Ofer, and Simon Baron-Cohen. "Systemizing Empathy: Teaching Adults with Aspergers Syndrome or High-Functioning Autism to Recognize Complex Emotions using Interactive Media." *Development and Psychopathology* (2006) 18: 591–617.

Herbert, Martha. "Autism: A Brain Disorder, or a Disorder that Affects the Brain?" *Clinical Neuropsychiatry* (2005) 2: 354–59.

Hix-Small, Kevin Marks, Jane Squires, and Robert Nickel. "Impact of Implementing Developmental Screening at 12 and 24 Months in a Pediatric Practice." *Pediatrics* (2007) 120: 381–89.

Howlin, Patricia, and Anna Moorf. "Diagnosis in Autism: A Survey of over 1200 Patients in the UK." *Autism* (1997) 1: 135–72.

Howlin, Patricia. "Outcome in High-Functioning Adults with Autism with and without Early Language Delays: Implications for the Differentiation between Autism and Asperger Syndrome." *Journal of Autism and Developmental Disorders* (2003) 33: 3–13.

Howlin Patricia, S. Goode, J. Hutton, and Michael Rutter. "Adult Outcome for Children with Autism." *Journal of Child Psychology and Psychiatry* (2004) 45:212–22.

Johnson, Chris Plauché, Scott Myers, and the Council on Children with Disabilities. "Identification and Evaluation of Children with Autism Spectrum Disorders." *Pediatrics* (2007) 120: 1183–215.

Kanner, Leo. "Autistic Disturbance of Affective Contact." *The Nervous Child* (1943) 2: 217–50.

Kirby David. *Evidence of Harm: Mercury in Vaccines and the Autism Epidemic—a Medical Controversy.* New York: St. Martin's Press, 2005.

Klin, Ami. "Defining and Quantifying the Social Phenotype in Autism." *American Journal of Psychiatry* (2002) 159: 895–908.

Lord, Catherine, Susan Risi, Pamela DiLavore, Cory Schulman, Audrey Thurm, and Andrew Pickles. "Autism from Two to Nine Years of Age." *Archives of General Psychiatry* (2006) 63: 694–701.

Lotter, Victor. "Epidemiology of Autistic Conditions in Young Children: I. Prevalence." *Social Psychiatry* (1966) 1: 124–37.

Lyons, Viktoria, and Michael Fitzgerald. "Humor in Autism and Asperger Syndrome." *Journal of Autism and Developmental Disorders* (2004) 34:521–31.

Mandell, David, Maytali Novak, and Cynthia Zubritsky. "Factors Associated with Age of Diagnosis among Children with Autism Spectrum Disorders." *Pediatrics* (2005) 116: 1480–86.

Myers, Scott, Chris Plauche Johnson, and the Council on Children with Disabilities. "Management of Children with Autism Spectrum Disorders." *Pediatrics* (2007) 120: 1162–68.

National Research Council, Committee on Interventions for Children with Autism. *Educating Children with Autism.* Washington, DC: National Academies Press, 2001.

Ozonoff, Sally, Beth Goodlin-Jones, and Marjorie Solomon. "Evidence-Based Assessment of Autism Spectrum Disorders in Children and Adolescents." *Journal of Clinical Child and Adolescent Psychology* (2005) 34: 523–40.

Report to the Legislature on the Principal Findings From the Epidemiology of Autism in California: A Comprehensive Pilot Study. Davis: University of California, Davis; 2002. Available at http://www.ucdmc.ucdavis.edu/mindinstitute/newsroom/studyfinal.pdf.

Richdale, Amanda. "Sleep Problems in Autism: Prevalence, Cause and Intervention." *Developmental Medicine and Child Neurology* (1999) 41: 60–66.

Rogers, Sally, and Laurie Vismara. "Evidence-Based Comprehensive Treatments for Early Autism." *Journal of Clinical Child and Adolescent Psychology* (2008) 37: 8–38.

Rogers, Sally, and Sally Ozonoff. "Annotation: What Do We Know about Sensory Dysgunction in Autism? A Critical Review of the Empirical Evidence." *Journal of Child Psychology and Psychiatry* (2005) 46:1255–68.

Schechter, R and JK Grether. "Continuing Increases in Autism Reported to California's Developmental Service System: Mercury in Retrograde." *Archives of General Psychiatry* (2008) 65: 19–24.

Schaffer, G. Bradley, and Nancy Mendelshon. "Genetics Evaluation for the Etiologic Diagnosis of Autism Spectrum Disorders." *Genetic Medicine* (2008) 10: 4–12.

Sperry, Virginia Walker. *Fragile Success: Ten Autistic Children: Childhood to Adulthood.* 2nd ed. Maryland: Paul Brookes, 2001.

Tammet, Daniel. *Born on a Blue Day: Inside the Extraordinary Mind of an Autistic Savant.* New York: Free Press, 2006.

Wakefield, Andrew, S. H. Murch, A. Anthony, et al. 1998. "Ileal-Lymphoid-Nodular Hyperplasia, Non-Specific Colitis, and Pervasive Developmental Disorders in Children." *Lancet* 351:637–41.

Wills, Sharifia, Maricel Cabanlit, Jeff Bennett, Paul Ashwood, David Amaral, and Judy Van De Water. "Autoantibodies in Autism Spectrum Disorders." *Annals of the New York Academy of Science* (2007) 1107: 79–91.

Wing, Lorna, S. R. Yeates, L. M. Brierly, and Judith Gould. "The Prevalence of Early Childhood Autism: Comparison of Administrative and Epidemiological Studies." *Psychological Medicine* (1976) 6: 89–100.

Wing, Lorna. "Asperger Syndrome: A Clinical Account." *Psychological Medicine* (1981) 11: 115–19.

World Health Organization. *International Statistical Classification of Diseases and Related Health Problems, 10th Revision.* Vols. 1–3. Geneva, Switzerland: World Health Organization, 1994.

Index

About the Author

LISA D. BENARON is a graduate of Yale Medical School and is board certi-
fied in Pediatrics, Internal Medicine, and Neurodevelopmental Disabilities.
She is the medical director of Far Northern Regional center, where she provides evaluations for individuals of all ages suspected of having an ASD. She
is a strong advocate of including the schools in the process of diagnosis. Dr.
Benaron served on the advisory committee for the California Department of
Developmental Services Best Practice Guidelines for Screening Diagnosis and
Assessment of ASDs and is currently on the advisory committee reviewing
evidence-based interventions for ASDs.